Preface

Welcome to the **Windows Operating System Interview Questions and Answers,** Windows Operating System stands as a cornerstone of the digital world, serving as the backbone for countless personal computers, enterprise environments, and data centres worldwide. Its rich history and evolution, extensive array of versions and editions, and complex components have made it an integral part of our daily lives and workspaces. To navigate the intricacies of this operating system, whether for personal use, professional IT management, or cybersecurity, a deep understanding of its core elements is essential.

This comprehensive set of interview questions and answers aims to guide you through the multifaceted landscape of Windows OS. Starting with a foundational overview of Windows and its historical journey, we delve into the various versions and editions that have shaped the way we interact with technology. Licensing and activation processes, which underpin the legal and functional aspects of Windows, are also explored.

Moving on, we dissect the intricate components that form the very heart of Windows. We examine the Windows Kernel and System Services, the distinction between User Mode and Kernel Mode, the essence of Processes and Threads, and the pivotal role of Windows Services and Drivers in ensuring seamless operations.

Windows is renowned for its robust and versatile file systems, and in this collection, we explore the intricacies of NTFS, FAT, and ReFS. We also delve into the nuances of file and directory management, file permissions, security, data compression, and encryption.

The Windows Registry is a critical aspect of the OS, acting as its centralized database for system and application settings. In this guide, we take a deep dive into the structure and hives of the registry, understanding how to work with registry keys and values, and its role in managing system configuration.

Table of Contents

Chapter 1 Introduction to Windows Operating Systems

Windows Operating System Overview

1. What is Windows OS?

Answer: Windows is an operating system developed by Microsoft that provides a graphical user interface (GUI) for personal computers and servers.

2. What are the different versions of Windows for desktop computers?

Answer: Some popular versions include Windows 10, Windows 8.1, Windows 7, and Windows Vista.

3. How does Windows differ from other operating systems like Linux or macOS?

Answer: Windows is known for its user-friendly GUI, while Linux is open-source and offers more flexibility. macOS is designed for Apple hardware and is Unix-based.

4. What is the Windows Registry, and what is its purpose?

Answer: The Windows Registry is a hierarchical database that stores configuration settings and options for the operating system and installed applications.

5. How do you access the Task Manager in Windows, and what is its main purpose?

Answer: You can access Task Manager by pressing Ctrl+Shift+Esc or Ctrl+Alt+Delete and selecting it. It is used to manage running processes and applications and monitor system performance.

6. Explain the Windows File System (NTFS).

Answer: NTFS (New Technology File System) is the default file system for Windows, known for its security features, file compression, and support for large file sizes.

7. What is the purpose of the Windows System Restore feature?

Answer: System Restore allows users to revert the system's configuration and settings to a previous state, helping to recover from system issues or software conflicts.

8. What is the Windows Control Panel used for?

Answer: The Control Panel provides a centralized location for configuring and managing various system settings, including hardware, software, and user accounts.

9. How do you create a user account in Windows, and what are the different types of user accounts?

Answer: User accounts can be created through the Control Panel or Settings app. Windows supports three main types of user accounts: Administrator, Standard, and Guest.

10. What is the purpose of the Windows Event Viewer?

Answer: Event Viewer is a tool that records system, security, and application events, helping users and administrators diagnose system issues and monitor system health.

11. What is the Windows Update service, and why is it essential?

Answer: Windows Update is responsible for delivering security updates, bug fixes, and feature enhancements to keep the operating system secure and up to date.

12. How can you troubleshoot network connectivity issues in Windows?

Answer: Troubleshooting network issues involves checking network settings, resetting network adapters, and using built-in tools like Ping, ipconfig, and tracert.

13. Explain the concept of BitLocker in Windows.

Answer: BitLocker is a disk encryption program that helps protect data on Windows devices by encrypting the entire drive.

14. What is the Windows Task Scheduler, and how can it be used?

Answer: Task Scheduler allows users to automate the execution of tasks or programs at specific times or in response to events, helping to streamline system management.

15. What is the Blue Screen of Death (BSOD), and how can you troubleshoot it?

Answer: BSOD is an error screen that appears when Windows encounters a critical error. To troubleshoot it, note the error code, check for recent hardware or software changes, and use online resources.

16. What is Windows PowerShell, and how does it differ from the Command Prompt?

Answer: PowerShell is a more powerful scripting and automation tool compared to the Command Prompt. It uses a more versatile scripting language and cmdlets for system management.

17. What is the purpose of Windows Defender, and how does it protect the system?

Answer: Windows Defender is an integrated antivirus and antimalware program that helps protect the system from threats by providing real-time scanning and threat detection.

18. How can you create a backup of files and folders in Windows, and what tools can you use?

Answer: You can create backups using tools like File History, Backup and Restore, or third-party backup software. These tools help protect data from accidental loss.

19. Explain the difference between 32-bit and 64-bit versions of Windows.

Answer: 32-bit Windows can address up to 4GB of RAM, while 64-bit Windows supports larger memory and is more efficient for modern hardware.

20. How can you enable Remote Desktop in Windows, and what is it used for?

Answer: To enable Remote Desktop, go to System Properties and enable the feature. Remote Desktop allows users to access and control a Windows system remotely, which is useful for remote administration and support.

History and Evolution of Windows

1. When was the first version of Windows released, and what was it called?

Answer: The first version of Windows, Windows 1.0, was released on November 20, 1985.

2. What was the primary purpose of Windows 1.0, and how did it differ from MS-DOS?

Answer: Windows 1.0 introduced a graphical user interface (GUI) to MS-DOS-based systems, making it easier for users to interact with their computers using a mouse and windows.

3. What was the first 32-bit version of Windows, and when was it released?

Answer: Windows 95 was the first 32-bit version of Windows, and it was released on August 24, 1995.

4. What was the significance of Windows 3.1 in the evolution of Windows?

Answer: Windows 3.1 was the first widely successful version of Windows and introduced features like TrueType fonts, multimedia support, and improved performance.

5. Which version of Windows introduced the Start menu, and in what year?

Answer: The Start menu was introduced in Windows 95, released in 1995.

6. When did Microsoft release Windows 98, and what were some of its key features?

Answer: Windows 98 was released on June 25, 1998. It featured improved hardware support, the Windows Driver Model (WDM), and the ability to browse the web using Internet Explorer.

7. What was Windows Me (Windows Millennium Edition), and why was it not well-received?

Answer: Windows Me was released in 2000 and was intended for home users. It was criticized for its instability and lack of significant improvements.

8. What was the major change introduced in Windows 2000, and in which year was it released?

Answer: Windows 2000, released in 2000, was a significant release as it merged the consumer and business lines of Windows, providing a more stable and secure platform.

9. Which Windows version replaced Windows 9x and was based on the Windows NT kernel?

Answer: Windows XP replaced Windows 9x and was based on the Windows NT kernel. It was released in 2001.

10. What is the significance of Windows Vista, and when was it released?

Answer: Windows Vista, released in 2007, introduced a new GUI, enhanced security features, and improvements in search functionality.

11. What is the Windows Aero user interface, and which version of Windows introduced it?

Answer: Windows Aero is a graphical user interface introduced in Windows Vista, featuring translucent windows, live thumbnails, and visual effects.

12. When was Windows 7 released, and what made it popular among users?

Answer: Windows 7 was released in 2009 and gained popularity due to its improved performance, stability, and user-friendly features.

13. What was Windows 8 known for, and how did it differ from previous versions?

Answer: Windows 8, released in 2012, featured a touch-optimized interface with live tiles but received criticism for its departure from the traditional Start menu.

14. What is the Windows NT family of operating systems, and how did it contribute to Windows' evolution?Answer: The Windows NT family includes versions like Windows NT 4.0, 2000, XP, and later. It brought stability, security, and support for multiple processors to the Windows platform.

15. When was Windows 10 released, and what are some of its key features?

Answer: Windows 10 was released in 2015 and introduced a unified platform for PCs, tablets, and smartphones, along with the return of the Start menu.

16. What is the Windows Insider Program, and how does it relate to Windows development?

Answer: The Windows Insider Program allows users to test pre-release versions of Windows and provide feedback to help improve the operating system.

17. How has Windows evolved to embrace cloud computing and services?

Answer: Windows has integrated cloud services, such as OneDrive and Azure, for data storage, synchronization, and access to cloud-based applications.

18. What is the Long-Term Servicing Channel (LTSC) version of Windows, and how does it differ from regular Windows releases?

Answer: LTSC versions of Windows are designed for critical systems and receive long-term support with minimal feature updates, focusing on stability.

19. What are some recent developments in Windows, such as the introduction of Windows 11, and what are their key features?

Answer: Windows 11, released in 2021, introduces a redesigned Start menu, enhanced gaming features, and improved window management.

20. How has the Windows operating system contributed to the growth and success of Microsoft as a company?Answer: Windows has been a cornerstone of Microsoft's success, helping the company establish itself as a leading technology provider and shaping the personal computing industry.

Windows Versions and Editions

1. What is the difference between a Windows version and a Windows edition?

Answer: A Windows version refers to the specific release of Windows (e.g., Windows 10), while a Windows edition refers to the variations of a version, each with different features (e.g., Windows 10 Home, Pro, Enterprise).

2. Name some popular versions of Windows for personal computers and their release years.

Answer: Examples include Windows 95 (1995), Windows XP (2001), Windows 7 (2009), Windows 8 (2012), Windows 10 (2015), and Windows 11 (2021).

3. What is the primary target audience for Windows Home editions, and what are their key features?

Answer: Windows Home editions are aimed at consumers. They offer essential features like the Start menu, Cortana, and Windows Store access.

4. Which Windows edition is designed for business and professional users, and what features differentiate it from Home editions?

Answer: Windows Pro is designed for business and professional users. It includes features like BitLocker, Hyper-V, Remote Desktop, and Group Policy management.

5. What is Windows Enterprise, and what additional features does it offer compared to Windows Pro?

Answer: Windows Enterprise is designed for large organizations. It includes features like Windows To Go, DirectAccess, and AppLocker for enhanced security and manageability.

6. Explain the significance of Windows Education editions and their primary target audience.

Answer: Windows Education editions are designed for educational institutions. They include features to support teachers and students, such as shared devices and Microsoft Classroom integration.

7. What is Windows S mode, and how does it differ from other Windows editions?

Answer: Windows 10 in S mode is a streamlined version that only allows apps from the Microsoft Store to be installed, enhancing security and performance.

8. Describe the purpose of Windows LTSC (Long-Term Servicing Channel) editions and who benefits from them.

Answer: LTSC editions are intended for critical systems that require long-term stability and minimal feature updates. They are often used in industrial and medical settings.

9. What are N and KN editions of Windows, and why do they exist?

Answer: N and KN editions are specialized versions of Windows without certain multimedia features, designed for regions where legal requirements necessitate their exclusion.

10. How do Windows Server editions differ from Windows client editions in terms of usage and features?Answer: Windows Server editions are designed for server environments, offering features like Active Directory, server roles, and remote desktop services for centralized management.

11. What is Windows IoT, and which industries or use cases typically rely on it?

Answer: Windows IoT (Internet of Things) is designed for embedded and IoT devices, including industries like manufacturing, healthcare, and retail.

12. When was Windows 10 S introduced, and what made it different from other Windows 10 editions?

Answer: Windows 10 S was introduced in 2017, designed to offer a secure and streamlined experience with only Microsoft Store apps.

13. Which Windows edition includes specialized features for creativity and content creation, and what are some of these features?

Answer: Windows 10 Creators Update introduced features like 3D Paint and enhanced gaming performance for creative users.

14. What is Windows 10X, and how does it differ from traditional Windows 10 editions?

Answer: Windows 10X was developed for dual-screen and foldable devices, featuring a simplified user interface and improved touch and pen input support.

15. How does Windows 11 differ from Windows 10, and what are some of its key features?

Answer: Windows 11 introduced a redesigned Start menu, new window management features, and enhanced gaming capabilities.

16. What are the main features of Windows Embedded editions and which industries often use them?

Answer: Windows Embedded editions offer customizable solutions for industries like retail, healthcare, and automotive, with features like lockdown and device management.

17. What is the purpose of Windows 365, and how does it relate to Windows editions?

Answer: Windows 365 is a cloud-based service that allows businesses to stream Windows desktops to their employees, providing flexibility and remote access to Windows editions.

18. Explain the Windows as a Service (WaaS) model and how it affects the release and update process for Windows editions.

Answer: WaaS is a model where Windows receives regular feature updates, ensuring that users have access to the latest features, security patches, and improvements.

19. What is the difference between Windows Home and Windows Home Single Language editions?

Answer: Windows Home Single Language editions are targeted at specific regions and come with a single language pre-installed, while Windows Home allows language selection.

20. How does Windows ARM-based editions differ from Windows editions for x86/x64 architecture, and why are they significant?

Answer: Windows ARM-based editions are designed for devices with ARM processors, providing longer battery life and improved efficiency compared to x86/x64 editions.

Licensing and Activation

1. What is software licensing, and why is it important for Windows?

Answer: Software licensing is the legal framework that governs how Windows can be used. It ensures compliance with Microsoft's terms and conditions.

2. What is the purpose of Windows activation, and when does it occur?

Answer: Windows activation is the process of validating the software's legitimacy. It typically occurs during the installation or when a significant hardware change is detected.

3. What is the difference between a Retail and OEM license for Windows?

Answer: Retail licenses are transferable between computers, while OEM licenses are tied to the hardware they are initially installed on and are non-transferable.

4. Explain the concept of Product Keys in Windows licensing.

Answer: Product Keys are alphanumeric codes that users enter during installation to activate Windows. They serve as proof of ownership.

5. What is Volume Licensing, and for whom is it suitable?

Answer: Volume Licensing is designed for organizations purchasing multiple licenses. It offers flexibility and cost savings for businesses, schools, and government entities.

6. How does the Genuine Advantage program relate to Windows activation and validation?

Answer: The Windows Genuine Advantage program aimed to reduce software piracy by requiring validation of genuine Windows installations.

7. What is Key Management Service (KMS), and how is it used for Windows activation?

Answer: KMS is a service that allows organizations to activate Windows on their own network. It requires a minimum number of clients to activate Windows.

8. How does Windows Activation work in Windows 10 and later versions compared to earlier Windows releases?

Answer: In Windows 10 and later, activation is often handled automatically through digital entitlement, based on hardware and previous activation status.

9. What is a Multiple Activation Key (MAK), and when is it commonly used in Windows activation?

Answer: A MAK is used for one-time activation of multiple computers. It's a method employed by organizations with a smaller number of machines.

10. What is the purpose of the Microsoft Activation Center, and when is it typically used?

Answer: The Microsoft Activation Center assists users and organizations in activating Windows, especially in cases where online activation is not feasible.

11. What is Windows Genuine Advantage (WGA), and why did it receive criticism from users?

Answer: WGA was a program designed to validate genuine Windows installations but was criticized for generating false positives and inconveniencing legitimate users.

12. What is the role of the Windows Digital License in activation, and how does it work?

Answer: The Windows Digital License (formerly known as a digital entitlement) links the activation status to the hardware, allowing for automatic reactivation.

13. What are the consequences of running a non-genuine (unlicensed) version of Windows?

Answer: Running a non-genuine version may result in reduced functionality, periodic reminders to activate, and ineligibility for updates and support.

14. How can Windows be activated in a scenario where the internet connection is not available?

Answer: Windows can be activated by phone using the Microsoft Activation Center when an internet connection is not available.

15. Explain the concept of Windows Genuine Advantage Notifications and its purpose.

Answer: Windows Genuine Advantage Notifications was a program that alerted users if their Windows installation was not genuine, prompting them to take action.

16. What is the purpose of the Windows Activation Technologies in recent Windows versions?

Answer: Windows Activation Technologies is designed to reduce software piracy by enforcing genuine software usage.

17. How does the digital licensing model simplify activation for users and organizations?

Answer: Digital licensing eliminates the need for entering product keys and enables automatic activation based on hardware and previous activation status.

18. What is the role of the Windows Product Activation (WPA) technology in Windows activation?

Answer: WPA is a technology that verifies the authenticity of Windows installations to prevent unauthorized use.

19. How can businesses manage their Windows activations efficiently when deploying Windows to multiple devices?

Answer: Businesses can use tools like the Volume Activation Management Tool (VAMT) to manage and monitor activations in a centralized manner.

20. Explain the difference between Windows activation and Windows validation.

Answer: Activation is the process of proving that Windows is genuine, while validation is the ongoing verification of Windows authenticity. Activation typically occurs once, while validation may happen regularly.

ONLINE RESOURCES

Practice Paper Link: https://forms.gle/6suqtG5GKb7J63dr6

QR Code:

Video Link: https://www.youtube.com/playlist?list=PLzlh_31VWEFqAd8JlYri0rF5l14cV1XoS

QR Code:

Chapter 2 Windows Components

Windows Kernel and System Services

1. What is the Windows kernel, and what is its primary function?

Answer: The Windows kernel is the core component of the Windows operating system, responsible for managing system resources and providing a foundation for running applications.

2. Explain the role of the Executive in the Windows kernel.

Answer: The Executive is a part of the kernel that manages processes, threads, and other essential system resources.

3. What is the Windows Executive's role in process management?

Answer: The Executive creates and manages processes, handles thread scheduling, and maintains the Object Manager namespace.

4. What are Windows system services, and why are they important?

Answer: Windows system services are background processes that provide essential operating system functionality. They are crucial for system stability and application support.

5. How does the Windows kernel manage memory in a multitasking environment?

Answer: The Windows kernel uses virtual memory and paging to allocate and manage physical and virtual memory for processes and the system.

6. What is the purpose of the Windows Plug and Play Manager, and how does it benefit users?

Answer: The Plug and Play Manager automates the detection and configuration of hardware devices, making it easier for users to add and remove devices.

7. What is the Windows File System Runtime Library, and how does it facilitate file operations?

Answer: The File System Runtime Library provides a set of functions for managing file I/O, including reading, writing, and file manipulation.

8. Explain the role of the Windows Security Reference Monitor in the kernel.

Answer: The Security Reference Monitor enforces access control to ensure that processes and users only access resources they are authorized to use.

9. What is the purpose of the Windows I/O Manager, and how does it interact with device drivers?

Answer: The I/O Manager abstracts communication with device drivers, simplifying I/O operations for applications and ensuring compatibility with various hardware.

10. What is the Windows Object Manager, and how does it manage system resources?

Answer: The Object Manager maintains an organized namespace for system objects, like files, processes, and synchronization objects, providing a uniform way to access them.

11. What is the role of the Windows Registry in system services, and how is it organized?

Answer: The Registry is a hierarchical database that stores configuration settings and information about system and application components.

12. How does Windows handle interposes communication (IPC) between processes and threads?

Answer: Windows provides various mechanisms for IPC, including named pipes, message passing, shared memory, and remote procedure calls (RPC).

13. What is the Windows Power Manager, and how does it optimize power consumption?

Answer: The Power Manager controls power policies and settings to optimize power consumption, extending battery life on laptops and reducing energy usage.

14. What is the Windows Task Scheduler, and how does it manage scheduled tasks and processes?

Answer: The Task Scheduler allows users to automate the execution of tasks, scripts, and programs at specified times or in response to events.

15. How does the Windows Performance Monitor assist in system monitoring and troubleshooting?

Answer: The Performance Monitor tracks various system metrics and allows users to create custom performance counters to diagnose and optimize system performance.

16. Explain the concept of a Windows service and how it differs from a regular application.

Answer:A Windows service is a background process that runs without user interaction and can be set to start automatically when the system boots. It operates independently of user sessions.

17. What is the role of the Windows Device Manager, and how does it assist in managing hardware components?

Answer: The Device Manager provides a centralized location for managing and configuring hardware devices, such as updating drivers and troubleshooting device issues.

18. How does the Windows Task Manager help users manage processes and system performance?

Answer: Task Manager allows users to view and manage running processes, monitor system performance, and terminate unresponsive applications.

19. What is the Windows Error Reporting service, and how does it benefit the operating system's reliability?Answer: The Windows Error Reporting service collects error information from users and sends it to Microsoft for analysis, helping identify and fix system issues.

20. How does the Windows Kernel Transaction Manager (KTM) support data integrity in file operations?

Answer:KTM enables applications to perform multiple file operations as a single transaction, ensuring that changes are either committed entirely or rolled back in case of failure.

21. Explain the role of the Windows Print Spooler service in managing print jobs.

Answer: The Print Spooler service manages print jobs by queuing them, managing print devices, and ensuring the orderly printing of documents.

22. What is the Windows Remote Procedure Call (RPC) service, and how does it facilitate interposes communication?

Answer: The RPC service allows applications to execute code on remote systems, enabling distributed and client-server communication.

23. How does Windows handle hardware interrupt requests, and what is the role of the Windows Hardware Abstraction Layer (HAL)?

Answer: Windows uses interrupt request lines (IRQs) to manage hardware interrupts, and the HAL abstracts hardware-specific details to ensure compatibility with different hardware platforms.

24. What is the Windows Management Instrumentation (WMI), and how does it assist in system management?Answer:WMI provides a standard interface for system management tasks, such as monitoring hardware, gathering system information, and configuring system settings.

25. How does Windows handle synchronization and concurrency control for multi-threaded processes and multi-core processors?

Answer: Windows provides synchronization mechanisms like mutexes, semaphores, and critical sections, and it utilizes the Windows Scheduler to manage thread execution on multi-core processors.

User Mode and Kernel Mode

1. What is the difference between User Mode and Kernel Mode in an operating system?

Answer: User Mode is a restricted mode where user applications run, while Kernel Mode is a privileged mode where the operating system's core functions operate.

2. What are the key responsibilities of User Mode in an operating system?

Answer: User Mode is responsible for running user applications, managing user processes, and handling user-level system calls.

3. What are the key responsibilities of Kernel Mode in an operating system?

Answer: Kernel Mode is responsible for executing critical system functions, managing hardware, and handling privileged system calls.

4. How does the operating system transition from User Mode to Kernel Mode?

Answer: The transition from User Mode to Kernel Mode occurs when a user application makes a system call, triggering a switch to Kernel Mode for the execution of the requested operation.

5. What is the primary reason for having distinct User Mode and Kernel Mode in an operating system?

Answer: Separating User Mode from Kernel Mode helps protect the integrity and stability of the operating system by preventing user applications from directly accessing hardware or executing privileged operations.

6. How does an operating system maintain memory protection between User Mode and Kernel Mode?

Answer: The operating system uses hardware features like Memory Management Units (MMUs) to enforce memory protection, ensuring that user processes cannot access kernel memory.

7. What is a system call, and how is it related to transitioning between User Mode and Kernel Mode?

Answer:A system call is a controlled way for user applications to request services or operations from the kernel. It triggers the transition from User Mode to Kernel Mode.

8. How does a context switch occur, and what is its role in managing User Mode and Kernel Mode transitions?

Answer:A context switch is the process of saving the current state of a running process in User Mode and loading the state of another process in Kernel Mode. It allows the operating system to manage multiple processes effectively.

9. What are the implications of running in Kernel Mode, in terms of hardware access and system control?

Answer: Kernel Mode has unrestricted access to hardware and can execute privileged instructions, control device drivers, and manage system resources.

10. What is the role of the System Control Block (SCB) or Process Control Block (PCB) in User Mode and Kernel Mode transitions?

Answer: The SCB or PCB contains essential information about a process, including its current state and execution context. It is used in context switches during mode transitions.

11. What is the Blue Screen of Death (BSOD) in Windows, and why does it appear in Kernel Mode errors?

Answer: The BSOD is a system error screen that appears when the operating system encounters a critical error in Kernel Mode, indicating a potentially severe issue that requires system diagnostics.

12. Can you explain the "ring" privilege levels in operating systems, and how do they relate to User Mode and Kernel Mode?

Answer: Rings represent different privilege levels in an operating system, with Ring 0 being the most privileged (Kernel Mode) and Ring 3 being the least privileged (User Mode). Ring transitions occur to switch between these levels.

13. How does a system call handler facilitate communication between User Mode and Kernel Mode?

Answer:A system call handler is a function within the kernel that processes system calls initiated from User Mode, providing the requested service or operation.

14. What are some common examples of system calls that initiate a transition from User Mode to Kernel Mode?Answer: Examples include file I/O operations, process creation and termination, memory allocation, and device control.

15. How does the operating system prevent user applications from directly accessing hardware devices in User Mode?

Answer: The operating system enforces hardware access control by allowing only Kernel Mode components to interact with hardware devices. User applications must make system calls to access hardware resources.

16. Explain how page table structures are used to enforce memory protection between User Mode and Kernel Mode.

Answer: Page table structures are used to map virtual addresses to physical memory addresses. Kernel-mode code has its own set of page tables, separate from those used by user-mode code, ensuring that they cannot directly access each other's memory.

17. What happens when a user application attempts to execute a privileged instruction in User Mode?

Answer: When a user application tries to execute a privileged instruction in User Mode, it triggers a hardware exception or trap, leading to a context switch to Kernel Mode to handle the exception.

18. How does a microkernel-based operating system architecture impact the separation of User Mode and Kernel Mode?

Answer: Microkernel-based architectures emphasize a minimalistic kernel in Kernel Mode, pushing many traditional operating system services and drivers into User Mode for modularity and security.

19. What are the potential security risks associated with transitioning between User Mode and Kernel Mode?Answer: Security risks include privilege escalation, denial-of-service attacks, and malicious system call exploitation. Proper security mechanisms are needed to mitigate these risks.

20. Can you describe how user-level threads (ULTs) and kernel-level threads (KLTs) relate to User Mode and Kernel Mode?

Answer:ULTs are managed entirely in User Mode, while KLTs are managed in Kernel Mode. ULTs may be implemented on top of KLTs, allowing user applications to create and manage threads without requiring Kernel Mode switches for thread management.

21. What is the role of a protection ring in an operating system's security model, and why are there typically multiple rings?

Answer: Protection rings define privilege levels in an operating system, with lower ring numbers indicating higher privilege. Multiple rings allow for different levels of access control, separation, and security.

22. How does virtualization technology impact the separation of User Mode and Kernel Mode in virtualized environments?

Answer: Virtualization technology introduces a hypervisor layer that provides multiple virtual machines (VMs), each with its own User Mode and Kernel Mode, isolated from the host operating system.

23. Explain the concept of a "trap door" or "back door" in the context of User Mode and Kernel Mode security.Answer:A trap door or back door is a hidden or undocumented method to gain unauthorized access to a system. In the context of security, it represents a security vulnerability that could potentially allow an attacker to bypass the User Mode-Kernel Mode separation.

24. What are some of the challenges in designing an operating system to manage User Mode and Kernel Mode effectively?

Answer: Challenges include balancing performance with security, handling hardware exceptions gracefully, and maintaining compatibility with a wide range of hardware devices.

25. How does the concept of context switching between User Mode and Kernel Mode affect system performance, and what strategies can be employed to minimize its impact?

Answer: Context switching introduces some overhead in terms of time and resources. Strategies to minimize its impact include optimizing scheduling algorithms, reducing the frequency of context switches, and utilizing efficient data structures for context storage.

Processes and Threads

1. What is a process in Windows, and how does it relate to applications?

Answer:A process is an independent program that runs in its own memory space. It includes the application code, data, and system resources needed for its execution.

2. What is the primary purpose of a process in an operating system?

Answer: The primary purpose of a process is to provide isolation and resource management for running applications. It ensures that one application cannot interfere with the memory or execution of another.

3. Can multiple processes run concurrently in Windows, and how does the operating system manage their execution?

Answer: Yes, multiple processes can run concurrently in Windows. The operating system schedules and manages their execution using the Windows Scheduler.

4. What is a thread, and how does it differ from a process?

Answer:A thread is the smallest unit of execution within a process. Threads within the same process share the same memory space and resources, making them more lightweight than processes.

5. What are the advantages of using threads within a process, as opposed to using multiple processes?

Answer: Threads within a process can share data and communicate more efficiently, reducing the overhead of inter-process communication. They are also more lightweight and consume fewer system resources.

6. What is the difference between a user-level thread and a kernel-level thread in Windows?

Answer: User-level threads are managed entirely by user-level libraries and are not visible to the kernel. Kernel-level threads are managed by the operating system kernel and can take full advantage of multi-core processors.

7. How does the Windows operating system create and manage threads within a process?

Answer: Windows provides API functions, such as CreateThread, to create and manage threads within a process. The operating system schedules and manages these threads using the Windows Scheduler.

8. What is the purpose of the Thread Local Storage (TLS) in Windows threads?

Answer: Thread Local Storage provides each thread within a process with its own data storage, allowing thread-specific data to be stored and accessed without conflicts.

9. Can a single process have multiple threads running concurrently on different processor cores?

Answer: Yes, a single process can have multiple threads running concurrently on different processor cores if the system is multi-core or multi-processor.

10. What is a thread pool, and why is it used in Windows applications?

Answer:A thread pool is a collection of threads that can be used by an application to perform tasks in parallel, reducing the overhead of creating and destroying threads for each task.

11. How does Windows handle thread synchronization and coordination in multi-threaded applications?

Answer: Windows provides synchronization mechanisms such as mutexes, semaphores, critical sections, and events to coordinate the execution of threads and prevent data conflicts.

12. What is the main function of the Windows Scheduler in managing processes and threads?

Answer: The Windows Scheduler is responsible for determining which threads and processes should execute and for how long, based on priority, time-slicing, and other factors.

13. What are the differences between foreground and background threads in Windows?

Answer: Foreground threads keep the application alive, and the application won't exit until all foreground threads have completed. Background threads do not prevent the application from exiting.

14. How does exception handling work in multi-threaded applications, and what are thread-specific exceptions?Answer: Exception handling in multi-threaded applications can capture exceptions raised in a specific thread. These are referred to as thread-specific exceptions.

15. What is a thread's execution context, and how does it affect context switching?

Answer:A thread's execution context includes its register values, program counter, and stack pointer. Context switching involves saving and restoring these values when switching between threads.

16. Can you explain the concept of thread priority and its significance in thread scheduling?

Answer: Thread priority determines the order in which threads are scheduled for execution. Threads with higher priority are given preference by the Windows Scheduler.

17. What is a deadlock in the context of multi-threaded applications, and how can it be prevented or resolved?Answer:A deadlock occurs when two or more threads are unable to proceed because they are waiting for resources held by each other. Deadlocks can be prevented through proper synchronization and resource allocation strategies.

18. What are the differences between pre-emptive and cooperative multi-threading in Windows?

Answer: Pre-emptive multi-threading allows the operating system to forcibly switch between threads, ensuring fairness and responsiveness. Cooperative multi-threading relies on threads voluntarily yielding control to other threads.

19. How does Windows support parallel processing and multi-threaded applications on multi-core processors?Answer: Windows can assign threads to multiple processor cores, allowing applications to take advantage of parallelism. The Windows Scheduler handles core assignment.

20. What is a critical section, and how does it help prevent data conflicts in multi-threaded applications?

Answer:A critical section is a region of code that only one thread can execute at a time. It helps protect shared resources from simultaneous access by multiple threads.

21. What is the purpose of thread-local storage in multi-threaded applications, and how is it accessed in Windows?Answer: Thread-local storage allows each thread to have its own copy of data. In Windows, it can be accessed using the TlsAlloc, TlsGetValue, and TlsSetValue functions.

22. How does thread prioritization work in Windows, and what factors influence a thread's priority?

Answer: Thread prioritization in Windows is influenced by factors like thread priority level, quantum length, and process priority class.

23. What is a thread pool in Windows, and how does it improve performance in multi-threaded applications?Answer:A thread pool is a collection of pre-allocated threads that can be used to execute tasks. It improves performance by reducing the overhead of thread creation and destruction.

24. What are user-mode and kernel-mode threads, and how do they differ in terms of functionality and privilege levels?

Answer: User-mode threads are managed by user-level libraries and are not as privileged as kernel-mode threads, which are managed by the operating system and have direct hardware access.

25. How does thread migration between processor cores affect performance in multi-threaded applications, and how is it controlled in Windows?

Answer: Thread migration can affect performance due to cache locality. Windows provides control over thread affinity to minimize migration.

26. Can you explain the concept of thread deadlock and provide an example of a situation that could lead to a deadlock?

Answer: Thread deadlock occurs when two or more threads are waiting for resources that are held by each other, resulting in a standstill. For example, if Thread A holds Resource X and waits for Resource Y, while Thread B holds Resource Y and waits for Resource X, a deadlock can occur.

27. What are thread handles in Windows, and how are they used in managing threads?

Answer: Thread handles are objects that represent threads in Windows. They are used to perform operations on threads, such as creating, suspending, resuming, or terminating them.

28. How does Windows handle thread prioritization when multiple threads are competing for execution time?Answer: Windows uses a priority-based scheduling algorithm, where threads with higher priority levels are given preference in execution. However, all threads are subject to time-slicing to ensure fairness.

29. What is the relationship between thread affinity and thread migration, and why is it important in multi-threaded applications?

Answer: Thread affinity controls the assignment of threads to specific processor cores. Managing affinity can minimize thread migration, which can impact cache performance and, thus, application speed.

30. How does Windows handle thread termination and resource cleanup when a thread finishes its execution?Answer: When a thread completes execution, Windows takes care of resource cleanup, including memory deallocation and the release of system resources. This ensures a clean termination process.

Windows Services and Drivers

1. What is a Windows service, and how does it differ from a regular application?

Answer:A Windows service is a background application that can run without user interaction. Unlike regular applications, services typically start automatically and can run even if no user is logged in.

2. What is the primary purpose of a Windows service in the operating system?

Answer: Windows services provide essential system functionality, such as managing hardware devices, network services, security, and background tasks.

3. Can you explain the difference between a local service and a network service in Windows?

Answer: Local services run with the least privileges on the local system, while network services may access network resources. Network services are typically more privileged and require network access permissions.

4. What is the Windows Service Control Manager (SCM), and what is its role in managing services?

Answer: The SCM is responsible for managing and controlling services. It starts, stops, and configures services, and it ensures they run correctly.

5. How do you access the Windows Services Control Manager (SCM) to view and manage services?

Answer: You can access the SCM through the "services.msc" console, which provides a graphical interface for viewing and configuring services.

6. Can a Windows service interact with the desktop, and under what circumstances is this allowed?

Answer: By default, services do not interact with the desktop to enhance security and stability. However, this feature can be enabled for specific services when necessary.

7. What is the difference between an automatic, manual, and disabled startup type for services?

Answer:

"Automatic" services start automatically when the system boots.

"Manual" services must be started manually by the user or an application.

"Disabled" services are prevented from starting and cannot be manually started.

8. How does the "Recovery" tab in service properties help manage service failures in Windows?

Answer: The "Recovery" tab allows you to define actions that should be taken if a service fails. You can specify whether the service should be restarted, the system should be rebooted, or a specific program should be run in response to a failure.

9. What is the Windows Event Log, and how is it related to services and service-related events?

Answer: The Windows Event Log is a centralized repository for recording system and service events. Services can write event log entries to provide information about their status and errors.

10. Can you explain the concept of service dependencies in Windows and why they are important?

Answer: Service dependencies specify which services a particular service depends on. This is crucial for ensuring that dependent services are started before the service that relies on them.

11. How do you configure a service to run with specific user credentials or permissions?

Answer: You can specify the user account and permissions under which a service should run in the service's properties, typically in the "Log On" tab.

12. What is the significance of the Windows Services Recovery Actions and what types of recovery actions are available?

Answer: Recovery actions define what happens when a service fails. Windows provides options such as restarting the service, restarting the computer, or running a specific program.

13. What is the difference between a Windows service and a Windows scheduled task?

Answer: Services run in the background, often continuously, and may perform system-level tasks. Scheduled tasks are specific jobs executed at scheduled times or intervals.

14. How can you programmatically interact with Windows services, for example, to start or stop them?

Answer: You can use the Windows Service Control Manager (SCM) API or command-line tools like sc or PowerShell cmdlets like Start-Service and Stop-Service to interact with services programmatically.

15. What are the various states a Windows service can be in, and what do they signify?

Answer: Windows services can be in states like "Running" (active and working), "Stopped" (not running), "Paused" (suspended but not terminated), and "Starting" or "Stopping" (currently being started or stopped).

16. What is the "Delayed Start" option for services, and when is it useful?

Answer: Delayed start allows a service to start after other critical services have started, reducing system boot time and ensuring a smoother boot process.

Windows Drivers:

1. What is a Windows driver, and how does it differ from a service?

Answer:A Windows driver is a software component that enables hardware devices to communicate with the operating system. Unlike services, drivers are tightly coupled with hardware and manage its operation.

2. What are the main types of Windows drivers, and how do they differ from one another?

Answer: Windows drivers include user-mode drivers, kernel-mode drivers, and file system drivers. User-mode drivers run in user space, kernel-mode drivers in kernel space, and file system drivers control file access.

3. How does Windows Plug and Play (PnP) work in relation to drivers and hardware devices?

Answer: PnP is a feature that automatically detects and installs drivers for new hardware devices, simplifying the process of adding or replacing hardware.

4. Can you explain the difference between a monolithic driver and a microkernel driver in Windows?

Answer:A monolithic driver combines all driver components in a single module. In contrast, a microkernel driver separates components into user and kernel mode for improved stability and security.

5. What are WHQL-certified drivers, and why are they important for hardware compatibility in Windows?Answer:WHQL (Windows Hardware Quality Labs) certification ensures that drivers meet Microsoft's standards for compatibility and reliability, reducing the risk of system instability or crashes.

6. How does Windows handle driver updates and installations, and how can users install or update drivers manually?

Answer: Windows can automatically download and install driver updates through Windows Update. Users can also manually install or update drivers through Device Manager or by downloading them from the manufacturer's website.

7. What is the role of the Windows Driver Model (WDM) in ensuring driver compatibility and stability?

Answer: The WDM standardizes driver development and allows for easier interoperability and compatibility with different Windows versions.

8. What is the purpose of the Device Manager in Windows, and how can it be used to manage drivers?

Answer: The Device Manager is used to view, manage, update, and troubleshoot hardware devices and their associated drivers in Windows.

9. How does Windows handle driver signing and driver signature enforcement for security and stability?

Answer: Windows requires drivers to be digitally signed to ensure their authenticity. Driver signature enforcement prevents the loading of unsigned or tampered drivers.

10. What is a driver package in Windows, and how does it simplify driver installation?

Answer:A driver package is a collection of driver files and installation metadata. It simplifies driver installation and allows for automated driver updates.

11. What is the Windows Hardware Abstraction Layer (HAL), and how does it facilitate driver development?Answer: The HAL abstracts hardware-specific details and provides a uniform interface for driver developers, making it easier to write hardware-independent drivers.

12. How does Windows handle driver versioning and provide compatibility with multiple hardware devices?Answer: Windows uses an INF file to define driver metadata and device compatibility, enabling a single driver to work with multiple hardware devices.

13. What is the Windows Driver Signature Enforcement policy, and how can it be modified by users or administrators?

Answer: Driver Signature Enforcement is a security feature that can be temporarily or permanently disabled by administrators, but it's recommended to keep it enabled for security.

14. Can you explain the role of the Windows Print Spooler service and its interaction with printer drivers?

Answer: The Print Spooler service manages print jobs and interfaces with printer drivers to send data to printers. It handles the printing process on behalf of applications.

ONLINE RESOURCES

Practice Paper Link: https://forms.gle/87YpdsBs3DwsRV3PA

QR Code :

Video Link: https://www.youtube.com/playlist?list=PLzlh_31VWEFpUeiz4FrASN1AU0es5WtcH

QR Code :

Chapter 3 File Systems and File Management

Windows File Systems (NTFS, FAT, ReFS)

1. What is NTFS, and why is it an improvement over older file systems like FAT?

Answer:NTFS is the New Technology File System used in Windows. It offers advanced features like file and folder permissions, encryption, compression, and journaling, making it more secure and robust compared to FAT.

2. What is file and folder compression in NTFS, and how does it work?

Answer:NTFS allows files and folders to be compressed to save disk space. It uses an algorithm to reduce the size of stored data, which is transparent to users.

3. Explain the concept of file and folder permissions in NTFS and how they enhance security.

Answer:NTFS provides access control through file and folder permissions, allowing administrators to specify who can read, write, modify, or execute files and folders. This enhances security and restricts unauthorized access.

4. What is NTFS journaling, and how does it benefit file system integrity and data recovery?

Answer:NTFS journaling logs file system changes, helping maintain file system integrity and simplifying data recovery after unexpected system crashes or power failures.

5. What is the Master File Table (MFT) in NTFS, and how does it organize file system metadata?

Answer: The MFT is a database in NTFS that stores metadata about files and directories. It organizes file attributes and file content pointers.

6. How does NTFS handle long file names and Unicode characters compared to FAT?

Answer:NTFS supports long file names and Unicode characters, while FAT has limitations on file name length and character encoding.

7. What is the maximum file size and volume size supported by NTFS?

Answer:NTFS supports extremely large file sizes (16 exabytes) and volume sizes (up to 256 terabytes).

8. How does NTFS handle file fragmentation, and what are the benefits of its file allocation strategy?

Answer:NTFS uses an efficient file allocation strategy to minimize fragmentation. It dynamically adjusts file allocation and optimizes disk usage.

9. Can you explain the concept of sparse files in NTFS and how they work?

Answer: Sparse files are files that contain large areas of zeros. NTFS allows these areas to be represented efficiently, saving disk space.

10. What is symbolic linking in NTFS, and how does it enable creating directory shortcuts?

Answer: Symbolic links are references to other files or directories. They allow for the creation of directory shortcuts, making it easier to navigate and organize files.

11. What are the different NTFS permission types, and how do they differ from one another?

Answer:NTFS provides various permission types, including Full Control, Modify, Read & Execute, Read, and Write, each granting different levels of access.

FAT (File Allocation Table):

1. What is FAT, and how does it differ from NTFS in terms of features and capabilities?

Answer:FAT is the File Allocation Table file system used in older Windows versions. It lacks the advanced features of NTFS, such as security, permissions, and journaling.

2. Can you explain the concept of the File Allocation Table (FAT) in the FAT file system?

Answer:FAT is a data structure that records information about the allocation of disk space to files and directories. It's used to keep track of clusters and their use.

3. What are the different versions of FAT, and how do they compare in terms of features and compatibility?Answer:FAT12, FAT16, and FAT32 are different versions of the FAT file system, with varying cluster sizes, file size limits, and compatibility.

4. What are the limitations of the FAT file system, particularly in terms of file size and volume size?

Answer:FAT has limitations on maximum file size (4 GB for FAT32) and volume size (2 TB for FAT32).

5. How does FAT handle file fragmentation, and why does it lead to performance issues on large volumes?

Answer:FAT does not manage file fragmentation efficiently, which can lead to performance issues on large volumes, as files are scattered across the disk.

6. What is the main advantage of using FAT over NTFS, and in what scenarios might FAT still be preferred?Answer:FAT is simple, compatible, and suitable for removable storage and older systems. It's preferred for certain devices like digital cameras and game consoles due to its broad compatibility.

ReFS (Resilient File System):

1. What is ReFS, and how does it aim to improve upon NTFS in Windows?

Answer: ReFS, the Resilient File System, is designed to address the limitations of NTFS, offering enhanced data integrity, scalability, and reliability.

2. How does ReFS improve data integrity and fault tolerance compared to NTFS?

Answer: ReFS includes features like checksums and integrity streams to detect and correct data corruption. It provides better fault tolerance and reliability.

3. What is block cloning in ReFS, and how does it optimize storage efficiency and performance?

Answer: Block cloning allows ReFS to reuse data blocks efficiently, reducing storage overhead and enhancing performance.

4. Can you explain the concept of data deduplication in ReFS and how it helps conserve storage space?

Answer: Data deduplication in ReFS identifies duplicate data blocks and stores them only once, conserving storage space.

5. How does ReFS handle file and directory structures, and what are the benefits of its storage architecture?Answer: ReFS simplifies file and directory structures, reducing the complexity of directory hierarchies and improving scalability.

6. What is the maximum file size and volume size supported by ReFS?

Answer: ReFS supports extremely large file sizes (up to 35 petabytes) and volume sizes (up to 18.4 million yottabytes).

7. How does ReFS support data scrubbing and automatic error correction to maintain data integrity?

Answer: ReFS uses scrubbing to detect and correct errors in stored data. It periodically scans and repairs data inconsistencies.

8. What is the integration between ReFS and the Windows Storage Spaces feature, and how does it enhance storage management?

Answer: ReFS is often used with Storage Spaces to provide a highly scalable and resilient storage solution. The combination offers enhanced manageability and protection.

9. How does ReFS handle the BitLocker encryption feature in Windows, and what are the security advantages?Answer: ReFS can work seamlessly with BitLocker encryption, offering enhanced data security and protection against unauthorized access.

10. What are the key differences between ReFS and NTFS in terms of scalability and data integrity?

Answer: ReFS offers better scalability, fault tolerance, and data integrity features compared to NTFS.

File and Directory Management

1. What is the primary purpose of a file system in an operating system like Windows?

Answer: The file system manages the organization, storage, and retrieval of files and directories, ensuring data persistence and accessibility.

2. Can you explain the difference between a file and a directory in Windows file systems?

Answer: Files are containers for data, while directories (folders) are organizational structures that contain files and other directories.

3. What is the Windows File Explorer, and how is it used for file and directory management?

Answer: Windows File Explorer is the graphical interface for managing files and directories. It allows users to create, move, copy, and delete files and directories.

4. How does the concept of a file extension in Windows help identify the type of a file?

Answer:A file extension, such as ".txt" or ".jpg," indicates the file type and is used by Windows to associate files with specific applications.

5. What are the different attributes that can be associated with files and directories in Windows, and what is their significance?

Answer: Attributes like "Read-Only," "Hidden," and "System" provide additional information about files and directories and can affect their behavior and visibility.

6. Can you explain the difference between a relative path and an absolute path when specifying file and directory locations?

Answer:A relative path is based on the current working directory, while an absolute path provides the full path from the root directory.

7. How does Windows handle long file names, and what are the limitations of file and path lengths?

Answer: Windows supports long file names (up to 260 characters) but has a maximum path length limitation of 260 characters.

8. What is the Recycle Bin in Windows, and how does it facilitate file recovery and deletion?

Answer: The Recycle Bin is a temporary storage area for deleted files. It allows users to restore deleted files and, if needed, permanently delete them.

9. How can you permanently delete a file in Windows without using the Recycle Bin?

Answer: You can permanently delete a file by holding down the "Shift" key while pressing the "Delete" key, bypassing the Recycle Bin.

10. What is file fragmentation, and how does it impact file access and system performance?

Answer: File fragmentation occurs when a file is divided into non-contiguous disk sectors. It can slow down file access and system performance.

11. How does the Windows search functionality work, and what are the search operators that can be used to refine searches?

Answer: Windows search indexes files and allows users to find them by using keywords, operators, and filters such as AND, OR, and NOT.

12. What are file permissions and access control lists (ACLs), and how are they used to secure files and directories?Answer: File permissions and ACLs determine who can access, modify, or delete files and directories. They are essential for securing data.

13. Can you explain the purpose of file timestamps in Windows, including the different types of timestamps?Answer: File timestamps include creation time, modification time, and access time. They provide information about a file's history and usage.

14. What is the difference between a file system and a file format, and how do they relate to each other?

Answer:A file system manages the structure and storage of files, while a file format specifies how data is stored within files. A file format is used within a file system to represent the file's content.

15. How does Windows handle file locking and file sharing among multiple users or applications?

Answer: Windows uses file locking mechanisms to prevent simultaneous write access by multiple users or applications, ensuring data integrity.

16. What is the "cut," "copy," and "paste" functionality used for in Windows file and directory management?Answer: These operations allow users to move or duplicate files and directories within or between directories.

17. How does Windows handle file system errors, and what is the purpose of the Check Disk (chkdsk) utility?Answer: Check Disk is used to scan and repair file system errors and bad sectors on a disk, ensuring file system integrity.

18. Can you explain the concept of symbolic links and hard links in Windows, and how do they differ?

Answer: Symbolic links are references to other files or directories, while hard links point to the same data as the original file. Hard links share the same file content, whereas symbolic links reference a target.

19. What is the purpose of a file property, and how can you view and modify file properties in Windows?

Answer: File properties contain information about a file, such as size, type, and location. You can view and modify them by right-clicking on a file and selecting "Properties."

20. How can you move or rename a file or directory in Windows using the Command Prompt or PowerShell?

Answer: You can use the "move" command (Cmd) or "Move-Item" cmdlet (PowerShell) to move or rename files and directories.

21. How does Windows handle file versioning and shadow copies, and what are their benefits for data recovery?Answer: Windows can create shadow copies, which are snapshots of files at specific points in time. They are used for data recovery and versioning.

22. What is the purpose of file compression, and how does it work in Windows?

Answer: File compression reduces the size of files to save disk space. Windows supports file compression through tools like NTFS compression and tools like "Compact" in PowerShell.

23. Can you explain the purpose of the "Recent Files" and "Recent Folders" features in Windows, and how do they help users access recent data?

Answer: These features provide quick access to recently accessed files and folders, making it easier for users to find and open their recent work.

24. How can you access and use the Windows command-line tools, such as "dir," "copy," "move," and "del," for file and directory management?

Answer: These command-line tools allow users to list files, copy, move, and delete files and directories from the Command Prompt.

25. What is the purpose of file archiving and compression utilities like "zip," "7-Zip," and "WinRAR," and how do they work in Windows?

Answer: These utilities are used to compress multiple files into a single archive file, reducing storage space and facilitating file sharing.

26. Can you explain the difference between a file copy and a file move operation in Windows?

Answer:A file copy operation duplicates a file to a new location, while a file move operation relocates a file from one location to another.

27. How does Windows handle file and folder access permissions, and how can you grant or restrict access to specific users or groups?

Answer: Windows uses access control lists (ACLs) and permissions to define who can access files and directories, with options to grant or deny access to users or groups.

28. What is the purpose of the "File History" feature in Windows, and how can it help users protect and recover their files?

Answer: File History is a backup and versioning feature that automatically backs up user files and allows for easy recovery of previous versions.

29. How does Windows handle file sorting and grouping in File Explorer, and what options are available for organizing files and folders?

Answer: Users can sort files by various criteria like name, date, and size, and group files by attributes like type or date to organize them effectively.

30. What are libraries in Windows, and how do they simplify file organization and access across multiple locations?

Answer: Libraries provide a way to access files and folders from different locations as a unified collection, making it easier to organize and access files.

File Permissions and Security

1. What are file permissions, and why are they important in an operating system?

Answer: File permissions define who can access, modify, and delete files and directories. They are essential for data security and access control.

2. Explain the three standard file permissions in Unix-like systems: read (r), write (w), and execute (x).

Answer: "Read" allows viewing file content, "write" allows modifying or creating files, and "execute" permits running a file as a program or script.

3. What are file permissions in Windows?

Answer: File permissions control who can access, modify, or execute files and folders on a Windows system.

4. Explain the difference between NTFS and share-level permissions.

Answer: NTFS permissions apply to individual files and folders, while share-level permissions control access to shared resources.

5. What are the basic NTFS permissions?

Answer: The basic NTFS permissions are Read, Write, and Execute (or Modify).

6. What is the difference between "Read" and "Read & Execute" permissions?

Answer: "Read" allows viewing file contents, while "Read & Execute" additionally allows running executable files.

7. How can you assign NTFS permissions to a user or group?

Answer: You can assign NTFS permissions through the Security tab of a file or folder's properties.

8. Explain the concept of inheritance in NTFS permissions.

Answer: Inheritance means that permissions applied to a parent folder are automatically passed down to its subfolders and files.

9. How do you break inheritance and set unique permissions on a folder in Windows?

Answer: You can break inheritance by going to the Advanced Security Settings and unchecking the "Inherit from parent" option.

10. What is the purpose of the "Traverse Folder" permission?

Answer: The "Traverse Folder" permission allows a user to navigate through folders to access the contents within.

11. What is the "Deny" permission and when should it be used?

Answer: The "Deny" permission explicitly denies a user access. It should be used sparingly to override specific permissions.

12. What is the Windows Security Identifier (SID)?

Answer: The SID is a unique identifier assigned to each user or group in Windows for security purposes.

13. How can you view the permissions assigned to a file or folder?

Answer: Right-click the file or folder, select Properties, and navigate to the Security tab.

14. Explain the purpose of the Windows built-in groups "Administrators" and "Users."

Answer: "Administrators" have full control over the system, while "Users" have more limited permissions.

15. What is UAC (User Account Control), and why is it important for security?

Answer: UAC is a Windows security feature that prompts users for permission when performing administrative tasks, reducing the risk of unauthorized changes.

16. What is EFS (Encrypting File System) in Windows?

Answer: EFS is a feature that allows files and folders to be encrypted to protect their contents from unauthorized access.

17. How do you enable and use BitLocker to encrypt an entire drive?

Answer: BitLocker is enabled through Control Panel or Group Policy, and it encrypts the entire drive to protect its data.

18. What are some best practices for securing file permissions in Windows?

Answer: Limit the use of "Deny" permissions, regularly audit permissions, and use groups to simplify management.

19. How can you protect against malware and ransomware attacks in Windows?

Answer: Keep the system and antivirus software up-to-date, use strong passwords, and educate users about safe online practices.

20. Explain the importance of regular data backups in Windows security.

Answer: Regular backups ensure that data can be restored in case of data loss due to various security incidents.

21. What is the principle of least privilege, and why is it important in Windows security?

Answer: The principle of least privilege means granting users the minimum permissions required to perform their tasks, reducing the risk of unauthorized access.

22. How can you audit file access and changes in Windows?

Answer: Enable auditing in Group Policy, set up auditing policies, and review the security event logs.

23. What is Active Directory, and how does it relate to user authentication in Windows?

Answer: Active Directory is a directory service used for user authentication, group management, and security in Windows environments.

24. Explain the difference between local user accounts and domain user accounts.

Answer: Local user accounts are specific to a single computer, while domain user accounts are managed centrally in an Active Directory domain.

25. What is Group Policy in Windows, and how can it be used to enforce security settings?

Answer: Group Policy allows administratorsto define and enforce security policies, application settings, and more across a network.

26. How can you enforce password policies using Group Policy?

Answer: Password policies can be enforced by configuring settings such as minimum length, complexity, and expiration in Group Policy.

27. Why is it important to regularly install Windows security updates and patches?

Answer: Security updates and patches fix vulnerabilities that could be exploited by attackers to compromise the system.

28. Explain the differences between NTLM and Kerberos authentication protocols in Windows.

Answer: NTLM is an older authentication protocol, while Kerberos is a more secure and modern alternative.

29. What is the Windows Firewall, and how does it enhance network security?

Answer: The Windows Firewall controls network traffic to and from a computer and helps protect against unauthorized access.

30. How does User Account Control (UAC) work, and how does it help prevent unauthorized system changes?

Answer: UAC prompts users for consent when performing tasks that require administrative privileges, reducing the risk of unauthorized changes.

31. Explain the role of antivirus and antimalware software in Windows security.

Answer: Antivirus and antimalware software help detect and remove malicious software to protect the system.

32. What is Secure Boot, and how does it contribute to Windows security?

Answer: Secure Boot is a feature that ensures only digitally signed, trusted components can start during the boot process, enhancing system security.

33. What are some security considerations when using Remote Desktop Services in Windows?

Answer: Implement network-level authentication, strong passwords, and limit remote access to authorized users.

34. How can you configure account lockout policies to enhance security in Windows?

Answer: Configure account lockout policies to lock out accounts temporarily after a specified number of failed login attempts, preventing brute force attacks.

35. Explain the role of Windows Defender in Windows security.

Answer: Windows Defender is Microsoft's built-in antivirus and antimalware solution, providing real-time protection against threats.

36. What is multifactor authentication (MFA), and how does it improve Windows security?

Answer: MFA requires users to provide multiple forms of authentication, such as a password and a mobile app code, adding an extra layer of security.

37. What is Credential Guard, and how does it protect user credentials in Windows?

Answer: Credential Guard is a feature that uses virtualization-based security to protect user credentials from theft by malware.

38. How does AppLocker enhance Windows security?

Answer: AppLocker is a feature that allows administrators to control which applications can run on a Windows system, reducing the risk of running malicious software.

39. What is Device Guard, and how does it improve security in Windows?

Answer: Device Guard is a security feature that uses hardware-based security to prevent the execution of unauthorized code on a system.

40. What is the Windows Security Center, and how does it help monitor and maintain system security?

Answer: The Windows Security Center provides a centralized location to view security status, update status, and take action to maintain system security.

41. Explain the concept of file integrity monitoring and its role in Windows security.

Answer: File integrity monitoring tracks changes to files and alerts administrators to potential unauthorized modifications or security breaches.

42. How can event logs in Windows be used to monitor and analyze security events?

Answer: Event logs record various system events, including security-related activities, and can be analyzed to detect and respond to security incidents.

Data Compression and Encryption

1. What is data compression, and why is it used in computing?

Answer: Data compression is the process of reducing the size of data to save storage space and transmission bandwidth. It is used to optimize data storage and transfer efficiency.

2. Explain the difference between lossless and lossy data compression techniques.

Answer: Lossless compression preserves all original data, while lossy compression sacrifices some data quality for higher compression ratios. Lossless compression is used when data integrity is critical, while lossy compression is suitable for multimedia data like images and audio.

3. What are some common lossless compression algorithms, and when might you use them?

Answer: Common lossless compression algorithms include ZIP, Gzip, and DEFLATE. They are used for text, executable files, and data where maintaining data integrity is essential.

4. How does encryption differ from compression, and why is it important for data security?

Answer: Encryption is the process of converting data into a coded form to protect its confidentiality. It is essential for safeguarding sensitive information during storage and transmission.

5. What is symmetric encryption, and how does it work?

Answer: Symmetric encryption uses the same key for both encryption and decryption. It is a fast method suitable for secure communication between trusted parties.

6. Explain the concept of public-key encryption and its advantages in secure data transmission.

Answer: Public-key encryption uses two keys: one for encryption and one for decryption. It enables secure communication with unknown or untrusted parties. The private key must remain secret, while the public key can be freely shared.

7. What is data at rest encryption, and why is it crucial for data security in storage devices?

Answer: Data at rest encryption involves encrypting data stored on devices like hard drives and solid-state drives. It is essential for protecting data from unauthorized access, especially in case of theft or data breaches.

8. How does data compression affect the effectiveness of encryption, and when might they be used together?

Answer: Data compression can be used before encryption to reduce the amount of data that needs to be encrypted and transmitted. This is beneficial when optimizing bandwidth and storage efficiency while maintaining data security.

9. Explain the term "data deduplication" and its relationship with data compression.

Answer: Data deduplication is the process of eliminating duplicate copies of data, which can lead to substantial data compression. It is commonly used in backup and storage systems to reduce storage requirements.

10. What are the potential security risks associated with data compression and encryption, and how can they be mitigated?

Answer: Security risks can include vulnerabilities in compression or encryption algorithms. To mitigate these risks, it's important to use well-established and trusted compression and encryption techniques and keep software and systems up to date. Regularly monitoring and auditing security practices is also crucial.

11. What is data compression in the context of Windows?

Answer: Data compression in Windows is the process of reducing the size of files and data to save storage space and improve transfer efficiency.

12. What are the common compression formats supported by Windows?

Answer: Windows supports popular compression formats like ZIP, GZIP, and CAB, and it has built-in tools for handling these formats.

13. How can you compress a folder or file in Windows using built-in tools?

Answer: You can compress a folder or file by right-clicking it, selecting "Send to," and choosing "Compressed (zipped) folder."

14. Explain the advantages and disadvantages of using file compression in Windows.

Answer: Advantages: Reduced storage space and faster file transfers. Disadvantages: Increased CPU usage for compression and decompression.

15. What is NTFS compression, and how does it differ from standard file compression?

Answer: NTFS compression is a file attribute that compresses files on an NTFS volume. It differs from standard file compression as it's transparent to users and doesn't require manual zipping/unzipping.

16. Can you access and modify files while they are compressed with NTFS compression?

Answer: Yes, you can access and modify files without decompressing them. The compression and decompression are transparent to users and applications.

17. Explain the concept of lossless and lossy compression.

Answer: Lossless compression retains all original data, while lossy compression sacrifices some data quality to achieve higher compression ratios.

18. What is the purpose of the Compact command in Windows?

Answer: The Compact command allows you to enable or disable compression on NTFS volumes, folders, or files.

19. What is data encryption in Windows, and why is it important?

Answer: Data encryption in Windows is the process of converting data into a secure format to prevent unauthorized access. It's essential for protecting sensitive information.

20. How does BitLocker encryption enhance data security in Windows?

Answer: BitLocker encrypts entire volumes and requires authentication to access the data, providing protection against unauthorized access.

21. Explain the difference between BitLocker and EFS (Encrypting File System).

Answer: BitLocker encrypts entire volumes, while EFS encrypts individual files and folders.

22. What are the methods for encrypting files and folders using EFS in Windows?

Answer: You can encrypt files and folders using EFS by right-clicking them, going to Properties, and selecting the "Advanced" button.

23. What is the significance of a recovery key in BitLocker encryption?

Answer: A recovery key is a crucial backup mechanism for unlocking a BitLocker-encrypted drive in case the user forgets their password or encounters issues.

24. How can you enable BitLocker on a Windows system?

Answer: BitLocker can be enabled through the Control Panel, Group Policy, or by using the Manage-bde command-line tool.

25. What are the different authentication methods available for BitLocker?

Answer: BitLocker supports various authentication methods, including a TPM (Trusted Platform Module), PIN, password, and USB key.

26. Explain the concept of data at rest and data in transit encryption in Windows.

Answer: Data at rest encryption protects data stored on disk, while data in transit encryption safeguards data during transfer over networks.

27. What is a digital certificate, and how is it used in data encryption in Windows?

Answer:A digital certificate is a cryptographic credential used for secure communication and authentication. In Windows, it's used to establish trust and enable secure connections.

28. How does a public key infrastructure (PKI) enhance data security in Windows?

Answer:A PKI provides the framework for managing digital certificates, enabling secure authentication and data encryption.

29. How can you import and manage certificates in Windows using the Certificate Manager?

Answer: Certificates can be imported and managed using the "certmgr.msc" tool, which provides a graphical interface for certificate-related tasks.

30. Explain the role of certificate stores in Windows.

Answer: Certificate stores are repositories for storing digital certificates, which are used for various security-related purposes.

31. What are SSL and TLS, and how do they contribute to data encryption in Windows?

Answer:SSL (Secure Sockets Layer) and TLS (Transport Layer Security) are cryptographic protocols used to secure communication over networks and the internet.

32. How can you configure SSL/TLS for securing web communications in Windows Server?

Answer: You can configure SSL/TLS for web communications by installing a certificate, enabling HTTPS, and configuring the web server (e.g., IIS).

33. How does encryption play a role in securing Remote Desktop Services in Windows?

Answer: Encryption is crucial for securing data transferred between a client and a remote desktop server in order to prevent eavesdropping.

34. What are IPsec (Internet Protocol Security) and SMB (Server Message Block) encryption, and how are they used in Windows?

Answer:IPsec is a protocol suite for securing IP communications, while SMB encryption is used to secure file sharing over the network.

35. How does the Windows Firewall enhance network security by allowing or blocking specific traffic?

Answer: The Windows Firewall filters network traffic by permitting or denying specific ports, applications, and services, thereby improving network security.

36. What is two-factor authentication (2FA), and how can it be implemented in Windows for enhanced security?

Answer:2FA requires users to provide two forms of authentication (e.g., password and SMS code), enhancing security by adding an extra layer of verification.

37. How does Secure Boot contribute to data and system security in Windows?

Answer: Secure Boot ensures that only trusted, signed components can be loaded during the boot process, preventing unauthorized code execution.

38. Explain the role of Windows Defender in Windows security.

Answer: Windows Defender is Microsoft's built-in antivirus and antimalware solution that provides real-time protection against threats.

39. What is application whitelisting, and how does it enhance data security in Windows?

Answer: Application whitelisting allows only approved applications to run on a system, reducing the risk of running malicious software.

40. How can Group Policy be used to enforce encryption and security settings in a Windows network?

Answer: Group Policy allows administrators to define and enforce security policies, including encryption settings, across a network.

41. How can event logs in Windows be used to monitor and analyze security events related to data encryption and protection?

Answer: Event logs record various security-related activities, and they can be analyzed to detect and respond to security incidents.

42. What is Mobile Device Management, and how does it contribute to data security in a Windows environment?

Answer:MDM solutions help manage and secure mobile devices used in the Windows ecosystem, ensuring data protection and compliance.

43. What is the Windows Security Center, and how does it help monitor and maintain data and system security?

Answer: The Windows Security Center provides a centralized location to view security status, update status.

ONLINE RESOURCES

Practice Paper Link: https://forms.gle/D5aGzpoXn5YBRMEK9

QR Code:

Video Link: https://www.youtube.com/playlist?list=PLzlh_31VWEFqTwNl_4muKAGq-SKyrURId

QR Code:

Chapter 4 Windows Registry and Configuration

Introduction to Windows Registry

1. What is the Windows Registry, and what role does it play in the Windows operating system?

Answer: The Windows Registry is a hierarchical database that stores configuration settings and options for the Windows operating system and installed applications. It is a critical component for system settings and preferences.

2. Where is the Windows Registry located, and what are its main hives or subtrees?

Answer: The Windows Registry is typically located in the "C:\Windows\System32\config" directory and is organized into several hives, including HKEY_CLASSES_ROOT, HKEY_CURRENT_USER, HKEY_LOCAL_MACHINE, HKEY_USERS, and HKEY_CURRENT_CONFIG.

3. What are registry keys and values, and how do they differ in the Windows Registry?

Answer: Registry keys are containers that can hold values and subkeys. Values are data entries that store configuration settings or information. Keys are used to organize and structure data.

4. Explain the concept of a registry path and its importance in accessing specific registry entries.

Answer: A registry path is a hierarchical sequence of keys separated by backslashes (e.g., "HKEY_LOCAL_MACHINE\Software\Microsoft\Windows"). It is essential for navigating the registry to locate specific entries.

5. How can the Windows Registry be accessed and modified, and what tools or utilities are commonly used for this purpose?

Answer: The Windows Registry can be accessed and modified using the Registry Editor (regedit.exe) and Command Prompt (reg.exe). Other third-party tools are available for advanced registry management.

6. What are the main categories of information stored in the Windows Registry, and why are they important?

Answer: The Windows Registry contains information about system hardware, software settings, user profiles, and preferences. These categories are crucial for configuring the operating system and installed applications.

7. What is the purpose of the "HKEY_CURRENT_USER" hive, and how does it relate to user-specific settings in Windows?

Answer: The "HKEY_CURRENT_USER" hive stores configuration settings specific to the currently logged-in user. It allows users to customize their Windows environment without affecting other users.

8. Can you explain the differences between a registry backup and a restore point in Windows?

Answer: A registry backup is a copy of the registry's state at a specific point in time, used for recovery. A restore point, on the other hand, is a system snapshot that includes not only the registry but also system files and settings. Restore points are used for system-wide recovery.

9. What precautions should be taken when editing the Windows Registry, and what are the potential risks of making incorrect changes?

Answer: When editing the Windows Registry, it's essential to create backups, make changes cautiously, and follow documentation or instructions. Incorrect changes can lead to system instability, errors, or data loss.

10. What is the Windows Registry's role in the boot process of the operating system, and how can it impact system performance?

Answer: The Windows Registry plays a vital role in the boot process, as it contains information about system drivers and services that load during startup. An inefficient or corrupted registry can lead to slow boot times and overall system performance issues.

11. What is the Windows Registry?

Answer: The Windows Registry is a hierarchical database used to store configuration settings and options for the Windows operating system and applications.

12. Where is the Windows Registry located on a Windows system?

Answer: The Windows Registry is stored in multiple files within the "C:\Windows\System32\config" directory.

13. What are the main purposes of the Windows Registry?

Answer: The Windows Registry is used to store system and application configuration settings, hardware information, user preferences, and more.

14. What are the five main Registry hives in Windows?

Answer: The five main Registry hives are HKEY_CLASSES_ROOT, HKEY_CURRENT_USER, HKEY_LOCAL_MACHINE, HKEY_USERS, and HKEY_CURRENT_CONFIG.

15. Explain the concept of Registry keys and values.

Answer: Registry keys are containers that store settings, while values are data entries within those keys that store configuration information.

16. How can you open the Windows Registry Editor?

Answer: You can open the Registry Editor by pressing Win + R, typing "regedit," and pressing Enter.

17. What is the difference between REG_SZ and REG_DWORD data types in the Registry?

Answer:REG_SZ stores string data, while REG_DWORD stores 32-bit integer data.

18. How can you back up the Windows Registry before making changes?

Answer: You can back up the Registry using the Registry Editor's "File" menu, which allows you to export the Registry to a .reg file.

19. Explain the importance of caution when editing the Registry.

Answer: Editing the Registry can affect the stability and functionality of your system, so it should be done with care. Incorrect changes can lead to system issues.

20. How can you restore the Registry to a previous state if something goes wrong?

Answer: You can restore the Registry using a previously created backup (.reg) file or use the System Restore feature in Windows.

21. What is the purpose of the HKEY_CLASSES_ROOT hive?

Answer:HKEY_CLASSES_ROOT contains information about file associations and OLE object class registration.

22. Explain the role of the HKEY_CURRENT_USER hive.

Answer:HKEY_CURRENT_USER stores configuration settings specific to the currently logged-in user.

23. What does the HKEY_LOCAL_MACHINE hive contain?

Answer: HKEY_LOCAL_MACHINE holds system-wide hardware and software settings and configuration data.

24. Describe the purpose of the HKEY_USERS hive.

Answer:HKEY_USERS contains profiles and settings for all user accounts on the computer.

25. What information is stored in the HKEY_CURRENT_CONFIG hive?

Answer:HKEY_CURRENT_CONFIG holds information related to the hardware profile currently in use.

26. Name a few Registry-related command-line tools in Windows.

Answer: Tools like "regedit," "reg," and "regedt32" are used for Registry management.

27. How can you use the "reg" command-line tool to manipulate the Registry?

Answer: The "reg" command allows you to query, add, delete, and modify Registry keys and values from the command line.

28. What is the purpose of the "System Restore" feature in relation to the Registry?

Answer: System Restore creates and manages snapshots of the Registry, allowing users to revert to a previous state if issues arise.

29. How often should you create Registry backups?

Answer: It's a good practice to create Registry backups before making significant system changes, but routine backups aren't typically necessary.

30. How can you secure the Registry to prevent unauthorized access and modifications?

Answer: You can set permissions and access controls on Registry keys and values to restrict access to authorized users.

31. Explain the role of the "regedt32" tool in Registry security.

Answer:"Regedt32" is an older Registry editor that allows for more granular control over Registry permissions.

32. What is the default Registry key for user profiles in the HKEY_USERS hive?

Answer: The default key for user profiles in HKEY_USERS is the Security Identifier (SID) of the user.

33. What is the difference between a Registry key and a Registry value?

Answer:A Registry key is a container that holds values, while a Registry value stores configuration data.

34. How can you troubleshoot and fix Registry errors in Windows?

Answer: You can use the Registry Editor to manually correct errors, or you can use system restore points to revert to a working state.

35. What are the file formats used by the Windows Registry?

Answer: The Windows Registry uses the .dat file format for its hive files, and .log and .sav files for transaction logs and backups.

36. How can you grant specific users or groups permissions to access and modify Registry keys?

Answer: You can use the Registry Editor to set permissions on individual keys or values within the Registry.

37. Explain the importance of limiting access to sensitive Registry keys.

Answer: Limiting access to sensitive keys helps protect system integrity and prevents unauthorized changes.

38. How does Group Policy use the Registry to manage Windows settings across a network?

Answer: Group Policy leverages Registry settings to control and enforce configurations on networked Windows machines.

39. What are some best practices for managing the Windows Registry?

Answer: Backup the Registry before making changes, use Group Policy for centralized management, and avoid unnecessary Registry tweaks.

40. When should you manually edit the Registry, and when should you avoid it?

Answer: Manually edit the Registry only when you have a specific need, and avoid it when there are alternative methods or if you're unsure of the impact.

Registry Structure and Hives

1. What is the Registry structure in the Windows operating system, and how is it organized?

Answer: The Registry structure is organized hierarchically, with keys and values stored in a tree-like structure. The structure is divided into hives, subkeys, and values.

2. What are Registry hives, and how do they relate to the overall structure of the Windows Registry?

Answer: Registry hives are the top-level containers that hold keys, subkeys, and values. They represent separate categories of system and user data, such as configuration settings and preferences.

3. Name the five main Registry hives in Windows and briefly describe their primary functions.

Answer: The five main Registry hives are:

HKEY_CLASSES_ROOT: Contains file association and COM object registration information.

HKEY_CURRENT_USER: Stores settings specific to the currently logged-in user.

HKEY_LOCAL_MACHINE: Holds system-wide settings and hardware information.

HKEY_USERS: Contains user profiles for all users on the system.

HKEY_CURRENT_CONFIG: Stores information about the current hardware configuration.

4. What is the purpose of the "HKEY_CLASSES_ROOT" hive in the Windows Registry, and what kind of data does it hold?

Answer: The "HKEY_CLASSES_ROOT" hive stores information related to file associations, including file type associations, COM object registrations, and OLE settings.

5. Explain the significance of the "HKEY_LOCAL_MACHINE" hive and its subkeys in the Windows Registry.

Answer: The "HKEY_LOCAL_MACHINE" hive contains system-wide settings, hardware information, and software configurations. Subkeys within it include "Software," which holds application-specific settings, and "System," which contains system settings.

6. How does the "HKEY_CURRENT_USER" hive differ from the "HKEY_USERS" hive in terms of user-specific Registry data?

Answer: The "HKEY_CURRENT_USER" hive contains settings specific to the currently logged-in user, while the "HKEY_USERS" hive holds user profiles for all users on the system.

7. What are the potential risks and consequences of making changes to Registry hives, and how can these risks be mitigated?

Answer: Making incorrect changes to Registry hives can lead to system instability, errors, or data loss. To mitigate these risks, it's important to create backups, make changes cautiously, and follow documentation or instructions.

8. How can you access and edit Registry hives in Windows, and what tools or utilities are commonly used for this purpose?

Answer: You can access and edit Registry hives using the Registry Editor (regedit.exe) or Command Prompt (reg.exe). There are also third-party tools available for advanced Registry management.

9. What is the "HKEY_CURRENT_CONFIG" hive's role in the Windows Registry, and how does it contribute to system configuration?

Answer: The "HKEY_CURRENT_CONFIG" hive stores information about the current hardware configuration, including settings for display devices and system resources.

10. How does the hierarchical structure of the Windows Registry hives help in organizing and managing system and user data?

Answer: The hierarchical structure enables logical organization of data, making it easier to locate, access, and manage specific settings and configurations. It also simplifies access control and permissions management.

11. What is the Windows Registry, and what is its primary purpose?

Answer: The Windows Registry is a hierarchical database used to store configuration settings and options for both the Windows operating system and applications.

12. Why is the Registry important in Windows?

Answer: The Registry is crucial as it stores critical configuration information, user settings, and application data, enabling the operating system and software to function as expected.

13. How is the Windows Registry organized?

Answer: The Registry is organized into a hierarchical structure of keys and values, similar to a tree, with each key containing configuration settings.

14. What are Registry hives, and how many primary hives are there in Windows?

Answer: Registry hives are high-level containers for organizing configuration data. There are five primary hives: HKEY_CLASSES_ROOT, HKEY_CURRENT_USER, HKEY_LOCAL_MACHINE, HKEY_USERS, and HKEY_CURRENT_CONFIG.

15. Explain the purpose of the HKEY_CLASSES_ROOT hive.

Answer:HKEY_CLASSES_ROOT contains information about file associations and OLE object class registration.

16. What kind of data is stored in the HKEY_CURRENT_USER hive?

Answer:HKEY_CURRENT_USER stores configuration settings specific to the currently logged-in user.

17. Describe the role of the HKEY_LOCAL_MACHINE hive.

Answer:HKEY_LOCAL_MACHINE holds system-wide hardware and software settings and configuration data.

18. What is the primary purpose of the HKEY_USERS hive?

Answer: HKEY_USERS contains profiles and settings for all user accounts on the computer.

19. What information is stored in the HKEY_CURRENT_CONFIG hive?

Answer:HKEY_CURRENT_CONFIG holds information related to the hardware profile currently in use.

20. What are Registry keys and Registry values?

Answer: Registry keys are containers that hold configuration settings, while Registry values store specific configuration data.

21. How can you differentiate between a Registry key and a Registry value when viewing the Registry?

Answer: In the Registry Editor, keys are displayed as folders, and values are shown as entries within those folders.

22. What are the common data types for Registry values?

Answer: Common data types for Registry values include REG_SZ (string), REG_DWORD (32-bit integer), REG_QWORD (64-bit integer), and REG_BINARY (binary data).

23. How can you open the Windows Registry Editor?

Answer: You can open the Registry Editor by pressing Win + R, typing "regedit," and pressing Enter.

24. What precautions should you take when editing the Registry?

Answer: It's essential to back up the Registry before making changes, double-check entries, and only modify keys/values when necessary, as incorrect changes can lead to system issues.

25. How can you back up the Registry before making changes?

Answer: You can back up the Registry using the Registry Editor's "File" menu, which allows you to export the Registry to a .reg file.

26. What is the Windows Registry used for when installing software?

Answer: During software installation, the Registry is used to store information about the software's installation path, components, and associated files.

27. Why is it a good practice to create Registry backups before making changes?

Answer: Creating Registry backups allows for easy recovery in case of errors or issues caused by changes, ensuring system stability.

28. How can you restore the Registry to a previous state using a backup?

Answer: You can restore the Registry by importing a previously created backup (.reg) file using the Registry Editor.

29. How can you secure the Registry to prevent unauthorized access and modifications?

Answer: You can set permissions and access controls on Registry keys and values to restrict access to authorized users or groups.

30. What is the "ACL" (Access Control List) in the context of Registry permissions?

Answer: The ACL is a list of permissions associated with a Registry key or value, specifying which users or groups have access and what actions they can perform.

31. What types of errors and issues might arise in the Registry?

Answer: Registry errors can include missing or corrupted entries, incorrect settings, and references to non-existent files or locations.

32. How can you troubleshoot and fix Registry errors in Windows?

Answer: You can use the Registry Editor to manually correct errors or use system restore points to revert to a working state.

33. What file formats are used by the Windows Registry?

Answer: The Windows Registry uses the .dat file format for its hive files and .log and .sav files for transaction logs and backups.

34. How does Group Policy use the Registry to manage Windows settings across a network?

Answer: Group Policy leverages Registry settings to control and enforce configurations on networked Windows machines.

35. What are some best practices for managing the Windows Registry?

Answer: Backup the Registry before making changes, use Group Policy for centralized management, and avoid unnecessary Registry tweaks or changes.

36. When should you manually edit the Registry, and when should you avoid it?

Answer: Manually edit the Registry only when you have a specific need, and avoid it when there are alternative methods or if you're unsure of the impact.

Working with Registry Keys and Values

1. What is a Registry key in the Windows Registry, and how is it used to organize information?

Answer: A Registry key is a container that can hold subkeys and values. It organizes related information, settings, and configuration data within the Windows Registry.

2. How are Registry keys named and structured, and what is the significance of backslashes in key names?

Answer: Registry keys are named with hierarchical paths, separated by backslashes (). For example, "HKEY_LOCAL_MACHINE\Software\Microsoft\Windows" represents a key path. Backslashes signify the hierarchy or structure of keys.

3. What is the role of a subkey within a Registry key, and how does it contribute to the organization of data?

Answer: A subkey is a container within a key that can hold additional subkeys or values. It is used to further organize and categorize information, creating a structured hierarchy.

4. What are Registry values, and how do they differ from Registry keys?

Answer: Registry values are data entries that store configuration settings, options, and information within a Registry key. Registry keys are containers that can hold values and subkeys.

5. Name and briefly describe some common types of Registry values used in the Windows Registry.

Answer: Common Registry value types include:

String: Stores text data.

DWORD: Holds 32-bit integer values.

Binary: Stores binary data.

Multi-String: Contains multiple text values.

QWORD: Holds 64-bit integer values.

6. How can you create a new Registry key or subkey, and why might you need to do so?

Answer: You can create new keys or subkeys using the Registry Editor or programmatic methods. You might create new keys to organize settings for an application or to add configuration options for a specific feature.

7. Explain the process of creating or modifying Registry values, and how can these values be used to configure applications?

Answer: Values can be created or modified using the Registry Editor or scripting. They are used to set specific configuration options, such as application behavior, preferences, or system settings.

8. What is the significance of data validation and data type in Registry values, and how can incorrect data types affect system stability?

Answer: Registry values have data types, and incorrect data types can lead to application errors or system instability. Data validation ensures that the data conforms to the expected format.

9. How can you delete a Registry key or value, and what precautions should be taken before making deletions?

Answer: Registry keys and values can be deleted using the Registry Editor. Before deleting, it's essential to create backups, as deletion is typically irreversible and can lead to system issues if done incorrectly.

10. What are the potential security implications of working with Registry keys and values, and how can data integrity be maintained?

Answer: Modifying Registry keys and values can impact system security and data integrity. To maintain integrity, follow best practices, make changes with proper permissions, and create backups to revert to a known good state in case of issues.

11. What is a Registry key in Windows?

Answer:A Registry key is a container within the Windows Registry that holds configuration settings and values.

12. How can you create a new Registry key?

Answer: In the Registry Editor, right-click the parent key, select "New," and choose "Key."

13. What is the significance of the "HKEY_LOCAL_MACHINE" key in the Registry?

Answer:HKEY_LOCAL_MACHINE holds system-wide configuration settings and hardware information.

14. How do you rename a Registry key?

Answer: Right-click the key, choose "Rename," and provide a new name.

15. What is the purpose of the "HKEY_CURRENT_USER" key?

Answer:HKEY_CURRENT_USER stores configuration settings specific to the currently logged-in user.

16. Can you delete a Registry key? If so, how?

Answer: Yes, you can delete a Registry key by right-clicking it and selecting "Delete."

17. What is the difference between a subkey and a root key in the Registry?

Answer:A root key is one of the primary hives, while a subkey is a key located within a hive.

18. How can you export a Registry key to a .reg file?

Answer: Right-click the key, select "Export," and choose a location to save the .reg file.

19. What is a Registry value in Windows?

Answer:A Registry value is an entry within a Registry key that stores configuration data.

20. How can you create a new Registry value?

Answer: In the Registry Editor, right-click the key, select "New," and choose the value type (e.g., DWORD, String Value).

21. Explain the purpose of a REG_SZ Registry value.

Answer:A REG_SZ value stores string data.

22. What is the significance of a REG_DWORD Registry value?

Answer:A REG_DWORD value stores 32-bit integer data.

23. How do you modify the data of an existing Registry value?

Answer: Right-click the value, select "Modify," and then edit the data in the dialog box.

24. How can you delete a Registry value?

Answer: Right-click the value and choose "Delete."

25. What is a default value in the Registry?

Answer: The default value is a value within a Registry key that is used when no other specific value matches a request.

26. How can you export a Registry value to a .reg file?

Answer: You can't export individual values; you can only export entire keys.

27. What are some common data types used in Registry values?

Answer: Common data types include REG_SZ (string), REG_DWORD (32-bit integer), REG_QWORD (64-bit integer), and REG_BINARY (binary data).

28. Explain the purpose of a REG_BINARY value.

Answer:A REG_BINARY value stores binary data, often used for hardware configurations.

29. How do you distinguish between REG_SZ and REG_EXPAND_SZ data types?

Answer:REG_SZ stores standard strings, while REG_EXPAND_SZ allows for environment variable expansion (e.g., %SystemRoot%).

30. When would you use a REG_MULTI_SZ value?

Answer:A REG_MULTI_SZ value is used for multi-string data, like multiple lines of text.

Registry Import and Export:

1. What is the purpose of exporting Registry keys and values?

Answer: Exporting Registry keys and values allows for creating backups and transferring configurations between systems.

2. How can you import a .reg file into the Registry?

Answer: Double-click the .reg file or use the "Import" option in the Registry Editor.

3. Explain the potential risks of importing .reg files.

Answer: Importing .reg files can make changes to the Registry, so it's crucial to ensure they come from trusted sources and are reviewed for accuracy.

4. How can you merge the contents of one .reg file into the Registry?

Answer: Right-click the .reg file and choose "Merge."

Registry Permissions:

1. What are Registry permissions, and why are they important?

Answer: Registry permissions control who can access and modify Registry keys and values, crucial for maintaining security and system integrity.

2. How can you set permissions on a Registry key?

Answer: Right-click the key, select "Permissions," and configure the access control list (ACL).

3. What is the difference between "Read" and "Full Control" permissions in the Registry?

Answer:"Read" allows viewing and querying the key, while "Full Control" grants complete control, including changing permissions.

4. How can you take ownership of a Registry key?

Answer: In the Permissions window, go to the "Owner" tab and select "Edit." Choose the new owner and check "Replace owner on sub containers and objects" if necessary.

Registry Best Practices:

1. What are some best practices for working with Registry keys and values?

Answer: Backup the Registry before making changes, document modifications, and avoid modifying keys/values without a specific need.

2. Why is it essential to be cautious when editing the Registry?

Answer: Editing the Registry incorrectly can lead to system instability and issues, making caution and backups critical.

Managing System Configuration

1. What is system configuration management, and why is it important in an operating system?

Answer: System configuration management involves the process of defining, modifying, and maintaining system settings to ensure optimal performance, security, and functionality. It is crucial for system stability and reliability.

2. How can environment variables be used to configure system settings and applications in Windows?

Answer: Environment variables store system-wide or user-specific configuration data that applications can reference. They are used to customize the behaviour of programs and system processes.

3. Explain the purpose of configuration files in system management, and provide examples of common configuration file formats.

Answer: Configuration files store settings and parameters that configure applications and services. Common configuration file formats include XML, INI, JSON, and YAML.

4. What are the potential challenges in managing system configurations, and how can version control systems (VCS) address these challenges?

Answer: Challenges in system configuration management include maintaining consistency, tracking changes, and ensuring that configurations are kept in sync. VCS solutions like Git can track changes, provide version history, and enable collaboration.

5. How can Group Policy be used to manage system settings in a Windows-based network environment?

Answer: Group Policy allows administrators to define and enforce policies for users and computers in an Active Directory network. It is used to configure security settings, software installation, and more.

6. What is the purpose of the Windows Registry in system configuration management, and how does it store configuration data?

Answer: The Windows Registry stores system and application settings. It is organized into hives, keys, subkeys, and values, each containing configuration data.

7. Explain the concept of system image backups and their role in system recovery and configuration management.

Answer: System image backups capture a snapshot of the entire system, including the operating system, applications, and settings. They are used for disaster recovery and restoring system configurations to a specific state.

8. What is the role of policy-based configuration management tools like Puppet and Ansible, and how do they automate system configuration tasks?

Answer: Policy-based configuration management tools automate system configuration tasks by defining desired states, automating deployments, and ensuring consistency across multiple systems.

9. How does the concept of infrastructure as code (IaC) apply to system configuration management, and what are the advantages of using IaC?

Answer: Infrastructure as code involves defining and managing infrastructure (including system configurations) using code. Advantages include automation, version control, scalability, and reproducibility.

10. What precautions should be taken when making system configuration changes to avoid system disruptions and maintain data integrity?

Answer: To avoid system disruptions, precautions include creating backups, documenting changes, testing in a non-production environment, and following change management processes. Data integrity can be maintained by using proper data validation and testing procedures.

11. What is System Configuration in Windows?

Answer: System Configuration, or "msconfig," is a utility in Windows that allows users to configure various system settings and startup programs.

12. How can you access System Configuration in Windows?

Answer: You can access System Configuration by typing "msconfig" into the Run dialog or the search bar.

13. What are the tabs available in the System Configuration utility?

Answer: The tabs include General, Boot, Services, Startup, and Tools.

14. Explain the purpose of the "General" tab in System Configuration.

Answer: The General tab allows you to select the startup mode, such as Normal startup, Diagnostic startup, or

Selective startup.

1. What is the "Boot" tab used for in System Configuration?

Answer: The Boot tab lets you configure boot options, including the default operating system and advanced boot settings.

2. How can you use the "Services" tab in System Configuration?

Answer: The Services tab allows you to enable or disable Windows services and control their startup type.

3. Explain the "Startup" tab in System Configuration.

Answer: The Startup tab displays a list of programs that start when your computer boots. You can enable or disable them here.

4. What are "Tools" in System Configuration used for?

Answer: The Tools tab provides quick access to various Windows diagnostic and administrative tools.

5. How do you disable a program from starting up with Windows in System Configuration?

Answer: In the Startup tab, uncheck the box next to the program you want to disable, then click "Apply."

6. What is the purpose of the "Selective startup" option in System Configuration?

Answer: Selective startup allows you to choose which services and startup items are enabled, useful for troubleshooting or optimizing performance.

7. What is the difference between "Normal startup" and "Diagnostic startup" in System Configuration?

Answer: Normal startup loads all drivers and services. Diagnostic startup loads only basic drivers and services for troubleshooting purposes.

8. How can you enable a previously disabled program in System Configuration?

Answer: In the Startup tab, check the box next to the program you want to enable, then click "Apply."

9. What is the significance of the "Advanced options" button in the "Boot" tab of System Configuration?

Answer: Advanced options allow you to configure settings like the number of processors and maximum memory used during boot.

10. How can you access Safe Mode through System Configuration?

Answer: You can access Safe Mode by selecting "Safe boot" on the Boot tab and choosing the desired Safe Mode option.

11. Explain the purpose of the "System Restore" button in System Configuration.

Answer: The System Restore button lets you open the System Restore utility to roll back your system to a previous state.

12. How can you start Windows in a clean boot state using System Configuration?

Answer: In the General tab, select "Selective startup" and uncheck "Load startup items."

13. What is the difference between System Configuration and the Task Manager in managing startup programs?

Answer: System Configuration provides a more detailed view and control of startup programs, while Task Manager offers basic information and the ability to disable or enable programs.

14. What is the role of the "Diagnostic startup" option in System Configuration?

Answer: Diagnostic startup loads only basic drivers and services, useful for identifying issues that might be caused by startup programs.

15. How do you apply changes made in System Configuration without restarting the computer?

Answer: Click "Apply" in System Configuration, but the changes won't take effect until you restart your computer.

16. What is the purpose of the "Command Prompt" option in the "Tools" tab of System Configuration?

Answer: The Command Prompt option provides quick access to a Command Prompt window with administrative privileges.

17. Explain the impact of disabling a Windows service in System Configuration.

Answer: Disabling a Windows service can affect the functionality of certain features or software that depend on that service. Be cautious when doing this.

18. How do you identify and manage third-party software in the "Startup" tab of System Configuration?

Answer: Third-party software in the "Startup" tab is usually listed by its name and publisher. You can enable or disable them as needed.

19. Can you configure the order in which startup programs load in System Configuration?

Answer: No, System Configuration doesn't allow you to set the load order of startup programs.

20. What is the "Boot Configuration Data (BCD)" in System Configuration used for?

Answer: The BCD is a store that contains boot configuration parameters and settings. You can edit it for advanced boot configuration.

21. How can you configure a dual-boot system using System Configuration?

Answer: In the "Boot" tab, you can set the default operating system and change the timeout value for choosing an OS during startup.

22. Explain the concept of "fast startup" in System Configuration.

Answer: Fast startup is a feature that combines elements of hibernation and shutdown to make your computer start faster. It's found in the "Shutdown settings" on the "Boot" tab.

23. What is the "Startup impact" column in the "Startup" tab of System Configuration used for?

Answer: It indicates how much a startup program impacts the system's boot time. High impact programs may slow down the boot process.

24. How do you create a system restore point using System Configuration?

Answer: In the "General" tab, click the "Create" button next to "System Restore" to create a restore point.

25. What happens when you select "Load system services" in System Configuration's "General" tab?

Answer: It loads Microsoft services and essential system components during startup.

26. What are the potential risks of disabling too many startup programs in System Configuration?

Answer: Disabling essential programs can lead to system instability, software malfunctions, or unexpected behaviour.

27. Explain how you can access the Event Viewer from System Configuration.

Answer: The Event Viewer can be accessed from the "Tools" tab, which provides a quick link to view system logs and events.

28. What is the "No GUI boot" option in System Configuration's "Boot" tab used for?

Answer: It disables the graphical user interface during the Windows boot process for a cleaner and faster startup.

29. How can you use System Configuration for troubleshooting a slow Windows startup?

Answer: You can use it to selectively disable startup programs and services to identify the cause of the slowdown.

30. Explain the "OS Boot Information" option in System Configuration's "Boot" tab.

Answer: It displays advanced boot debugging information. It's useful for diagnosing boot-related issues.

31. What should you do if your computer becomes unbootable after making changes in System Configuration?

Answer: You can start Windows in Safe Mode or use a System Restore point to revert the changes.

32. What is the purpose of the "Timeout" setting in the "Boot" tab of System Configuration?

Answer: It sets the amount of time Windows waits for a user to select an operating system during boot.

33. How can you create a custom boot entry in System Configuration for advanced boot options?

Answer: You can use the "bcdedit" command in Command Prompt to create custom boot entries.

34. What is the "Last Known Good Configuration" option in System Configuration used for?

Answer: It allows you to start Windows using a previously known good configuration in case of system problems.

35. Explain the difference between "Automatic" and "Manual" startup types for services in System Configuration.

Answer: Automatic services start with Windows. Manual services only start when needed by other programs.

36. What precautions should you take when using System Configuration for system management?

Answer: Be cautious when disabling services and startup programs, as it can affect the stability and functionality of your system. Always create a system restore point before making significant changes.

ONLINE RESOURCES

Practice Paper Link: https://forms.gle/JvqD6fEDmTyv2Wfx9

QR Code:

Video Link: https://www.youtube.com/playlist?list=PLzlh_31VWEFpo9PFaPd2wDiw1-6o7lNrI

QR Code:

Chapter 5 User and Group Management

User Accounts and Profiles

1. What is a user account, and why are user accounts important in an operating system?

Answer: A user account is a set of credentials that allow a user to access a computer or network. It is important for user authentication, access control, and personalization.

2. Explain the difference between a local user account and a domain user account in a Windows-based network environment.

Answer: A local user account is specific to a single computer, while a domain user account is part of a network domain, allowing access to multiple computers within that domain.

3. What are user profiles, and how do they enhance the user experience in an operating system?

Answer: User profiles store user-specific settings, preferences, and data, allowing users to customize their computing environment and maintain personalization.

4. What is the role of a user group, and how does it simplify user account management and access control?

Answer: A user group is a collection of user accounts with similar access permissions. They simplify account management by applying permissions to multiple users at once.

5. How can you create a new user account in Windows, and what information is typically required when creating one?

Answer: New user accounts can be created using the User Accounts section in Control Panel. Typically, you need to provide a username, password, and specify group memberships and user type (administrator or standard user).

6. Explain the purpose of user profiles and the differences between local and roaming profiles in Windows.

Answer: User profiles store personal settings and data. Local profiles are specific to a single computer, while roaming profiles allow users to have consistent settings across multiple computers on a network.

7. What are the security considerations when managing user accounts, and how can strong password policies enhance security?

Answer: Security considerations include setting strong, complex passwords, regularly updating passwords, and implementing policies for account lockouts and password changes. Strong password policies enhance security by making it more challenging for unauthorized users to gain access.

8. How can administrators manage user accounts in a network domain using Active Directory in Windows Server?

Answer: Active Directory allows administrators to create, modify, and manage user accounts, groups, and organizational units (OUs) across a network domain.

9. What is the purpose of user permissions and access control in the context of user accounts, and how do they impact data security?

Answer: User permissions and access control determine what a user can and cannot do within the system. They impact data security by limiting access to sensitive files and resources.

10. What are the potential issues and solutions related to user profiles in a network environment, especially when using roaming profiles?

Answer: Issues can include slow login times and profile corruption. Solutions may involve optimizing profile size, using folder redirection, or employing profile management tools to address these challenges.

11. What is a user account in Windows?

Answer: A user account is a collection of settings and information that defines a user's identity and privileges on a Windows system.

12. How do you create a new user account in Windows?

Answer: You can create a new user account through the Control Panel or Settings app, under "User Accounts" or "Accounts," respectively.

13. Explain the difference between a local user account and a Microsoft account.

Answer: A local user account is specific to a single computer, while a Microsoft account is associated with an email address and can be used on multiple devices.

14. What is a user profile in Windows?

Answer: A user profile is a collection of settings, preferences, and data associated with a user account, which customizes the user's Windows experience.

15. How can you manage user accounts and profiles in Windows?

Answer: User accounts and profiles can be managed through the Control Panel, Settings app, or Computer Management tool.

16. What is the purpose of the "User Account Control (UAC)" feature in Windows?

Answer: UAC is a security feature that helps prevent unauthorized changes to your computer by notifying you when a program tries to make changes that require administrative permissions.

17. Explain the steps to change a user account's password in Windows.

Answer: You can change a user account password by navigating to "User Accounts" in the Control Panel or "Accounts" in Settings and selecting the user account.

18. What is the significance of a user's security identifier (SID) in Windows?

Answer: A SID is a unique identifier assigned to each user account and group in Windows, allowing Windows to control access and manage security.

19. How can you switch between user accounts in Windows?

Answer: You can switch between user accounts by selecting the user's name from the Start menu or using keyboard shortcuts like "Ctrl+Alt+Del."

20. Explain the concept of a "roaming profile" in Windows.

Answer: A roaming profile allows users to access their customized desktop and settings on any computer within a network when properly configured.

21. What is a "default user profile" in Windows, and how is it used?

Answer: The default user profile serves as a template for creating new user profiles, providing initial settings and configurations.

22. How can you delete a user account in Windows?

Answer: User accounts can be deleted through the Control Panel or Settings app under "User Accounts" or "Accounts."

23. What is the purpose of the "Guest" account in Windows?

Answer: The Guest account provides limited access to the computer, allowing users to access basic features without creating a full user account.

24. Explain the steps to enable or disable the Guest account in Windows.

Answer: You can enable or disable the Guest account in the Control Panel under "User Accounts" or in the Local Security Policy.

25. What is "User Account Control (UAC) virtualization" in Windows?

Answer: UAC virtualization allows legacy applications to write to system-protected folders without administrative privileges.

26. How do you manage user account permissions and access rights in Windows?

Answer: Permissions and access rights can be managed through the Security and Sharing tabs of file and folder properties.

27. What is the "Administrator" account in Windows, and how is it different from other user accounts?

Answer: The Administrator account has full control over the computer and can perform administrative tasks. It is not subject to UAC prompts.

28. How can you change the account type of a user account (e.g., from Standard to Administrator) in Windows?

Answer: Account types can be changed through the Control Panel or Settings app in the "User Accounts" or "Accounts" sections.

29. What is a "user group" in Windows, and how does it relate to user accounts?

Answer: User groups are collections of user accounts with similar permissions. They simplify the process of managing access rights and permissions.

30. Explain the purpose of the "User State Migration Tool (USMT)" in Windows.

Answer: USMT is a Microsoft utility that allows users to transfer user accounts and profiles from one computer to another, ideal for migration scenarios.

31. How can you configure parental controls for a user account in Windows?

Answer: Parental controls can be configured through the Control Panel or Settings app under the "Family & other users" section.

32. What is the purpose of a "picture password" or "PIN" in Windows for user account login?

Answer: These options provide alternative and more convenient ways to log in to a user account, especially on touch-enabled devices.

33. Explain how to set up a Microsoft account in Windows for user authentication.

Answer: You can set up a Microsoft account by signing up for an Outlook.com email address or linking an existing email to a Microsoft account.

34. How do you reset a user account password in Windows if you forget it?

Answer: You can reset a forgotten password using a recovery email or phone number associated with the Microsoft account.

35. What are "user account profiles" and "system profiles" in Windows?

Answer: User account profiles are for individual user settings, while system profiles store settings and configurations for all users on a system.

36. Explain the "Fast User Switching" feature in Windows and how it works.

Answer: Fast User Switching allows multiple users to be logged in simultaneously, and users can switch between accounts without logging off.

37. How can you manage Windows user accounts and profiles on a domain network?

Answer: User accounts and profiles on a domain network can be managed through Active Directory and Group Policy.

38. What is the "net user" command in Windows, and how is it used to manage user accounts?

Answer: The "net user" command is used to create, modify, and delete user accounts via the Command Prompt.

39. Explain the concept of "mandatory profiles" in Windows.

Answer: Mandatory profiles are user profiles that serve as templates, and any changes made by users are not saved. They are often used in a corporate environment.

40. How can you configure user account password policies in Windows?

Answer: Password policies can be configured through Group Policy or Local Security Policy to enforce password complexity and expiration rules.

41. What is "User Profile Service" in Windows, and why is it essential?

Answer: The User Profile Service manages the loading and unloading of user profiles, ensuring that users' settings and data are preserved correctly.

42. Explain the process of migrating a user profile from one computer to another in Windows.

Answer: User profiles can be migrated using the User State Migration Tool (USMT) or manually by copying the user profile folder.

43. How can you change the name of a user account in Windows without creating a new account?

Answer: You can change the account name in the Control Panel or Settings app under "User Accounts" or "Accounts."

44. What are "group policies" in Windows, and how do they impact user accounts and profiles?

Answer: Group policies are used to configure and control user and computer settings, affecting the behavior and security of user accounts and profiles.

45. Explain the concept of "user account control settings" and how they influence account security.

Answer: User Account Control settings determine the level of notification and consent required for changes that may impact system security.

46. What are the different user account types available in Windows, and what are their roles?

Answer: User account types include Administrator, Standard, Guest, and Child. They define the level of access and control over the system.

47. How do you customize the appearance and settings of a user account profile in Windows?

Answer: User profile settings, such as desktop background and theme, can be customized through the Control Panel or Settings app.

48. What is a "user account control password" in Windows, and how is it used?

Answer: A user account control password is required when making changes to system settings that require administrative privileges.

49. Explain the purpose of "Fast Startup" and how it affects user accounts and profiles.

Answer: Fast Startup is a feature that speeds up the boot process. It can impact how user profiles are loaded during startup.

50. How do you prevent unauthorized access to a user account in Windows?

Answer: You can secure a user account with a strong password, enable two-factor authentication, and apply proper security policies through Group Policy.

Group Accounts and Permissions

1. What is a group account, and why are they used in an operating system?

Answer: A group account is a collection of user accounts that share common permissions and access rights. They are used to simplify access control and permissions management.

2. Explain the differences between a local group and a global group in Windows Server environments.

Answer: In Windows Server, a local group is specific to a single computer, while a global group can include members from multiple domains within the forest. Global groups are often used for permissions management across domains.

3. How can you create and manage group accounts in Windows, and what are the advantages of using groups for access control?

Answer: Group accounts can be created and managed using the Local Users and Groups tool or Active Directory in Windows Server. The advantages of using groups include simplifying permissions assignment and making management more efficient.

4. What are group policies, and how do they help in enforcing and controlling system settings in a network environment?

Answer: Group policies are a way to define and enforce security settings, configurations, and restrictions across user accounts and computers in a network domain. They ensure consistency and security compliance.

5. Explain the concept of role-based access control (RBAC) and how it relates to group accounts and permissions.

Answer: RBAC involves assigning permissions based on user roles or groups. Group accounts are used to create roles, and permissions are assigned to these groups to ensure that users in the same role have consistent access rights.

6. What is an access control list (ACL), and how is it used to define permissions for objects in an operating system?

Answer: An ACL is a list of permissions attached to an object (e.g., files, directories, resources) that specifies which users or groups have access and what type of access (read, write, execute) they are allowed.

7. What are the potential security considerations when managing group accounts and permissions, and how can these risks be mitigated?

Answer: Security considerations include avoiding over-privileging users, regularly reviewing and auditing permissions, and adhering to the principle of least privilege. Risks can be mitigated through proper access management and regular security audits.

8. How does the nesting of groups work, and what are the advantages and challenges of using nested groups in permissions management?

Answer: Nesting groups involves placing a group inside another group. Advantages include flexibility and efficiency in managing access. Challenges can arise if nesting is too complex, making it harder to track and manage permissions.

9. What is the purpose of dynamic access control in Windows Server, and how does it enhance access control and permissions management?

Answer: Dynamic access control allows administrators to define access policies based on attributes, classifications, and conditions. It enhances access control by providing a more granular and context-aware approach to permissions.

10. How do you use effective permissions to determine a user's access rights to a specific resource, and why is this important for access control?

Answer: Effective permissions show the combined access rights granted to a user through direct assignments and group memberships. This is important for understanding a user's actual access and for troubleshooting permissions issues.

11. What are group accounts in Windows?

Answer: Group accounts in Windows are collections of user accounts that are treated as a single entity for assigning permissions and access rights.

12. Explain the difference between local and domain groups in Windows.

Answer: Local groups are specific to a single computer, while domain groups are created in an Active Directory domain and can be used across multiple computers.

13. How do you create a new group account in Windows?

Answer: You can create a new group account using the "Local Users and Groups" or "Active Directory Users and Computers" management tools.

14. What is the purpose of group membership in Windows?

Answer: Group membership simplifies the management of permissions and access control by allowing multiple users to share common settings and privileges.

15. How can you add a user to a group in Windows?

Answer: Users can be added to a group through the "Member Of" tab in the user's properties or by using the "net localgroup" command.

16. What is the "Administrators" group in Windows, and what permissions does it grant?

Answer: The Administrators group has elevated privileges, allowing members to perform administrative tasks, such as installing software and configuring system settings.

17. Explain the purpose of "Security Groups" in Active Directory.

Answer: Security Groups are used in Active Directory to manage access control and permissions for resources like files, folders, and printers.

18. What is the "Power Users" group in Windows, and what are its permissions?

Answer: The Power Users group has fewer permissions than Administrators but more than Standard Users, allowing users to install software and manage some system settings.

19. How can you view the members of a group in Windows?

Answer: You can view the members of a group by opening the group's properties or using the "net localgroup" or "net group" commands.

20. Explain the difference between a "global group" and a "local group" in Active Directory.

Answer:A global group can contain users from the same domain, while a local group can include users and groups from the local computer.

21. What is the "Remote Desktop Users" group in Windows used for?

Answer: The Remote Desktop Users group allows members to access a computer remotely using Remote Desktop Protocol (RDP).

22. How do you change group membership for a user account in Windows?

Answer: You can modify group membership by accessing the user's properties and making changes in the "Member Of" tab.

23. What are "Distribution Groups" in Active Directory, and how are they different from security groups?

Answer: Distribution Groups are used for sending email to a group of users. Security groups control access and permissions.

24. Explain the purpose of the "Guests" group in Windows.

Answer: The Guests group provides limited access to a computer, granting permissions to perform only basic tasks.

25. What is the "net group" command in Windows, and how is it used to manage group accounts?

Answer: The "net group" command allows you to create, modify, and delete group accounts from the Command Prompt.

26. How can you restrict a user from accessing a particular resource using group permissions?

Answer: You can deny access to a user by either removing them from the group with access or explicitly setting Deny permissions for the resource.

27. Explain the concept of "Nested Groups" in Windows.

Answer: Nested groups are groups that contain other groups as members. This hierarchical structure simplifies permissions management.

28. What is the purpose of "Domain Local Groups" in Active Directory?

Answer: Domain Local Groups are used to assign permissions within a specific domain, and they can include members from other domains.

29. Explain the difference between "Explicit" and "Implicit" permissions in Windows.

Answer: Explicit permissions are directly assigned to a resource, while implicit permissions are inherited from parent folders or groups.

30. How do you secure a shared folder by assigning group permissions?

Answer: You can specify which groups have access to a shared folder and define their level of access (read, write, etc.) in the folder's properties.

31. What is the purpose of the "Backup Operators" group in Windows, and what permissions does it grant?

Answer: The Backup Operators group has permissions to back up and restore files and directories, but it doesn't have full administrative control.

32. Explain the "Group Policy" feature in Windows and its role in managing group permissions.

Answer: Group Policy allows administrators to define and enforce a wide range of settings and permissions for users and computers within an Active Directory environment.

33. How can you check a user's effective permissions for a resource in Windows?

Answer: You can use the "Effective Access" tab in the resource's properties to determine the permissions a user has based on group membership.

34. What is the "net localgroup" command in Windows, and how does it relate to local group management?

Answer: The "net localgroup" command allows you to manage local groups on a computer using the Command Prompt.

35. How do you create a group policy to apply specific settings to a group of users in Active Directory?

Answer: Group policies can be created and linked to organizational units (OUs) in Active Directory, affecting the users and computers within those OUs.

36. What is the "net group" command's syntax for adding a user to a group?

Answer: The syntax is: **net group <groupname><username> /add**.

37. Explain the concept of "group scope" in Active Directory, including Universal, Global, and Domain Local groups.

Answer: Group scope defines where a group can be used in Active Directory. Universal groups can be used in any domain, Global groups in the same domain, and Domain Local groups for access control within a domain.

38. What is the "Authenticated Users" group in Windows, and how does it impact security settings?

Answer: Authenticated Users includes all users with valid logon credentials. It is often used to grant basic access rights to authenticated users.

39. How can you prevent a group of users from accessing a specific folder in Windows?

Answer: You can deny permissions to that folder for the group, ensuring they can't access it.

40. How do you delegate administrative tasks using group accounts in Windows?

Answer: You can grant administrative permissions to a group and then add users to that group to delegate tasks.

41. What is the "net group" command's syntax for listing the members of a group?

Answer: The syntax is: **net group <groupname> /domain**.

42. Explain the concept of "resource-based access policies" and how they are used with group accounts.

Answer: Resource-based access policies allow you to define access control policies directly on the resource, simplifying management and eliminating the need for complex group structures.

43. How can you configure group policies for restricting software installations for a group of users?

Answer: Group policies can be configured to restrict software installations by specifying software restriction rules and permissions for the group.

44. What is the "Account Operators" group in Windows, and what permissions does it grant?

Answer: The Account Operators group has limited permissions to manage user accounts, groups, and their properties.

45. Explain how you can audit group membership changes and permissions in Windows.

Answer: Auditing can be set up through Group Policy to log and track changes to group memberships and permission settings.

46. What is the "Authenticated Users" group in Active Directory, and how is it used for permissions?

Answer: Authenticated Users includes all users and computers with valid logon credentials and is used to grant basic access rights to authenticated entities.

47. How do you handle conflicts in group permissions in Windows when a user belongs to multiple groups?

Answer: Windows uses an order of precedence to determine a user's effective permissions based on the combination of groups they belong to.

48. Explain the concept of "group policy inheritance" in Windows.

Answer: Group policy inheritance determines how group policies are applied to objects in Active Directory, with the closest organizational unit taking precedence.

49. How do you grant permissions to a group to access a shared printer in Windows?

Answer: You can assign the group appropriate permissions on the printer's properties, allowing members to print.

50. What is the purpose of "Service Accounts" in Windows, and how are they different from user accounts?

Answer: Service accounts are used by Windows services and applications to run tasks, often with minimal user interaction. They are not associated with individual users.

Managing User Authentication

1. What is user authentication, and why is it a critical component of operating systems and network security?

Answer: User authentication is the process of verifying the identity of a user or entity before granting access to a system or network. It is essential for safeguarding data and resources from unauthorized access.

2. Explain the concept of multi-factor authentication (MFA), and how does it enhance security over traditional username and password authentication?

Answer*:* Multi-factor authentication requires users to provide at least two forms of authentication, such as something they know (password), something they have (a token or smartphone), or something they are (biometric data). MFA adds an extra layer of security, making it more difficult for unauthorized users to gain access.

3. What is the role of the Active Directory in user authentication in a Windows network environment, and how does it manage user credentials?

Answer*:* Active Directory is a directory service in Windows Server that manages user accounts, group memberships, and authentication. It stores and verifies user credentials, such as usernames and passwords.

4. How can a single sign-on (SSO) solution simplify user authentication for users across multiple applications and services?

Answer*:* SSO allows users to log in once and gain access to multiple applications and services without needing to re-enter their credentials. It enhances user experience and reduces the need to remember multiple passwords.

5. What are the security risks associated with password-based authentication, and what best practices can mitigate these risks?

Answer*:* Risks include password cracking and phishing attacks. Best practices include using strong, unique passwords, enabling account lockout policies, and implementing password expiration and complexity requirements.

6. Explain the difference between centralized and decentralized authentication, and what are the advantages and disadvantages of each approach?

Answer*:* Centralized authentication involves a single authority for authentication, while decentralized authentication allows multiple entities to manage authentication independently. Centralized authentication provides consistency and ease of management, but it can also be a single point of failure. Decentralized authentication offers autonomy but can lead to inconsistencies and added complexity.

7. What is the purpose of biometric authentication, and what are some common biometric methods used in user authentication?

Answer*:* Biometric authentication uses physical or behavioural characteristics to verify identity. Common methods include fingerprint recognition, facial recognition, and iris scanning.

8. How do single-factor and two-factor authentication differ, and when might each be used in user authentication?

Answer*:* Single-factor authentication requires one form of authentication (e.g., a password), while two-factor authentication requires at least two forms (e.g., a password and a token or biometric scan). Two-factor authentication is typically used for sensitive or high-security applications.

9. What is the role of identity and access management (IAM) systems in user authentication and authorization, and how do they improve security and compliance?

Answer*:* IAM systems manage user identities, access rights, and permissions. They improve security by providing centralized control, auditing, and compliance monitoring.

10. What precautions should organizations take to ensure secure and robust user authentication, and how can user training and awareness play a role in this process?

Answer: Precautions include regularly updating authentication methods, monitoring for suspicious activities, and educating users about secure practices. User training and awareness can help prevent social engineering attacks and improve overall security.

11. What is user authentication in the context of computer security?

Answer: User authentication is the process of verifying the identity of a user, typically through a username and password, to grant access to a system or resource.

12. Why is user authentication important for computer security?

Answer: User authentication is crucial for ensuring that only authorized users can access systems and data, preventing unauthorized access and data breaches.

13. What are the common methods of user authentication in computing?

Answer: Common methods include password-based authentication, biometrics (fingerprint, face, etc.), smart cards, tokens, and multi-factor authentication (MFA).

14. Explain the concept of multi-factor authentication (MFA).

Answer:MFA is a security method that requires users to provide two or more different factors to authenticate, such as something they know (password) and something they have (smartphone or token).

15. What are the advantages of using MFA for user authentication?

Answer:MFA significantly enhances security by adding an extra layer of protection, making it more challenging for attackers to gain access.

16. How can you enforce strong password policies for user authentication?

Answer: Strong password policies may require longer and complex passwords, regular password changes, and password history restrictions.

17. What is the role of a password hashing algorithm in user authentication?

Answer:A password hashing algorithm securely stores and verifies passwords without storing the actual password. It protects against password theft.

18. Explain the risks associated with using simple, easily guessable passwords for user authentication.

Answer: Simple passwords are susceptible to brute-force attacks and can lead to unauthorized access, data breaches, and security vulnerabilities.

19. What is a CAPTCHA, and how does it relate to user authentication?

Answer:CAPTCHA (Completely Automated Public Turing test to tell Computers and Humans Apart) is a challenge-response test used to verify that the user is a human, not a bot, during authentication.

20. How can you prevent password cracking in user authentication?

Answer: Password cracking can be prevented by using strong, unique passwords, implementing account lockout policies, and employing secure password hashing techniques.

21. What is the purpose of account lockout policies in user authentication?

Answer: Account lockout policies temporarily disable an account after a certain number of failed login attempts to prevent brute-force attacks.

22. Explain the concept of "time-based one-time passwords" (TOTP) in user authentication.

Answer:TOTP is a form of MFA that generates a unique, time-limited code based on a shared secret and the current time.

23. How does biometric authentication work, and what are its advantages and disadvantages?

Answer: Biometric authentication uses unique physical or behavioural traits (e.g., fingerprints, faces) for user verification. It's highly secure but can be less convenient.

24. What are "public key certificates" and how are they used in user authentication?

Answer: Public key certificates are digital certificates that bind a user's public key to their identity, allowing secure authentication and data encryption.

25. Explain the difference between single sign-on (SSO) and username/password authentication.

Answer:SSO allows users to access multiple systems with one set of credentials, while username/password authentication requires separate credentials for each system.

26. What are the risks associated with using "Remember Me" features for user authentication on websites?

Answer:"Remember Me" features can pose security risks by storing login credentials in cookies, making them vulnerable to theft if the device is compromised.

27. What is "social engineering," and how does it relate to user authentication?

Answer: Social engineering is a tactic used by attackers to manipulate individuals into revealing confidential information, such as passwords, posing a risk to user authentication.

28. How can you secure user authentication in a remote work environment?

Answer: Securing remote work involves implementing secure VPNs, strong authentication methods, and access controls to protect against unauthorized access.

29. What is the difference between "two-step verification" and "two-factor authentication" in user authentication?

Answer: Two-step verification typically involves using a username and password, followed by a second verification method. Two-factor authentication involves two independent factors for authentication.

30. Explain the role of "session management" in web-based user authentication.

Answer: Session management ensures that a user remains authenticated during their session and can access resources without repeatedly re-entering credentials.

31. How can you prevent account takeover attacks in user authentication?

Answer: Preventing account takeovers may involve monitoring for unusual activities, implementing strong authentication, and using threat detection systems.

32. What is "password salting," and why is it important for user authentication?

Answer: Password salting is the practice of adding a unique random value to a password before hashing it. It prevents rainbow table attacks and increases security.

33. Explain the concept of "zero trust" in user authentication and network security.

Answer: Zero trust security assumes that no one, whether inside or outside the network, should be trusted by default and enforces strict access controls and authentication.

34. How can you securely store and manage user authentication data in a database?

Answer: Secure storage involves using strong hashing algorithms, salts, and encryption to protect user credentials in the database.

35. What is "Single Sign-On (SSO)," and how does it simplify user authentication?

Answer:SSO allows users to access multiple systems and applications with a single set of credentials, reducing the need to remember multiple usernames and passwords.

36. Explain the concept of "session hijacking" in user authentication.

Answer: Session hijacking occurs when an attacker takes over an established session to impersonate a user, typically by stealing session cookies or tokens.

37. What are the benefits of using a password manager for user authentication?

Answer: Password managers generate and securely store complex, unique passwords, reducing the risk of password-related security incidents.

38. How do you protect user authentication against "brute force" attacks?

Answer: Protection against brute-force attacks includes implementing account lockout policies, using CAPTCHAs, and deploying rate limiting and intrusion detection systems.

39. Explain the role of "Kerberos" in network authentication and security.

Answer: Kerberos is a network authentication protocol that provides secure authentication for users and services, commonly used in Windows environments.

40. How do you handle forgotten passwords for user accounts while maintaining security?

Answer: Forgotten passwords can be reset through secure password reset processes, often involving email verification, security questions, or multi-factor authentication.

41. What is "OAuth" and "OpenID Connect," and how do they relate to user authentication for web applications?

Answer:OAuth is an authorization protocol, and OpenID Connect is an identity layer on top of OAuth, both used for web-based authentication and authorization.

42. Explain the process of token-based authentication in web applications.

Answer: Token-based authentication involves issuing tokens to users after they authenticate, which are then used for subsequent requests to access protected resources.

43. What is the purpose of "Single Logout" (SLO) in user authentication for single sign-on systems?

Answer:SLO allows users to log out from multiple connected applications simultaneously, improving user experience and security.

44. How do you protect user authentication against "replay attacks"?

Answer: Protection against replay attacks involves using time-based tokens and ensuring that data exchanged between the client and server is not re-used.

45. Explain the concept of "Identity as a Service" (IDaaS) in user authentication.

Answer:IDaaS provides identity and access management services via the cloud, allowing organizations to manage user authentication and authorization more efficiently.

46. What is the role of "Access Control Lists" (ACLs) in user authentication and authorization?

Answer:ACLs are used to define which users or groups have access to specific resources and what actions they can perform.

47. How can you implement strong authentication methods for remote access to corporate networks?

Answer: Strong authentication methods for remote access may include MFA, VPNs, secure tokens, and secure remote desktop protocols.

48. What are "Security Assertion Markup Language" (SAML) and "OpenID" in user authentication and authorization?

Answer:SAML and OpenID are protocols for exchanging authentication and authorization data between parties, commonly used in single sign-on and identity federation.

49. Explain the difference between "login" and "logout" in user authentication terminology.

Answer:"Login" is the process of gaining access, while "logout" is the process of ending a user's authenticated session and revoking access.

50. What is the role of "active directory" in user authentication for Windows-based networks?

Answer: Active Directory is a directory service and identity management system used for user authentication, access control, and network administration in Windows environments.

Local and Domain User Management

1. Explain the difference between a local user account and a domain user account in a Windows network environment.

Answer: A local user account is specific to a single computer and is not part of a network domain. A domain user account, on the other hand, is part of a network domain and can access resources across multiple computers within that domain.

2. How can you create a new local user account on a Windows computer, and what information is typically required during the account creation process?

Answer: You can create a local user account through the Computer Management tool. Typically, you need to provide a username, password, and specify group memberships (e.g., Administrators, Users).

3. What is Active Directory, and how does it facilitate the management of domain user accounts in a Windows Server network environment?

Answer: Active Directory is a directory service in Windows Server that centralizes the management of user accounts, groups, and network resources. It simplifies the administration of domain user accounts and provides security features.

4. Explain the process of adding a new domain user account in Active Directory, including the required information and permissions.

Answer: To add a new domain user account, an administrator typically needs to provide a username, password, and specify group memberships. Appropriate permissions in Active Directory are required to perform this task.

5. What are user profiles, and how do they differ for local and domain user accounts in terms of storage and personalization?

Answer: User profiles store personal settings, preferences, and data. Local user profiles are specific to a single computer, while domain user profiles can roam across multiple computers in a network domain.

6. How can you disable or delete a user account, and what are the implications of doing so, especially in a domain environment?

Answer: You can disable a user account to temporarily prevent its use or delete it to permanently remove it. Disabling an account is a security measure, and deleting an account may impact access to resources and data.

7. What are security groups and distribution groups in Active Directory, and how are they used for managing domain user accounts and permissions?

Answer: Security groups are used to manage permissions and access control, while distribution groups are used for email distribution. Both types of groups can contain domain user accounts and simplify access management.

8. Explain the concept of account lockout policies and their role in protecting user accounts against unauthorized access.

Answer: Account lockout policies define rules for locking out user accounts after a certain number of failed login attempts. They protect accounts from brute-force attacks and unauthorized access.

9. What is the purpose of home directories for user accounts, and how can they be configured in Windows, especially in a domain environment?

Answer: Home directories provide users with a dedicated storage area for their files and data. They can be configured through Active Directory, Group Policy, or local user profile settings.

10. What steps should be taken to ensure that user accounts, both local and domain, are secure and compliant with organizational policies, and how can regular auditing and monitoring help in this process?

Answer: Secure user accounts by implementing strong password policies, regularly reviewing permissions, and auditing account activity. Monitoring user accounts and access can help detect and respond to security issues and compliance violations.

11. What is the difference between local user accounts and domain user accounts in Windows?

Answer: Local user accounts are specific to a single computer, while domain user accounts are managed centrally within an Active Directory domain and can be used across multiple computers.

12. How do you create a new local user account in Windows?

Answer: You can create a new local user account through the "Local Users and Groups" tool in Computer Management.

13. What is the purpose of domain user accounts in Windows networks?

Answer: Domain user accounts provide a centralized method for managing and granting access to resources across multiple computers in a network.

14. How can you create a new domain user account in Windows Server using Active Directory Users and Computers?

Answer: To create a domain user account, open "Active Directory Users and Computers," right-click on the desired organizational unit, and select "New" > "User."

15. Explain the concept of a user's "profile" in Windows and how it differs between local and domain accounts.

Answer:A user's profile in Windows stores personal settings, files, and preferences. Local profiles are specific to a single computer, while domain profiles can roam across computers within a domain.

16. How can you set up a roaming profile for a domain user in Windows Server?

Answer: To set up a roaming profile, specify the profile path in the user's profile properties in Active Directory Users and Computers.

17. What is the "Default User Profile" in Windows, and how is it used?

Answer: The Default User Profile serves as a template for creating new user profiles, providing initial settings and configurations.

18. Explain the process of migrating a user profile from a local account to a domain account in Windows.

Answer: You can use the User State Migration Tool (USMT) or manually transfer user profile data when migrating from a local to a domain account.

19. How do you change a user's account type (e.g., from Standard to Administrator) in Windows?

Answer: You can change a user's account type through the Control Panel or Settings app by modifying their account properties.

20. What is the "Local Security Policy" in Windows, and how is it used in user management?

Answer: The Local Security Policy allows administrators to configure security settings, including user rights and permissions on a local computer.

21. How can you reset a user's password for a domain account in Windows Server?

Answer: To reset a domain user's password, open Active Directory Users and Computers, right-click the user, and select "Reset Password."

22. Explain the purpose of "Group Policy" in user management for both local and domain user accounts.

Answer: Group Policy is used to define and enforce various settings and configurations for user accounts, both at the local and domain level.

23. What is the "User Profile Service" in Windows, and why is it important for user management?

Answer: The User Profile Service manages the loading and unloading of user profiles, ensuring that users' settings and data are preserved correctly.

24. How do you delegate user account management tasks in Active Directory to non-administrative users?

Answer: Delegation can be achieved through custom Active Directory security permissions or using the "Delegate Control" wizard.

25. Explain the difference between a "user group" and a "security group" in Active Directory.

Answer: User groups are used for organizing users, while security groups are used to control access to resources and apply permissions.

26. How do you enable or disable a user account in Active Directory?

Answer: To enable or disable a user account, open Active Directory Users and Computers, right-click the user, and select "Enable Account" or "Disable Account."

27. What is the "Guest" account in Windows, and how can it be managed for local and domain accounts?

Answer: The Guest account provides limited access to the computer. It can be enabled or disabled for local accounts, and its use can be controlled through Group Policy for domain accounts.

28. Explain the difference between "profile migration" and "profile management" in user accounts.

Answer: Profile migration refers to the transfer of user profiles between computers, while profile management involves maintaining and configuring user profiles.

29. How can you enforce password policies for domain user accounts in Windows Server?

Answer: Password policies can be configured through Group Policy to enforce password complexity and expiration rules for domain users.

30. What is the "Administrator" account in Windows, and how does it differ from other user accounts?

Answer: The Administrator account has full control over the computer and can perform administrative tasks. It is not subject to User Account Control (UAC) prompts.

31. Explain the concept of "service accounts" and their role in user account management.

Answer: Service accounts are used by Windows services and applications to run tasks, often with minimal user interaction. They are not associated with individual users.

32. How do you perform a bulk import of user accounts in Active Directory using a CSV file?

Answer: Bulk imports can be accomplished through tools like PowerShell scripts or the "Import-CSV" cmdlet.

33. What is "user account provisioning," and why is it important for user management in organizations?

Answer: User account provisioning involves the automated creation, modification, and deletion of user accounts, streamlining the user lifecycle management process.

34. Explain the concept of "User Principal Name" (UPN) and its significance for user authentication.

Answer:A UPN is an alternative to a user's domain\username and is in the format user@domain.com. It simplifies user login and is commonly used for email addresses.

35. How can you monitor and audit user account changes and activities in Active Directory?

Answer: Monitoring and auditing can be enabled through Active Directory's auditing policies and reviewing security event logs.

36. What is the purpose of "Organizational Units" (OUs) in Active Directory, and how are they used in user management?

Answer:OUs are used to organize and manage user accounts and other objects within Active Directory, simplifying administrative tasks and applying Group Policy.

37. Explain the "net user" command in Windows and how it is used for user management.

Answer: The "net user" command allows you to create, modify, and delete user accounts from the Command Prompt.

38. What is the "User Principal Name (UPN) Suffix" in Active Directory, and how is it configured for user accounts?

Answer: UPN suffixes allow users to log in with email-style usernames. They can be configured in Active Directory Domains and Trusts.

39. How can you migrate user profiles from one domain to another in Windows?

Answer: User profile migration can be performed using the User State Migration Tool (USMT) or manually by copying the profile data.

40. Explain the concept of "fine-grained password policies" in Windows Server and how they affect user accounts.

Answer: Fine-grained password policies allow you to apply different password policies to specific users or groups within a domain.

41. What is the "net group" command in Windows, and how is it used to manage group memberships for user accounts?

Answer: The "net group" command allows you to create, modify, and manage group memberships for user accounts from the Command Prompt.

42. How can you configure user account attributes like "user logon name" and "user logon name (pre-Windows 2000)" in Active Directory?

Answer: These attributes can be configured in the user's properties within Active Directory Users and Computers.

43. Explain the concept of "account lockout policies" and how they prevent unauthorized access to user accounts.

Answer: Account lockout policies temporarily disable an account after a specified number of failed login attempts, preventing unauthorized access.

44. What is the "net user" command's syntax for creating a new user account from the Command Prompt?

Answer: The syntax is: **net user <username><password> /add**.

45. How do you perform bulk modifications to user accounts in Active Directory using PowerShell scripts?

Answer: PowerShell scripts can be used to automate bulk modifications, such as changing attributes or group memberships for user accounts.

46. What is "User Account Control (UAC)" in Windows, and how does it impact user account management for administrators?

Answer: UAC is a security feature that prompts administrators for consent or credentials when performing tasks that require administrative privileges.

47. How can you recover a deleted user account in Active Directory, and what precautions should be taken?

Answer: Deleted user accounts can be recovered from the Active Directory Recycle Bin or through backup and restore procedures. Precautions include verifying the recovery process.

48. Explain the concept of "group nesting" in Active Directory and how it impacts user account management.

Answer: Group nesting involves including one group within another. It simplifies user account management by controlling access through higher-level groups.

49. What is the "user account control password" in Windows, and how is it used to secure user accounts?

Answer: The user account control password is required for making changes to user accounts that require administrative privileges, providing an additional layer of security.

50. How can you enforce password policies for local user accounts on a Windows computer not joined to a domain?

Answer: Local password policies can be set through the "Local Security Policy" or the "Secpol.msc" tool on standalone Windows computers.

ONLINE RESOURCES

Practice Paper Link: https://forms.gle/bh3SdaXcT45s4bP48

QR Code:

Video Link: https://www.youtube.com/playlist?list=PLzlh_31VWEFou_X2dK5vqoy4Wl8kvm_bZ

QR Code:

Chapter 6 Networking in Windows

Windows Networking Concepts

1. What is a network in the context of Windows operating systems, and why is networking essential in modern computing environments?

Answer: A network in Windows refers to the interconnection of computers and devices for the purpose of sharing resources and information. Networking is essential for communication, resource sharing, and efficient data exchange in today's interconnected world.

2. Explain the significance of an IP address in Windows networking, and what are the key differences between IPv4 and IPv6 addresses?

Answer: An IP address uniquely identifies a device on a network. IPv4 addresses are 32-bit numeric addresses, while IPv6 addresses are 128-bit alphanumeric addresses designed to accommodate the growing number of devices on the internet.

3. What is the role of a subnet mask, and how does it help in routing and addressing within a Windows network?

Answer: A subnet mask is used to divide an IP address into a network address and a host address. It helps in routing data to the correct subnet and determining which part of an IP address identifies the network and which part identifies the host.

4. How does the Domain Name System (DNS) work in Windows networking, and what is its function in translating human-readable domain names to IP addresses?

Answer: DNS translates human-readable domain names (e.g., www.example.com) into IP addresses (e.g., 192.168.1.1). It functions as a distributed database system to resolve domain names to their corresponding IP addresses.

5. Explain the concept of a DHCP server in Windows networking and its role in dynamically assigning IP addresses to devices on a network.

Answer: A DHCP (Dynamic Host Configuration Protocol) server automatically assigns IP addresses, subnet masks, and other network configuration information to devices when they connect to a network, simplifying network administration.

6. What are workgroups and domains in Windows networking, and how do they differ in terms of user account and resource management?

Answer: A workgroup is a small peer-to-peer network where each computer manages its user accounts and resources independently. A domain is a centralized network environment where a Windows Server, known as a domain controller, manages user accounts and resources.

7. What is the purpose of a firewall in Windows networking, and how does it enhance network security by controlling incoming and outgoing network traffic?

Answer: A firewall is a network security device or software that filters and controls network traffic. It enhances security by allowing or blocking specific traffic based on predefined rules, helping to protect against unauthorized access and threats.

8. Explain the concept of a Virtual Private Network (VPN) and how it can be used to establish secure connections between remote locations or users in a Windows network.

Answer: A VPN is a technology that creates a secure, encrypted tunnel over a public network (usually the internet) to connect remote locations or users to the main network. It allows for secure data transmission and remote access to resources.

9. What is a network protocol, and how do protocols like TCP/IP, HTTP, and FTP play crucial roles in enabling communication and data transfer in Windows networking?

Answer: A network protocol is a set of rules governing communication between devices on a network. TCP/IP is the foundational protocol suite for the internet and local networks. HTTP is used for web communication, and FTP is used for file transfers.

10. How can network monitoring and diagnostic tools, such as Wireshark and Ping, assist in troubleshooting and maintaining the health of a Windows network?

Answer: Network monitoring tools like Wireshark capture and analyze network traffic, helping diagnose network issues. Ping is used to test network connectivity. These tools are vital for maintaining network performance and resolving problems.

11. What is a network in the context of Windows networking?

Answer:A network in Windows networking is a collection of computers and devices that are interconnected and can share resources and communicate with each other.

12. Explain the purpose of an IP address in Windows networking.

Answer: An IP address is a unique numerical label assigned to each device on a network to identify and locate it, enabling communication between devices.

13. What is the key role of the Domain Name System (DNS) in Windows networking?

Answer:DNS resolves human-readable domain names to IP addresses, making it easier for users to access websites and resources by name.

14. How does Dynamic Host Configuration Protocol (DHCP) simplify IP address management in Windows networks?

Answer:DHCP automatically assigns and manages IP addresses for devices on a network, reducing the need for manual configuration.

15. Explain the difference between a local and a public IP address in Windows networking.

Answer:A local IP address is used within a private network, while a public IP address is used to identify a device on the internet.

16. What is the purpose of the Default Gateway in Windows networking, and how is it configured?

Answer: The Default Gateway is a device that connects a local network to other networks, such as the internet. It is configured in network settings to enable internet access.

17. How do you set up a static IP address for a Windows computer on a network?

Answer:A static IP address can be configured in the computer's network settings by specifying the IP address, subnet mask, default gateway, and DNS servers manually.

18. Explain the concept of a subnet mask and its role in Windows networking.

Answer:A subnet mask defines the network and host portions of an IP address, allowing devices to determine if they are on the same local network.

19. What is Network Address Translation (NAT) in Windows networking, and why is it used?

Answer:NAT is a method used to allow multiple devices on a local network to share a single public IP address for internet access.

20. How does the Windows Firewall contribute to network security in Windows networking?

Answer: Windows Firewall controls inbound and outbound network traffic to protect the computer from unauthorized access and malware.

21. What is a MAC address, and how does it relate to IP addresses in Windows networking?

Answer:A MAC address is a hardware-based address assigned to network interface cards. It is used at the data link layer to identify devices within a local network.

22. Explain the concept of port forwarding in Windows networking and its role in network configuration.

Answer: Port forwarding redirects network traffic from a specific port on a router to a specific device or server within the local network, allowing external access.

23. What is a router in Windows networking, and how does it facilitate communication between local and external networks?

Answer:A router is a network device that connects different networks and forwards data between them, enabling communication between local and external networks.

24. What are the differences between a hub, switch, and router in Windows networking?

Answer:A hub operates at the physical layer and simply broadcasts data to all devices. A switch operates at the data link layer and routes data to specific devices. A router connects different networks.

25. How does Windows implement network discovery, and what is its purpose?

Answer: Network discovery is a feature that allows Windows computers to identify and communicate with other devices on the same network, making shared resources visible.

26. Explain the concept of a local area network (LAN) and its typical size in Windows networking.

Answer:A LAN is a network of interconnected devices within a relatively small geographic area, such as a home or office, typically with a range of a few kilometers.

27. What is a Wide Area Network (WAN) in Windows networking, and how does it differ from a LAN?

Answer:A WAN is a network that covers a larger geographical area, often spanning cities or even countries, connecting multiple LANs.

28. How can you configure a virtual private network (VPN) in Windows to secure network connections over the internet?

Answer:VPN settings can be configured in Windows to create a secure, encrypted connection over the internet, typically to access resources on a private network.

29. What is a subnet in Windows networking, and how does it help with network organization and management?

Answer:A subnet is a logical division of an IP network that allows for more efficient organization and management of network resources.

30. How do you share files and printers on a Windows network, and what is the role of file and printer sharing permissions?

Answer: File and printer sharing is configured in the Network and Sharing Center, and permissions are set to control who can access shared resources.

31. What is a network protocol, and how do protocols like TCP/IP function in Windows networking?

Answer:A network protocol is a set of rules governing communication between devices. TCP/IP is the fundamental protocol suite used for internet communication in Windows.

32. Explain the concept of a network segment in Windows networking and how it affects data traffic.

Answer:A network segment is a portion of a network that is isolated from the rest, affecting data traffic by creating separate collision domains.

33. What is a domain controller in Windows networking, and how does it relate to Active Directory?

Answer:A domain controller is a server that authenticates users and enforces security policies within an Active Directory domain.

34. How do you configure a static route in Windows to manage network traffic?

Answer: Static routes can be configured in Windows to specify how network traffic is directed to a particular destination.

35. Explain the concept of Network Load Balancing (NLB) in Windows and its benefits for server availability.

Answer:NLB allows multiple servers to share the load, ensuring high availability and redundancy for network services.

36. What is the purpose of a subnet calculator in Windows networking, and how can it help with IP address management?

Answer:A subnet calculator assists in IP address management by calculating subnets, IP ranges, and other network parameters.

37. How can you troubleshoot network connectivity issues in Windows, and what tools are available for this purpose?

Answer: Troubleshooting network issues involves using tools like ping, tracert, ipconfig, and network monitoring tools to identify and resolve problems.

38. Explain the concept of a network gateway and its role in routing traffic between networks.

Answer:A network gateway is a device that connects one network to another, facilitating the flow of data between networks.

39. What is the purpose of the Windows Hosts file in network configuration, and how is it used to resolve domain names?

Answer: The Hosts file is used to map domain names to IP addresses, providing a local method of DNS resolution.

40. How does the Network Location Awareness (NLA) service in Windows help identify network profiles and configure network settings?

Answer:NLA identifies the type of network a computer is connected to and configures appropriate settings, such as firewall rules and sharing options.

41. What is a network switch in Windows networking, and how does it improve network performance compared to a hub?

Answer:A network switch operates at the data link layer and routes data to specific devices, unlike a hub, which simply broadcasts data.

42. Explain the concept of a network mask and its role in subnetting.

Answer:A network mask is used to divide an IP address into network and host portions, enabling subnetting and defining network boundaries.

43. How can you secure a wireless network in Windows using encryption and access controls?

Answer: Wireless network security can be enhanced by using encryption methods like WPA3, setting strong passphrases, and enabling MAC address filtering.

44. What is a network bridge in Windows networking, and how does it connect two separate network segments?

Answer:A network bridge connects two or more network segments, allowing them to function as a single network and share resources.

45. Explain the difference between an IP address and a subnet mask and how they work together in Windows networking.

Answer: An IP address is used to identify a device on a network, while a subnet mask determines the network and host portions of the IP address.

46. What is a network share in Windows, and how can it be used to collaborate and share resources with others on a network?

Answer:A network share allows users to make files and folders accessible to others on the same network, enabling collaboration and resource sharing.

47. How do you configure a virtual switch in Windows Hyper-V for virtual machine networking?

Answer:A virtual switch can be configured in Hyper-V to connect virtual machines to physical networks and other VMs.

48. Explain the concept of a network proxy in Windows and how it can be used to filter and control internet access.

Answer:A network proxy serves as an intermediary server that can filter, cache, and control internet traffic, enhancing security and performance.

49. How can you diagnose and resolve issues related to IP conflicts in a Windows network?

Answer:IP conflicts can be diagnosed and resolved by checking for duplicate IP addresses and ensuring that DHCP is correctly configured.

50. What is the purpose of a network sniffer (packet analyser) in Windows networking, and how is it used for network troubleshooting and analysis?

Answer:A network sniffer captures and analyses network traffic to troubleshoot problems, identify network issues, and monitor performance.

TCP/IP Networking and Configuration

1. **What is TCP/IP, and why is it considered the foundation of the internet and modern networking?**

Answer: TCP/IP (Transmission Control Protocol/Internet Protocol) is a suite of protocols that enables data transmission and communication between devices on the internet and local networks. It's fundamental to network communication because it ensures reliable and standardized data transmission.

2. Explain the purpose of an IP address and the differences between IPv4 and IPv6.

Answer: An IP address is a unique identifier for devices on a network. IPv4 uses 32-bit addresses, while IPv6 uses 128-bit addresses to accommodate the growing number of devices on the internet.

3. What is a subnet mask, and how does it assist in IP address management and network segmentation?

Answer: A subnet mask is used to divide an IP address into network and host portions. It assists in IP address management by determining the network segment and host within that segment, enabling efficient network routing and addressing.

4. How does DNS (Domain Name System) work in mapping domain names to IP addresses, and why is it crucial in web browsing and network communication?

Answer: DNS translates human-readable domain names into IP addresses. It's crucial because it makes it easier for users to access websites and services by using domain names rather than numeric IP addresses.

5. Explain the role of DHCP (Dynamic Host Configuration Protocol) in IP address allocation and configuration within a network.

Answer: DHCP automates the allocation of IP addresses, subnet masks, and other network configuration settings to devices, reducing administrative overhead and ensuring efficient IP address usage.

6. What is NAT (Network Address Translation), and how does it facilitate the sharing of a single public IP address among multiple devices in a local network?

Answer: NAT allows multiple devices in a local network to share a single public IP address by mapping internal IP addresses to the public address. It enhances security and conserves public IP addresses.

7. What is the purpose of a default gateway in TCP/IP networking, and how does it affect routing and internet access for devices in a network?

Answer: The default gateway is a router or device that serves as an exit point to other networks, including the internet. It directs traffic between the local network and external networks, enabling internet access.

8. Explain the concept of ports in TCP/IP communication and how they assist in identifying specific services and applications on a device.

Answer: Ports are used to distinguish different services and applications on a device. They facilitate data routing and allow multiple services to run on a single device. Common examples include port 80 for HTTP and port 22 for SSH.

9. What is a subnet, and how does subnetting contribute to efficient IP address allocation and network segmentation?

Answer: A subnet is a portion of a larger network. Subnetting divides a network into smaller, more manageable segments, reducing broadcast traffic and aiding in IP address management.

10. How does ARP (Address Resolution Protocol) work, and what is its role in mapping IP addresses to physical MAC addresses on a local network?

Answer: ARP resolves an IP address to a MAC address in local network communication. When a device needs to communicate with another on the same network, it uses ARP to find the corresponding MAC address, allowing data transmission at the physical layer.

11. What does TCP/IP stand for, and what is its role in networking?

Answer:TCP/IP stands for Transmission Control Protocol/Internet Protocol and is the foundation of the internet, responsible for data transmission and addressing.

12. Explain the difference between TCP and UDP in the TCP/IP suite.

Answer:TCP (Transmission Control Protocol) provides reliable, connection-oriented communication, while UDP (User Datagram Protocol) offers connectionless, fast data transmission.

13. What is an IP address, and why is it essential in networking?

Answer: An IP address is a unique numerical label assigned to devices in a network, allowing them to communicate and be identified.

14. What are the two main versions of IP addresses, and how do they differ?

Answer: The two main versions are IPv4 (32-bit) and IPv6 (128-bit). IPv6 was introduced to address the exhaustion of IPv4 addresses and offers more space.

15. How is subnetting used in IP addressing, and what does a subnet mask do?

Answer: Subnetting divides a large IP network into smaller, more manageable segments. A subnet mask determines the network and host portions of an IP address.

16. What is a default gateway in TCP/IP networking, and why is it important?

Answer: The default gateway is a device that connects a local network to other networks. It plays a crucial role in routing traffic outside the local network.

17. Explain the purpose of DNS in TCP/IP networking.

Answer:DNS (Domain Name System) resolves domain names to IP addresses, making it easier for users to access websites and resources by name.

18. What is DHCP, and how does it simplify IP address management in networks?

Answer:DHCP (Dynamic Host Configuration Protocol) automatically assigns and manages IP addresses, making it easier to configure devices on a network.

19. How do you configure a static IP address in Windows, and when would you use one?

Answer:A static IP address can be configured manually in network settings and is often used for servers or devices requiring a consistent address.

20. What is a MAC address, and how does it differ from an IP address?

Answer:A MAC (Media Access Control) address is a unique hardware address assigned to a network interface, while an IP address identifies devices on a network.

21. How do you use the "ping" command in Windows to test network connectivity?

Answer: The "ping" command is used to send ICMP echo requests to a remote host and check if it responds, helping diagnose network issues.

22. What is NAT (Network Address Translation), and why is it used in networking?

Answer:NAT allows multiple devices in a local network to share a single public IP address for internet access, providing an extra layer of security.

23. Explain the function of a router in TCP/IP networking.

Answer:A router is a device that connects different networks, facilitating data traffic between them, and is essential for connecting local networks to the internet.

24. What is a network firewall, and how does it enhance network security?

Answer:A network firewall is a security device or software that filters and controls network traffic, protecting the network from unauthorized access and threats.

25. What are TCP and UDP ports, and how are they used in networking?

Answer:TCP and UDP ports are used to distinguish different services on a device. Ports help route incoming data to the correct application.

26. How does Network Address Translation (NAT) impact the availability of IPv4 addresses?

Answer:NAT helps conserve IPv4 addresses by allowing multiple devices on a local network to share a single public IP address for internet access.

27. Explain the concept of a network socket in TCP/IP networking.

Answer:A network socket is a combination of an IP address and port number, enabling communication between devices over a network.

28. What is the role of the subnet mask in IP addressing, and how is it represented?

Answer:A subnet mask defines the network and host portions of an IP address. It is represented as a series of binary 1s followed by 0s.

29. What is a DHCP lease, and how does it work?

Answer:A DHCP lease is a temporary assignment of an IP address to a device. The lease duration determines how long the IP address is valid.

30. How do you troubleshoot network issues using the "ipconfig" command in Windows?

Answer: The "ipconfig" command provides information about network configuration, including IP addresses, gateway, and DNS servers, helping diagnose network problems.

31. Explain the concept of IP routing in TCP/IP networking.

Answer:IP routing is the process of determining the path that network traffic should take from the source to the destination, typically performed by routers.

32. What is a static route, and when might you use one in IP routing?

Answer:A static route is a manually configured route that defines how network traffic should be directed. It is used when specific routes need to be defined.

33. What is the "tracert" command, and how does it help trace the path of network packets?

Answer: The "tracert" command traces the route network packets take from the source to the destination, helping diagnose network path issues.

34. Explain the purpose of a DNS resolver and its role in DNS resolution.

Answer:A DNS resolver is responsible for sending DNS queries to DNS servers and obtaining IP addresses associated with domain names.

35. What is a loopback address in TCP/IP, and how is it used?

Answer:A loopback address, typically represented as 127.0.0.1, is used for self-testing network applications and is used to communicate with the local host.

36. What are public and private IP addresses, and how do they relate to network address translation (NAT)?

Answer: Public IP addresses are used for devices accessible on the internet, while private IP addresses are used within local networks, with NAT providing a bridge between them.

37. How do you configure a Windows computer to use a custom DNS server for name resolution?

Answer: Custom DNS server settings can be configured in the network adapter's properties to specify a preferred DNS server.

38. What is a gateway address, and how is it different from a default gateway?

Answer:A gateway address can refer to any device that connects networks. A default gateway is the specific gateway used for routing traffic outside the local network.

39. Explain the significance of an IPv6 address in the transition from IPv4 to IPv6.

Answer:IPv6 addresses provide a vast address space to accommodate the growing number of devices connected to the internet, addressing the limitations of IPv4.

40. What is the purpose of the "netstat" command, and how does it help monitor network connections?

Answer: The "netstat" command displays network statistics and active network connections, helping identify network usage and issues.

41. What is a MAC address table, and how is it used in network switches?

Answer:A MAC address table is a database that associates MAC addresses with switch ports, helping switches make informed decisions about data traffic.

42. Explain the concept of a network mask in CIDR notation and its role in IP addressing.

Answer:CIDR (Classless Inter-Domain Routing) notation represents a network mask in the form of IP address/prefix length, enabling flexible network segmentation.

43. What is a public key infrastructure (PKI) in the context of TCP/IP networking, and how is it used for security?

Answer:PKI is a framework that uses asymmetric cryptography to secure communications, including activities like encryption, digital signatures, and secure key exchange.

44. How do you configure a static route on a Windows server or router for directing network traffic?

Answer:A static route can be manually configured in the server or router's settings to specify the destination and next hop for traffic.

45. What is the "netsh" command, and how is it used for network configuration in Windows?

Answer: The "netsh" command allows users to configure and manage network settings from the command prompt, including firewall rules and network interface settings.

46. Explain the concept of a subnet calculator, and how can it assist with network management?

Answer:A subnet calculator is a tool that helps calculate subnets, IP ranges, and other network parameters, simplifying network design and management.

47. What is an APIPA (Automatic Private IP Address) address, and when does a Windows device use it?

Answer:APIPA is a self-assigned IP address used by Windows devices when they cannot obtain an IP address from a DHCP server. It is used for local network communication.

48. What is a TCP three-way handshake, and how does it establish a connection between two devices?

Answer: The TCP three-way handshake is a process where two devices exchange synchronized messages to establish a reliable connection.

49. Explain the concept of a broadcast address in TCP/IP networking.

Answer:A broadcast address is used to send data to all devices on a local network simultaneously, typically ending in .255 for IPv4 networks.

50. What is a network topological diagram, and why is it important for network administrators?

Answer:A network topological diagram is a visual representation of a network's structure and connections, helping administrators plan and troubleshoot network configurations.

Network Protocols and Services

1. What is a network protocol, and why are protocols essential for effective communication in computer networks?

Answer: A network protocol is a set of rules and conventions that govern data communication and interactions between devices on a network. Protocols are essential for ensuring data is transmitted accurately and efficiently.

2. Explain the role of the HTTP protocol in web communication, and how does it work in requesting and delivering web pages?

Answer: HTTP (Hypertext Transfer Protocol) is used for transferring web pages and other resources on the World Wide Web. It allows a client (browser) to request web content from a server, and the server responds with the requested data.

3. What is the purpose of the FTP protocol, and how does it facilitate the transfer of files between computers on a network?

Answer: FTP (File Transfer Protocol) is used for transferring files between computers on a network. It provides commands for uploading and downloading files to and from a server.

4. Explain the difference between TCP and UDP, and when would you choose one over the other for network communication?

Answer: TCP (Transmission Control Protocol) provides reliable, connection-oriented communication, making it suitable for applications where data integrity is critical. UDP (User Datagram Protocol) offers lightweight, connectionless communication and is used for applications that prioritize speed over reliability.

5. What is SMTP, and how does it function in the context of sending and receiving email messages?

Answer*:* SMTP (Simple Mail Transfer Protocol) is used to send email messages. It facilitates the transmission of emails from the sender's client or server to the recipient's email server.

6. Explain the role of the DNS (Domain Name System) in translating domain names to IP addresses, and why it is a crucial component of internet communication.

Answer*:* DNS translates human-readable domain names (e.g., www.example.com) to IP addresses (e.g., 192.168.1.1), making it easier for users to access websites and services by name rather than IP address.

7. What is DHCP, and how does it simplify IP address configuration in a network, especially for dynamic and temporary connections?

Answer*:* DHCP (Dynamic Host Configuration Protocol) automatically assigns IP addresses, subnet masks, and other network settings to devices when they connect to a network. It simplifies IP address management, especially for devices with changing or temporary connections.

8. Explain the role of SSH (Secure Shell) and its significance in providing secure remote access to networked devices and servers.

Answer*:* SSH is a network protocol that provides secure remote access and management of networked devices and servers. It encrypts data to protect against eavesdropping and unauthorized access.

9. What is SNMP (Simple Network Management Protocol), and how is it used for monitoring and managing network devices and services?

Answer*:* SNMP is used for the management and monitoring of network devices and services. It allows administrators to collect information, set configurations, and receive alerts from network devices, such as routers and switches.

10. Explain the concept of NAT (Network Address Translation) and its role in conserving public IP addresses and providing a level of network security.

Answer*:* NAT allows multiple devices in a private network to share a single public IP address for internet access. It helps conserve public IP addresses and acts as a basic form of firewall, as it hides internal device details from external networks.

11. What is a network protocol, and why are they essential in networking?

Answer: Network protocols are sets of rules that govern communication between devices on a network. They ensure data is transmitted reliably and consistently.

12. Explain the difference between TCP and UDP protocols and when each is used.

Answer:TCP (Transmission Control Protocol) is connection-oriented and provides reliable data transmission, while UDP (User Datagram Protocol) is connectionless and focuses on speed and simplicity.

13. What is the purpose of the HTTP protocol in web communication?

Answer:HTTP (Hypertext Transfer Protocol) is used for transmitting web content, allowing web browsers to request and display web pages.

14. What are common ports associated with HTTP and HTTPS, and why are they significant?

Answer:HTTP typically uses port 80, while HTTPS uses port 443. Ports allow different services to share a single IP address.

15. Explain the role of DNS (Domain Name System) in network communication.

Answer:DNS resolves human-readable domain names into IP addresses, enabling users to access websites and services using names instead of numerical addresses.

16. What is SMTP, and how does it facilitate email communication?

Answer:SMTP (Simple Mail Transfer Protocol) is used to send and relay email messages between mail servers.

How does IMAP differ from POP3 in email retrieval, and which is more commonly used?

Answer:IMAP (Internet Message Access Protocol) allows users to access and manage email on the mail server, while POP3 (Post Office Protocol) downloads emails to the client device. IMAP is more commonly used.

17. Explain the concept of a firewall in network security, and how does it work?

Answer:A firewall is a security device or software that filters network traffic, allowing or blocking data based on predefined rules.

18. What is FTP, and how is it used for file transfer in a network?

Answer:FTP (File Transfer Protocol) is used to transfer files between computers on a network or over the internet.

19. What is SNMP, and what role does it play in network management?

Answer:SNMP (Simple Network Management Protocol) allows network administrators to monitor and manage network devices, collecting information and adjusting settings.

20. Explain the function of the RDP protocol in Windows networking.

Answer:RDP (Remote Desktop Protocol) allows users to connect to and control remote Windows computers, making it possible to work on a remote machine as if it were local.

21. What is the SMB protocol, and how does it enable file and printer sharing in Windows networks?

Answer:SMB (Server Message Block) is a network file sharing protocol used by Windows for sharing files, printers, and resources.

22. Explain the concept of Telnet and its role in remote terminal access.

Answer: Telnet is a network protocol used for remote terminal access to control and manage remote devices over a network.

23. What is DHCP, and how does it simplify IP address configuration in networks?

Answer:DHCP (Dynamic Host Configuration Protocol) automatically assigns and manages IP addresses for devices on a network, reducing manual configuration.

24. What is NAT (Network Address Translation), and why is it essential for internet connectivity in local networks?

Answer:NAT allows multiple devices in a local network to share a single public IP address, enabling them to access the internet while adding a layer of security.

25. What is LDAP, and how does it relate to directory services in Windows networks?

Answer:LDAP (Lightweight Directory Access Protocol) is used to access and manage directory services like Active Directory, which stores user and resource information in Windows networks.

26. Explain the concept of VPN (Virtual Private Network) and its role in secure remote access.

Answer:VPNs provide secure, encrypted connections over public networks, enabling remote users to access private network resources.

27. What is ICMP, and how does it support network diagnostics and error reporting?

Answer:ICMP (Internet Control Message Protocol) is used to send error messages and perform network diagnostics, such as with the "ping" command.

28. What is the purpose of the DNSSEC protocol in DNS, and how does it enhance security?

Answer:DNSSEC (Domain Name System Security Extensions) adds cryptographic security to DNS, ensuring the authenticity and integrity of DNS data.

29. What is WINS, and how does it help resolve NetBIOS names to IP addresses in Windows networks?

Answer:WINS (Windows Internet Name Service) is a legacy system for resolving NetBIOS names to IP addresses, primarily used in older Windows networks.

30. Explain the function of the NTP protocol in network time synchronization.

Answer:NTP (Network Time Protocol) is used to synchronize the clocks of devices on a network, ensuring accurate timekeeping.

31. What is the role of HTTPS in web security, and how does it provide encryption for data transmission?

Answer:HTTPS (Hypertext Transfer Protocol Secure) uses encryption to secure data transmission between web clients and servers, ensuring confidentiality and integrity.

32. What is the SMB/CIFS protocol, and how does it relate to file and printer sharing in Windows networks?

Answer:SMB/CIFS is an extended version of the SMB protocol, used in Windows for sharing files, printers, and resources in a networked environment.

33. What is ICMPv6, and how does it differ from ICMP for IPv4 in network diagnostics?

Answer:ICMPv6 is the equivalent of ICMP for IPv6, providing similar network diagnostics but with improvements for the new protocol.

34. Explain the purpose of the BGP protocol in routing for the internet.

Answer:BGP (Border Gateway Protocol) is used by internet service providers to exchange routing information, making it vital for internet routing and stability.

35. What is ARP, and how does it map IP addresses to MAC addresses in a local network?

Answer:ARP (Address Resolution Protocol) maps IP addresses to MAC addresses, allowing devices to communicate within the same local network.

36. What is SIP, and how does it enable voice and video communication in VoIP (Voice over IP) networks?

Answer: SIP (Session Initiation Protocol) is used to initiate and manage real-time voice and video communication sessions in VoIP networks.

37. What is TLS, and how does it provide secure communication over the internet, especially for web browsers?

Answer: TLS (Transport Layer Security) encrypts data transmitted over the internet, ensuring secure and private communication, such as in HTTPS connections.

38. Explain the role of SNMP traps in network management and monitoring.

Answer: SNMP traps are notifications sent by network devices to a management station, informing it of specific events or conditions in the network.

39. What is IGMP, and how does it support multicasting in network communications?

Answer: IGMP (Internet Group Management Protocol) is used by devices to join and leave multicast groups, allowing efficient delivery of data to multiple recipients.

40. What is FTPS, and how does it provide secure file transfer over FTP (File Transfer Protocol)?

Answer: FTPS is an extension of FTP that adds encryption to secure file transfer, making it suitable for sensitive data transmission.

41. Explain the concept of a network bridge, and how is it used in network configuration?

Answer: A network bridge connects two or more network segments, allowing them to function as a single network, share resources, and communicate.

42. What is SNMPv3, and how does it enhance SNMP security compared to earlier versions?

Answer: SNMPv3 adds authentication and encryption to SNMP messages, making network management more secure by protecting against unauthorized access and data tampering.

43. What is PPP, and how does it enable secure point-to-point communication, such as in VPNs?

Answer: PPP (Point-to-Point Protocol) is a data link layer protocol used for establishing secure connections between two devices, making it suitable for VPNs.

44. Explain the concept of a proxy server and its role in network security and web content filtering.

Answer: A proxy server acts as an intermediary between clients and servers, providing security, privacy, and content filtering services.

45. What is GRE, and how does it create virtual private networks over the internet or other networks?

Answer: GRE (Generic Routing Encapsulation) is used to encapsulate various network layer protocols, allowing the creation of virtual private networks.

46. What is SSH, and how does it provide secure remote access and command execution on remote servers?

Answer: SSH (Secure Shell) is a protocol used for secure remote access and administration of network devices and servers.

47. Explain the concept of multicast routing, and how does it differ from unicast and broadcast routing?

Answer: Multicast routing enables data to be sent to multiple recipients, similar to broadcasting, but in a more efficient and controlled manner.

48. What is RADIUS, and how does it facilitate centralized authentication, authorization, and accounting for network access?

Answer:RADIUS (Remote Authentication Dial-In User Service) is used to centralize user authentication and authorization for network access, with accounting features for tracking usage.

49. What is the DNS cache, and how does it improve domain name resolution efficiency?

Answer: The DNS cache is a temporary storage of DNS query results, speeding up domain name resolution by reducing the need to repeatedly query authoritative DNS servers.

Troubleshooting Network Issues

1. What is the first step you would take when a user reports they cannot access the internet?

Answer: The first step is to check the physical connectivity, including cables, switches, and routers. Often, the issue is a simple connection problem.

2. A user reports slow network performance. What steps would you take to diagnose and resolve this issue?

Answer: To diagnose slow network performance, I would start by checking the network bandwidth, monitoring network traffic, and identifying potential bottlenecks, such as high resource usage on servers or network congestion.

3. How do you troubleshoot when a user can't connect to a specific website while other websites work fine?

Answer: I would first check the user's internet connection and ensure the website is accessible from other devices. If the problem persists, I would investigate DNS issues, firewall rules, or potential problems on the website's end.

4. A user experiences intermittent connectivity issues. How would you go about diagnosing and resolving these problems?

Answer: Intermittent connectivity issues can be challenging. I would start by checking for interference, signal strength, and environmental factors in the case of wireless connections. Additionally, I would monitor network logs for any recurring patterns.

5. What are common tools or utilities you would use to troubleshoot network problems, and why are they valuable?

Answer: Common tools include ping, traceroute, netstat, and Wireshark. These tools help diagnose connectivity, routing, and traffic issues by providing insights into network behaviour.

6. A user's computer cannot obtain an IP address from the DHCP server. How would you address this issue?

Answer: I would verify that the DHCP server is operational, check for IP address conflicts, ensure the network cable is connected, and troubleshoot the DHCP client settings on the user's computer.

7. What steps would you take to troubleshoot a network that experiences frequent packet loss?

Answer: To address packet loss, I would investigate the quality of the network connection, inspect switches and routers for errors, and monitor network traffic for congestion or heavy utilization. Traceroute and ping tests can help identify the location of packet loss.

8. A user's email client cannot connect to the mail server. How would you determine the cause of this issue?

Answer: I would first check the email server's status and configurations. Then, I would review the email client settings, test connectivity to the mail server, and inspect firewalls or security software that may be blocking the connection.

9. What is the purpose of a loopback address (127.0.0.1), and how can it be used in troubleshooting network issues?

Answer: A loopback address allows a computer to communicate with itself. It's valuable for testing network stack functionality, ensuring network protocols and drivers are functioning correctly, and verifying software installations.

10. A user reports frequent disconnections from a remote office via a VPN. How would you troubleshoot this issue?

Answer: I would begin by checking the stability of the internet connection at both ends, verify VPN configurations, and examine logs for VPN errors. If necessary, I would consider adjusting VPN settings and firewall rules for improved stability.

11. What are common signs that indicate network connectivity issues on a Windows computer?

Answer: Signs may include the inability to access websites, server or resource unavailability, slow data transfer, or frequent disconnections.

12. How do you start troubleshooting network problems on a Windows computer?

Answer: Begin by checking physical connections, verifying network settings, and testing connectivity using tools like "ping" or "ipconfig."

13. What does the "Limited or no connectivity" error message in Windows indicate, and how would you address it?

Answer: This error often suggests a DHCP or IP configuration issue. It can be resolved by checking DHCP settings, renewing the IP address, or addressing any network conflicts.

14. Explain the purpose of the "ipconfig" command in troubleshooting network issues.

Answer:"ipconfig" displays IP configuration information, including the IP address, subnet mask, default gateway, and DNS servers, helping diagnose connectivity problems.

15. What is the "ping" command, and how can it be used to test network connectivity?

Answer:"ping" sends ICMP echo requests to a remote host and checks for responses, helping verify network connectivity and assess latency.

16. What does the "Request Timed Out" response in a "ping" test indicate, and how can it be addressed?

Answer:"Request Timed Out" suggests the target host didn't respond to the ping. It may indicate a firewall blocking ICMP or a connectivity problem with the host.

17. Explain the purpose of a loopback address (127.0.0.1) and how it can help in network troubleshooting.

Answer: The loopback address allows a computer to send data to itself for testing network stack functionality and diagnosing issues.

18. What are the common causes of "DNS Server Not Responding" errors in Windows, and how can you troubleshoot them?

Answer: Causes may include DNS server outages, misconfigured DNS settings, or DNS cache issues. Troubleshoot by checking DNS server availability, verifying settings, and flushing the DNS cache.

19. How can you troubleshoot "Limited Connectivity" or "No Internet Access" issues on a Windows computer connected to a wireless network?

Answer: Troubleshoot by checking signal strength, resetting the wireless adapter, verifying wireless security settings, and power cycling the router.

20. Explain the steps to diagnose and resolve issues when a Windows computer cannot obtain an IP address via DHCP.

Answer: Verify DHCP server availability, check network cable connections, renew the IP lease, and ensure the DHCP client service is running.

21. What is the "Unidentified Network" issue in Windows, and how can you troubleshoot and resolve it?

Answer:"Unidentified Network" occurs when Windows cannot determine the network type. Troubleshoot by checking adapter settings, disabling IPv6, and resetting network configurations.

22. How can you diagnose and address issues with a Windows computer that can't connect to a specific website or server while other sites are accessible?

Answer: Troubleshoot by clearing browser cache, checking DNS settings, and attempting to access the site from another device or network.

23. Explain the steps to resolve "Windows IP Configuration" errors like "Media Disconnected" or "Autoconfiguration IPv4 Address."

Answer: Troubleshoot by checking network cable connections, adapter settings, and using the "ipconfig" command to release and renew the IP lease.

24. What does the "Network Cable Unplugged" error message indicate, and how can you troubleshoot it?

Answer: This error suggests a physical connection issue. Troubleshoot by checking cable connections, testing with a known working cable, or inspecting the network port.

25. How can you troubleshoot issues with Windows network shares not accessible by other devices on the same network?

Answer: Troubleshoot by verifying share permissions, checking network discovery settings, ensuring appropriate firewall rules, and confirming user access rights.

26. Explain the steps to troubleshoot slow network performance on a Windows computer.

Answer: Troubleshoot by checking for background network activity, evaluating the bandwidth of the network connection, and considering possible software or hardware issues.

27. What is a DNS cache, and how can you clear it to resolve DNS-related issues on a Windows computer?

Answer:A DNS cache stores DNS query results to speed up future lookups. Clear it using the "ipconfig /flushdns" command to address DNS resolution problems.

28. How can you troubleshoot issues when a Windows computer loses Wi-Fi connectivity intermittently?

Answer: Troubleshoot by updating wireless adapter drivers, changing Wi-Fi channels, checking for interference, and ensuring the power-saving settings do not affect the adapter.

29. Explain the purpose of "Network Reset" in Windows, and when should it be used to resolve network issues?

Answer:"Network Reset" reinstalls network adapters, settings, and protocols to their default state. Use it when all other troubleshooting methods fail.

30. What is the purpose of the Windows "Network Troubleshooter," and how can it assist in resolving network issues?

Answer: The "Network Troubleshooter" is a built-in tool that can automatically diagnose and fix common network problems by following its recommendations.

31. How can you troubleshoot issues when a Windows computer cannot connect to a wireless network, even with the correct SSID and passphrase?

Answer: Troubleshoot by verifying passphrase accuracy, checking the wireless adapter's power settings, and updating wireless adapter drivers.

32. Explain the concept of "Traceroute" (or "tracert") and how it helps diagnose network path issues.

Answer:"Traceroute" is a command-line tool that traces the route network packets take to a destination, helping identify network path issues or delays.

33. What are some common causes of slow internet connectivity on a Windows computer, and how can you troubleshoot and improve it?

Answer: Causes may include network congestion, outdated hardware, or software interference. Troubleshoot by checking speed with online tests, updating hardware, and optimizing software.

34. How can you diagnose and resolve issues when a Windows computer is not able to connect to a specific network share or server?

Answer: Troubleshoot by checking share permissions, verifying credentials, and ensuring network discovery and firewall settings are correct.

35. Explain the concept of "Network Isolation" and how it can be used for troubleshooting network issues.

Answer: Network isolation involves systematically disconnecting components of a network to pinpoint the source of a problem, helping identify and resolve issues.

36. What are common causes of DNS resolution failures, and how can you troubleshoot and resolve them in Windows?

Answer: Causes may include misconfigured DNS settings, server issues, or DNS cache problems. Troubleshoot by checking settings, testing with different DNS servers, and clearing the DNS cache.

37. How can you diagnose and resolve issues with Windows network adapters that are not recognized or not functioning correctly?

Answer: Troubleshoot by checking device manager for driver issues, updating drivers, disabling and re-enabling the adapter, or testing with a different adapter.

38. Explain the steps to diagnose and address network issues when a Windows computer cannot connect to the internet, but the local network is accessible.

Answer: Troubleshoot by checking DNS settings, testing other devices, verifying the gateway, or contacting the Internet Service Provider (ISP) for issues on their end.

39. What are the common signs of a DNS cache poisoning attack, and how can you protect against it?

Answer: Signs may include incorrect DNS resolution and redirection to malicious sites. Protect against it by using DNSSEC and regularly clearing the DNS cache.

40. How can you troubleshoot network issues related to IP address conflicts on a Windows network?

Answer: Troubleshoot by checking for duplicate IP addresses, ensuring DHCP is correctly configured, and releasing and renewing IP leases.

41. Explain the concept of a "Network Diagram" and how it can assist in troubleshooting network issues.

Answer: A network diagram is a visual representation of a network's layout, helping administrators identify and resolve problems more effectively.

42. What are common causes of intermittent network disconnects on a Windows computer, and how can you troubleshoot and resolve them?

Answer: Causes may include interference, driver issues, or router problems. Troubleshoot by updating drivers, checking wireless settings, and monitoring for interference.

43. What is the "ARP cache," and how can you clear it to address network connectivity issues?

Answer: The ARP cache stores IP-to-MAC address mappings. Clear it using the "arp -d" command to resolve ARP-related network problems.

44. How can you troubleshoot issues when a Windows computer cannot access network resources even though it's connected to the network?

Answer: Troubleshoot by checking permissions, verifying network share settings, and ensuring proper network discovery and firewall configurations.

45. Explain the concept of a "Network Monitor" or "Packet Capture" tool and how it assists in troubleshooting network issues.

Answer: Network monitor tools capture and analyse network traffic, helping diagnose problems and monitor network performance.

46. What are common causes of slow file transfer speeds on a Windows network, and how can you improve them?

Answer: Causes may include network congestion, outdated hardware, or inefficient protocols. Troubleshoot by optimizing network settings, upgrading hardware, and using efficient file transfer methods.

47. How can you diagnose and address issues with Windows computers that are unable to access network printers?

Answer: Troubleshoot by checking printer sharing settings, permissions, and ensuring that the printer is correctly configured on the network.

48. Explain the purpose of a "Ping Plotter" tool and how it helps in diagnosing network issues over time.

Answer: Ping Plotter is a tool that continuously pings a host and visualizes the results over time, helping to identify intermittent network problems.

49. What is a "Trunk Line" in network troubleshooting, and how does it relate to VLANs (Virtual LANs)?

Answer:A trunk line carries data for multiple VLANs over a single physical connection. Troubleshoot by checking VLAN configurations and trunk line settings.

50. How can you troubleshoot network issues when a Windows computer cannot obtain an IP address via DHCP even though the server appears to be functioning correctly?

Answer: Troubleshoot by verifying DHCP settings, checking the DHCP server's event logs, and diagnosing issues on the network that may prevent DHCP communication.

ONLINE RESOURCES

Practice Paper Link: https://forms.gle/QKXurLweD67wGv6BA

QR Code:

Video Link: https://www.youtube.com/playlist?list=PLzlh_31VWEFqJYVteDLCTUIa-YtXJfu36

QR Code:

Chapter 7 Windows Security and Permissions

Windows Security Models

1. What is the Windows Security Model, and why is it important in the context of the Windows operating system?

Answer: The Windows Security Model is a framework that defines how resources are protected and accessed within the Windows operating system. It is vital for maintaining the integrity, confidentiality, and availability of data and resources.

2. Explain the concept of discretionary access control (DAC) in the Windows Security Model. How does it allow users to control resource access?

Answer:DAC enables resource owners to define and control access permissions for their resources. Users have the discretion to grant or deny access to their files and directories, allowing for flexibility in access management.

3. What is the role of an access control list (ACL) in the Windows Security Model, and how does it work in defining and managing resource permissions?

Answer: An ACL is a list of permissions associated with an object (e.g., a file or folder). It specifies which users or groups have access and the type of access they are granted (e.g., read, write, execute).

4. Explain the principle of least privilege (POLP) in the context of Windows Security. How does it enhance security and access control?

Answer: The principle of least privilege dictates that users and processes should only have the minimum level of access required to perform their tasks. It enhances security by reducing the potential impact of security breaches.

5. What is the role of mandatory access control (MAC) in the Windows Security Model, and how does it differ from discretionary access control?

Answer:MAC enforces access control policies based on security labels assigned to resources and users. Unlike DAC, where resource owners have control, MAC is centrally managed and enforces strict access rules, often used in government and military contexts.

6. How does the Windows Security Identifier (SID) function in user authentication and access control, and what is its significance in the Windows Security Model?

Answer:SIDs uniquely identify user and group accounts in the Windows Security Model. They are used to check access permissions and grant or deny resource access.

7. What is role-based access control (RBAC), and how does it improve resource access management in the Windows Security Model?

Answer:RBAC is a security model where permissions are assigned based on a user's role or job function rather than their individual identity. It simplifies access management and ensures consistent access policies.

8. What are the security advantages and challenges of using encryption in the Windows Security Model, and how does it enhance data protection?

Answer: Encryption enhances data protection by securing data in transit and at rest. However, challenges include managing encryption keys and ensuring secure encryption practices are followed.

9. What is user authentication, and how does it relate to the Windows Security Model in verifying the identity of users?

Answer: User authentication is the process of verifying a user's identity to ensure they have the right to access resources. It is a fundamental aspect of the Windows Security Model, ensuring that only authorized users gain access.

10. How does auditing and logging play a role in the Windows Security Model, and what are the benefits of monitoring and reviewing security logs?

Answer: Auditing and logging record security-related events and access attempts. Regularly reviewing security logs helps in identifying and responding to security incidents, tracking system behaviour, and ensuring compliance with security policies.

11. What is a security model in the context of Windows operating systems?

Answer:A security model defines how security is implemented and managed in a Windows environment, including access control, authentication, and auditing.

12. Explain the basic components of the Windows security model.

Answer: The components include user accounts, security identifiers (SIDs), security groups, access control lists (ACLs), and security policies.

13. What is the principle of least privilege, and how does it relate to Windows security models?

Answer: The principle of least privilege means granting users only the permissions they need to perform their tasks, reducing the risk of unauthorized access and misuse of resources.

14. How does Windows use security identifiers (SIDs) to uniquely identify users and groups?

Answer:SIDs are unique identifiers assigned to each user and group in a Windows environment, allowing for accurate identification and access control.

15. What is the purpose of access control lists (ACLs) in Windows security?

Answer:ACLs specify permissions for users and groups on Windows resources, determining who can access, modify, or delete them.

16. Explain the difference between discretionary access control and mandatory access control in Windows security models.

Answer: Discretionary access control allows resource owners to determine access, while mandatory access control enforces access based on security labels.

17. What is the concept of role-based access control (RBAC) in Windows security models, and how does it simplify access management?

Answer:RBAC assigns permissions to roles rather than individual users, streamlining access control administration and ensuring consistency.

18. What is the purpose of User Account Control (UAC) in Windows, and how does it enhance security?

Answer:UAC helps prevent unauthorized changes to a system by requiring administrator approval for certain actions, reducing the risk of malware infection.

19. Explain how the Windows Registry is used to store security-related configuration settings.

Answer: The Windows Registry stores security policies, user rights assignments, and other security-related settings, allowing for centralized configuration.

20. What are the differences between user-level and kernel-level security models in Windows?

Answer: User-level security models manage access control and authentication at the user level, while kernel-level models focus on protecting the operating system and system resources.

21. How does Windows use the concept of trust relationships between domains to manage access across a network?

Answer: Trust relationships establish connections between domains, allowing users and resources from one domain to be recognized and accessed by another.

22. Explain the purpose of Windows Group Policy and how it is used to enforce security settings across a network.

Answer: Group Policy is used to define and enforce security and configuration settings for users and computers in a Windows network, ensuring consistency and security.

23. What is the difference between Windows Security Policies and Security Templates, and how are they used to enforce security standards?

Answer: Security policies define security rules, while security templates provide predefined configurations. Both are used to enforce security standards, with templates serving as preconfigured settings.

24. How does the Windows security model ensure data confidentiality, integrity, and availability?

Answer: Through access controls, encryption, auditing, and user authentication, the Windows security model protects data from unauthorized access, tampering, and loss.

25. What is Windows BitLocker, and how does it enhance data security?

Answer: BitLocker is a full-disk encryption tool in Windows that encrypts the entire system drive to protect data at rest.

26. Explain the purpose of the Windows Security Account Manager (SAM) database and its role in user authentication.

Answer:SAM stores user account information and is used for local authentication on standalone Windows computers.

27. How does the Windows security model protect against common security threats like malware, viruses, and phishing attacks?

Answer: Security measures such as antivirus software, firewalls, user training, and UAC help safeguard against these threats.

28. What is the principle of defense-in-depth, and how is it applied in Windows security models?

Answer: Defense-in-depth involves using multiple layers of security controls to protect against a variety of threats, including network security, host security, and application security.

29. Explain the concept of logon scripts and how they can be used to enhance security in Windows.

Answer: Logon scripts are used to automate tasks and enforce security policies when users log in to a Windows system, helping ensure consistent configurations.

30. What is the significance of Microsoft's Security Development Lifecycle (SDL) in Windows security models?

Answer:SDL is a set of practices used to develop secure software, helping identify and eliminate vulnerabilities during the development process.

31. How does Windows SmartScreen help protect against malicious downloads and unsafe websites?

Answer:uses reputation-based filtering to warn users about potentially unsafe downloads and websites.

32. What is AppLocker, and how is it used to control which applications can run on Windows systems?

Answer: AppLocker is a Windows feature that enforces application control policies to specify which applications are allowed to run on a system.

33. Explain the purpose of Windows Defender and how it contributes to the security of Windows systems.

Answer: Windows Defender is an anti-malware tool that helps protect against viruses, spyware, and other threats, enhancing the security of Windows systems.

34. What is the concept of secure boot in Windows, and how does it prevent unauthorized operating system modifications?

Answer: Secure boot ensures that only signed and trusted software components are loaded during the system boot process, preventing unauthorized modifications.

35. How does Windows Firewall enhance network security, and what are some common firewall configurations?

Answer: Windows Firewall filters network traffic, helping block unwanted incoming and outgoing connections. Common configurations include blocking specific ports and allowing specific applications.

36. Explain how Windows BitLocker can be used to secure removable storage devices like USB drives.

Answer: BitLocker To Go extends BitLocker encryption to removable storage devices, ensuring data security even on USB drives.

37. What is the purpose of the Windows Credential Manager, and how does it improve user authentication and credential management?

Answer: Credential Manager stores and manages credentials securely, making it easier for users to access resources without repeatedly entering login details.

38. How does Windows Defender SmartScreen protect against phishing attacks and deceptive websites?

Answer: SmartScreen checks the reputation of websites and warns users if a site is known for phishing or other deceptive practices.

39. Explain the role of User Rights Assignments in Windows security policies and how they affect user permissions.

Answer: User Rights Assignments define what actions users can perform on a Windows system, such as logging in as a service or shutting down the system.

40. What is Windows Security Identifier (SID) filtering, and how is it used in Active Directory trusts to enhance security?

Answer:SID filtering is a security measure used to protect against certain trust-based attacks in Active Directory by filtering out SIDs from incoming trust authentication.

41. How does Windows use security templates to apply security settings to multiple computers within an organization?

Answer: Security templates contain predefined security configurations that can be applied to multiple Windows computers to ensure uniform security settings.

42. Explain how Windows Firewall with Advanced Security allows for more granular control of firewall rules and settings.

Answer: Windows Firewall with Advanced Security provides enhanced control over inbound and outbound traffic, allowing administrators to create custom rules and configure advanced settings.

43. What is the Windows Security Identifier (SID) history feature, and how does it facilitate security during domain migration and restructuring?

Answer:SID history allows users to retain access to resources during domain migrations by associating old SIDs with new SIDs, preserving access rights.

44. Explain the concept of User Account Control (UAC) virtualization in Windows, and how it protects legacy applications.

Answer:UAC virtualization enables older applications to run with limited privileges to prevent compatibility issues and maintain system security.

45. How does the Group Policy Object (GPO) security model work in Windows, and how is it used to enforce security policies across a domain?

Answer:GPOs define and enforce security policies across a domain, allowing administrators to control user and computer configurations.

46. What is the "Trusted Platform Module" (TPM) in Windows, and how does it enhance system security?

Answer:TPM is a hardware-based security component that provides secure storage of cryptographic keys and enables features like BitLocker encryption.

47. Explain the concept of user authentication methods in Windows, including password-based, smart card, and biometric authentication.

Answer: Windows supports various authentication methods, including traditional passwords, smart cards, and biometrics, each with its own strengths and weaknesses.

48. What is Windows Information Protection (WIP), and how does it safeguard data on Windows devices?

Answer:WIP helps protect corporate data by separating personal and work-related data, encrypting business data, and enforcing access controls.

49. How does Windows use role-based access control (RBAC) to define user permissions based on their roles and responsibilities?

Answer:RBAC assigns specific permissions to user roles, making access management more efficient and ensuring that users have only the access they need.

50. Explain how Windows Network Access Protection (NAP) enforces security policies for devices connecting to a network.

Answer:NAP checks the health and compliance of devices connecting to a network, allowing or denying access based on security policy adherence.

User Rights and Permissions

1. What are User Rights and Permissions in the context of Windows operating systems, and how do they differ?

Answer: User Rights are system-wide privileges that allow users to perform various actions on a system, such as shutting down the computer. Permissions, on the other hand, are specific access rules assigned to objects like files and folders.

2. Explain the difference between "User Rights" and "Permissions" in terms of scope and functionality.

Answer: User Rights are system-wide and control actions a user can perform, while Permissions apply to specific objects (files, folders, etc.) and define who can access, modify, or delete those objects.

3. What is the purpose of the "Take Ownership" User Right in Windows, and when might it be necessary to exercise this right?

Answer: The "Take Ownership" User Right allows a user to take ownership of a file or folder, enabling them to modify permissions. It's typically used by administrators to troubleshoot or regain access to resources.

4. Explain how effective permissions are determined for a user attempting to access a file in a Windows file system.

Answer: Effective permissions are calculated based on a combination of explicit and inherited permissions, considering both allow and deny rules. The most restrictive permission prevails in case of conflicts.

5. What is the purpose of the "Log on as a service" User Right, and which types of accounts and services might require this right?

Answer: The "Log on as a service" User Right allows accounts to log in as a service or perform background tasks. Service accounts, such as those used by database or web servers, require this right.

6. How do you grant specific permissions to a user or group in Windows, and what is the process for assigning different permission levels (e.g., Read, Write, Full Control) to resources?

Answer: You can assign permissions through the Properties dialog of a resource, such as a file or folder. By adding users or groups and specifying their access levels (Read, Write, etc.), you grant the desired permissions.

7. What is the purpose of the "Deny" permission, and how does it interact with other permissions when set on a resource?

Answer: The "Deny" permission explicitly denies access even if other permissions allow it. It takes precedence over "Allow" permissions and is typically used to restrict access in exceptional cases.

8. Explain the concept of inheritance in Windows file permissions, and how does it impact the consistency and management of permissions within a directory structure?

Answer: Inheritance allows permissions to propagate from a parent object to its child objects. It simplifies permission management by ensuring consistency within a directory structure, but it can also be customized if needed.

9. What are "Special Permissions" in Windows, and why might they be necessary to define when standard permissions are insufficient?

Answer: Special Permissions are detailed access rights that provide more fine-grained control over resource access. They are useful when standard permissions do not precisely match the desired access requirements.

10. How can Group Policy be used to enforce security settings, User Rights, and permissions across multiple computers in a Windows domain environment?

Answer: Group Policy is a centralized method for configuring and enforcing security settings, including User Rights and permissions, across multiple computers in a Windows domain. It ensures consistency and adherence to security policies.

11. What is the difference between user rights and permissions in Windows?

Answer: User rights define what users can do on a system, while permissions specify what actions they can perform on files, folders, and objects.

12. Explain the concept of "least privilege" in user rights and permissions.

Answer:"Least privilege" means granting users the minimum level of access necessary to perform their tasks, reducing the risk of unauthorized actions.

13. What are some common examples of user rights in Windows, and how do they affect system behavior?

Answer: Examples include "Log on locally," "Shut down the system," and "Change the system time." These user rights control system-level actions.

14. How do you view the user rights assigned to a user or group on a Windows system?

Answer: You can view user rights using the "Local Security Policy" or the "Group Policy Management Console."

15. Explain the purpose of the "Log on as a service" user right in Windows, and how is it managed?

Answer:"Log on as a service" allows specified accounts to run services on a system. It's managed through the "Local Security Policy" or Group Policy.

16. What is the "Deny logon locally" user right, and how does it differ from "Allow logon locally"?

Answer:"Deny logon locally" prevents specific users or groups from logging on locally, while "Allow logon locally" permits specified users.

17. What is the "Act as part of the operating system" user right, and why is it crucial for system security?

Answer: This right allows specified accounts to perform tasks on behalf of the operating system, which is essential for security and system integrity.

18. Explain the purpose of the "Shut down the system" user right in Windows.

Answer:"Shut down the system" allows users to shut down the system, making it important for administrative and maintenance tasks.

19. What is the "Change the system time" user right, and how can it impact system security?

Answer: This right allows users to modify the system time. Granting it should be done carefully to prevent security issues like time-based attacks.

20. How are user rights assigned and managed in a Windows domain environment?

Answer: User rights in a domain environment are assigned and managed through Group Policy settings, ensuring consistent permissions across the network.

21. Explain the concept of "effective permissions" in Windows file and folder permissions.

Answer: Effective permissions are the combination of all permissions granted and denied to a user, determining what actions they can perform on a resource.

22. What are the fundamental types of permissions in Windows file and folder security?

Answer: The fundamental types of permissions are "Read," "Write," "Execute," "List," "Modify," "Full Control," and "Special Permissions."

23. What is the difference between "Share" and "NTFS" permissions in Windows file security?

Answer: Share permissions control network access to shared resources, while NTFS permissions define file and folder access on the local system.

24. How do you check the effective permissions for a user or group on a Windows file or folder?

Answer: You can check effective permissions by using the "Security" tab in the file or folder's properties and the "Advanced" button.

25. Explain how the "Inheritance" feature works in Windows file and folder permissions.

Answer: Inheritance allows permissions set at a higher-level folder to flow down to its subfolders and files, simplifying access control.

26. What is the purpose of "explicit permissions" in Windows file and folder security?

Answer: Explicit permissions are permissions that are specifically set for a resource, overriding any inherited permissions.

27. How can you prevent inheritance and set custom permissions for a file or folder in Windows?

Answer: You can prevent inheritance by disabling it on the "Advanced Security Settings" tab of a file or folder and then configuring custom permissions.

28. Explain the "Share Permissions" tab and the "Security" tab on a shared folder in Windows.

Answer: The "Share Permissions" tab controls network access to the shared folder, while the "Security" tab sets NTFS permissions for local access.

29. What is the difference between "Read" and "List" permissions in Windows file and folder security?

Answer:"Read" permissions allow reading and executing files, while "List" permissions permit viewing folder contents but not file content.

30. What are "Special Permissions" in Windows file and folder security, and how do they differ from standard permissions?

Answer: Special permissions are fine-grained permissions that allow precise control over actions, providing more detailed access control than standard permissions.

31. Explain how "Effective Access" is determined for a user or group in Windows file and folder permissions.

Answer: Effective access is determined by combining permissions from both NTFS permissions and share permissions, resulting in the most restrictive access.

32. What is the purpose of the "Read and Execute" permission, and how does it affect file and folder access?

Answer:"Read and Execute" permission allows reading and executing files, making it suitable for applications and scripts.

33. How do you audit file and folder access in Windows, and what is the purpose of auditing?

Answer: Auditing is enabled in the "Security" tab of a file or folder's properties, allowing administrators to track and review access to resources.

34. What is the "Effective Permissions" tab in Windows file and folder security, and how is it used?

Answer: The "Effective Permissions" tab helps users and administrators determine what actions they can perform on a file or folder based on their group memberships and permissions.

35. Explain how "Deny" permissions work in Windows file and folder security and when they should be used.

Answer:"Deny" permissions explicitly block a user or group from performing a specified action, and they should be used sparingly to override other permissions.

36. What is the purpose of the "Change" permission in Windows file and folder security?

Answer: The "Change" permission allows users to read, write, and delete files, but not change folder permissions or ownership.

37. How do you assign ownership of a file or folder in Windows, and why is ownership important for access control?

Answer: Ownership can be assigned in the "Security" tab, and it's crucial for controlling access and resolving permission conflicts.

38. Explain the concept of "effective access" testing in Windows, and how is it useful for users and administrators?

Answer: Effective access testing helps users and administrators determine the permissions they effectively have on a resource without performing real actions.

39. What are "share-level permissions," and how do they interact with NTFS permissions on shared folders in Windows?

Answer: Share-level permissions control network access, while NTFS permissions determine local access. Both are evaluated, with the most restrictive permissions applied.

40. How can you recover from a situation where you've locked yourself out of a file or folder due to incorrect permissions in Windows?

Answer: Recovery can be done through the Administrator account or by taking ownership of the resource, then reconfiguring the permissions.

41. Explain the concept of "File System Access Control Lists" (FACLs) and their role in Windows file and folder security.

Answer:FACLs are data structures that control access to resources, listing permissions for users and groups, and determining who can perform specific actions.

42. What is the "Traverse Folder/Execute File" permission, and when is it necessary for access to subfolders?

Answer:"Traverse Folder/Execute File" permission allows a user to navigate into a folder to access its subfolders, making it important for folder access.

43. How can you prevent unauthorized changes to file and folder permissions in Windows?

Answer: Prevent unauthorized changes by limiting who can modify permissions and regularly auditing changes to permissions.

44. What is the purpose of "List Folder Contents" permission in Windows file and folder security?

Answer:"List Folder Contents" allows users to view the contents of a folder without being able to open or read files directly.

45. Explain the role of the Windows "Creator Owner" and "Creator Group" in file and folder security.

Answer:"Creator Owner" and "Creator Group" are placeholders for the user or group that creates a file or folder, allowing them to specify permissions for their creations.

46. How do you use Group Policy to manage user rights and permissions across a Windows network?

Answer: Group Policy allows administrators to define and enforce security settings for user rights, permissions, and access controls across a network.

47. What are the benefits and limitations of using inherited permissions in Windows file and folder security?

Answer: Inherited permissions simplify access control but may grant excessive access to subfolders and files. Careful planning is needed to balance security.

48. Explain the concept of "effective access denial" and how it's determined in Windows security models.

Answer: Effective access denial is the result of a combination of permissions, including explicit "Deny" permissions, leading to a restriction of access.

49. What is the "Delete" permission, and how does it affect file and folder management in Windows?

Answer: The "Delete" permission allows users to delete files and folders, but it's distinct from "Modify" or "Write" permissions.

50. How can you audit and review user rights and permissions in Windows for compliance and security purposes?

Answer: Audit user rights and permissions by using auditing tools, reviewing logs, and regularly assessing permissions to ensure compliance and security.

Windows Firewall and Security Software

1. What is Windows Firewall, and how does it contribute to the security of a Windows operating system?

Answer: Windows Firewall is a built-in security feature in Windows that controls incoming and outgoing network traffic. It helps protect the system by allowing or blocking connections based on defined rules.

2. Explain the difference between inbound and outbound rules in Windows Firewall, and how are they configured to enhance security?

Answer: Inbound rules control incoming network traffic, while outbound rules manage outgoing traffic. These rules are configured to specify which applications or services are allowed to communicate with the network, enhancing security by restricting unauthorized access.

3. What is the purpose of security software, and how does it complement the protection provided by Windows Firewall?

Answer: Security software, such as antivirus and anti-malware programs, complements Windows Firewall by providing protection against various types of threats, including viruses, malware, and other malicious software that may bypass or exploit firewall rules.

4. How often should you update security software, and what are the risks of using outdated security definitions or signatures?

Answer: Security software should be updated regularly, ideally daily. Outdated definitions or signatures can leave a system vulnerable to new threats, as the software won't recognize or block them.

5. Explain the role of a personal firewall in the context of security software, and how does it protect against unauthorized access and data leakage?

Answer: A personal firewall, often included in security software, monitors network traffic and protects against unauthorized access and data leakage by controlling the communication between a device and the network.

6. What is the difference between signature-based and behavior-based threat detection in security software, and why is a combination of both methods important?

Answer: Signature-based detection relies on known patterns of threats, while behavior-based detection identifies abnormal activities. A combination is important because it covers both known and unknown threats, enhancing security.

7. How can a Windows user configure Windows Firewall to allow specific applications or services to communicate through it?

Answer: Users can configure Windows Firewall by creating custom inbound and outbound rules to allow specific applications or services. They define the program or port, action (allow or block), and scope (e.g., local network or public).

8. What are the benefits and challenges of using third-party security software over Windows Defender, the built-in antivirus program in Windows?

Answer: Third-party security software often offers additional features and may provide more comprehensive protection. However, it can be resource-intensive and may require regular updates and maintenance.

9. Explain the concept of "sandboxing" in security software and how it protects a system from potentially harmful or untrusted applications.

Answer: Sandboxing involves running untrusted or potentially harmful applications in an isolated environment, separate from the rest of the system. This containment prevents these applications from causing harm.

10. What is the role of a firewall in a network security context, and how does it differ from the Windows Firewall installed on individual computers?

Answer:A network firewall is typically a hardware or software device that protects an entire network from unauthorized access and threats. It differs from the Windows Firewall, which is focused on individual computer protection. Network firewalls control traffic at the network perimeter, while Windows Firewall operates at the endpoint level.

11. What is the Windows Firewall, and what is its primary purpose?

Answer: Windows Firewall is a security feature in Windows that filters incoming and outgoing network traffic to protect the system from unauthorized access and threats.

12. Explain the difference between an inbound rule and an outbound rule in Windows Firewall.

Answer: Inbound rules control incoming network traffic, while outbound rules manage outgoing traffic, allowing or blocking specific actions based on defined criteria.

13. How do you enable or disable the Windows Firewall on a Windows system?

Answer: You can enable or disable Windows Firewall through the Control Panel or using Group Policy settings.

14. What is the purpose of a firewall rule, and how is it used to control network traffic in Windows Firewall?

Answer:A firewall rule defines how traffic should be treated based on specific criteria, allowing or blocking connections.

15. Explain the difference between a stateful firewall and a stateless firewall.

Answer:A stateful firewall tracks the state of active connections and allows related responses, while a stateless firewall filters packets based on predefined rules without tracking connection states.

16. What is the Windows Defender Firewall, and how does it differ from the traditional Windows Firewall?

Answer: Windows Defender Firewall is a more advanced version of Windows Firewall integrated with Windows Security, providing additional features such as application-level filtering.

17. How does Windows Firewall protect against common network threats like port scanning and unauthorized access?

Answer: Windows Firewall can block incoming traffic on specific ports, preventing port scanning and unauthorized access attempts.

18. Explain how Windows Firewall can be configured to allow specific programs or applications to communicate over the network.

Answer: You can create inbound and outbound rules to permit specific programs to communicate, allowing them to bypass the firewall.

19. What are the potential risks of disabling the Windows Firewall, and in what situations might you need to do it?

Answer: Disabling the Windows Firewall exposes the system to network threats. You might disable it for troubleshooting, but it's generally not recommended.

20. How can you use Group Policy to manage Windows Firewall settings across a network of Windows computers?

Answer: Group Policy allows administrators to define and enforce firewall rules and settings across multiple computers, ensuring consistency.

21. Explain the role of Windows Firewall with Advanced Security and how it extends the capabilities of the standard Windows Firewall.

Answer: Windows Firewall with Advanced Security provides advanced features such as advanced rule configuration, connection security rules, and IPsec settings.

22. What is a "firewall profile" in Windows Firewall, and how does it tailor firewall settings for different network environments?

Answer:A firewall profile contains specific settings for different network environments, such as public, private, and domain networks, adapting firewall behavior accordingly.

23. How can you configure Windows Firewall rules to allow specific IP addresses or ranges of IP addresses?

Answer: You can create custom firewall rules specifying IP addresses or IP address ranges to allow or block traffic from specific sources.

24. Explain the purpose of "outbound connection rules" in Windows Firewall, and why they are important.

Answer: Outbound connection rules control which applications or services can initiate outgoing network connections, helping prevent malicious software from sending data.

25. What is a "firewall log" in Windows Firewall, and how is it useful for monitoring and troubleshooting network traffic?

Answer:A firewall log records information about incoming and outgoing traffic, helping administrators monitor and troubleshoot network activity.

26. How does Windows Firewall handle ICMP (Internet Control Message Protocol) traffic, and what are the security implications?

Answer: Windows Firewall can be configured to allow or block ICMP traffic. Allowing ICMP can help with network diagnostics, but it may also expose the system to certain attacks.

27. Explain how to configure Windows Firewall to allow or block traffic on specific ports, and why port-based rules are important for network security.

Answer: Port-based rules specify which ports and protocols should be allowed or blocked, providing granular control over network traffic.

28. What is a "firewall exception" in Windows Firewall, and how does it affect the way certain applications interact with the firewall?

Answer:A firewall exception allows specific applications or services to bypass the firewall rules, ensuring they can communicate without interruption.

29. What is the purpose of "connection security rules" in Windows Firewall with Advanced Security, and how do they enhance network security?

Answer: Connection security rules enforce encryption and authentication requirements for network connections, enhancing security between systems.

30. Explain how Windows Firewall can be used to protect against Distributed Denial of Service (DDoS) attacks.

Answer: Windows Firewall can be configured to block or limit traffic from known malicious sources, helping mitigate DDoS attacks.

31. What is a "firewall state table," and how does it help in managing and monitoring network connections?

Answer:A firewall state table keeps track of active network connections, helping the firewall manage and monitor connection states.

32. What is Windows Defender, and how does it provide real-time protection against malware and other threats?

Answer: Windows Defender is an antivirus and antimalware software integrated into Windows, providing real-time protection against malicious software.

33. Explain how Windows Defender SmartScreen helps protect against unsafe websites and downloads.

Answer: SmartScreen checks the reputation of websites and downloaded files, warning users about potentially unsafe content.

34. How can you configure Windows Defender to schedule regular scans for malware on a Windows system?

Answer: Scheduled scans in Windows Defender can be configured through Windows Security settings, allowing automated malware scanning.

35. What is the Windows Defender Offline scan, and how does it help in removing advanced malware?

Answer: Windows Defender Offline is a bootable tool that runs before Windows starts, allowing it to detect and remove malware that might evade regular scans.

36. What is the Windows Security Center, and how does it provide a centralized view of security-related information in Windows?

Answer: Windows Security Center provides a central dashboard for monitoring and managing security settings, including Windows Firewall, Windows Defender, and other security features.

37. Explain the purpose of Windows Firewall with Advanced Security's "connection security rules" and "authentication exemptions."

Answer: Connection security rules enforce specific security requirements, while authentication exemptions allow exceptions to these rules.

38. What is the Windows Firewall "edge traversal" setting, and how does it affect network traffic?

Answer: Edge traversal allows incoming network traffic to pass through the firewall when it reaches the edge of the network, ensuring it doesn't get blocked.

39. How can you configure Windows Firewall to allow specific remote desktop or terminal services connections to a Windows computer?

Answer: You can create inbound rules to allow remote desktop or terminal services connections based on your requirements.

40. Explain the concept of a "firewall profile" and how it adapts firewall settings for different types of networks.

Answer: A firewall profile is a set of firewall rules and settings tailored to specific network types, such as public, private, and domain networks.

41. What are "Action Center" notifications in Windows, and how do they inform users about security and maintenance issues?

Answer: Action Center provides notifications about security and maintenance issues, including Windows Firewall and antivirus alerts.

42. How can you use Windows Firewall to secure a public Wi-Fi connection while maintaining a more permissive configuration at home?

Answer: You can switch between different firewall profiles based on your network location to adapt to the level of security required.

43. Explain the concept of "firewall logging" and how it helps in monitoring and diagnosing network traffic.

Answer: Firewall logging records information about network traffic, helping administrators monitor and diagnose issues or security threats.

44. What are some common reasons for Windows Firewall blocking legitimate network traffic, and how can these issues be resolved?

Answer: Common reasons include incorrect firewall rules or settings. Troubleshoot by reviewing rules, event logs, and testing connections.

45. How does Windows Firewall interact with third-party security software, and what considerations should be made when using both?

Answer: Third-party security software may include its own firewall. Consider compatibility, potential conflicts, and whether to disable one firewall if using another.

46. Explain the concept of "firewall stealth mode" and how it enhances security by making a system less visible to network scans.

Answer: Stealth mode suppresses responses to certain network scans, making the system less detectable to potential attackers.

47. What is a "firewall stateful packet inspection" and how does it help in identifying and blocking malicious traffic?

Answer: Stateful packet inspection analyzes network traffic and tracks connection states, allowing the firewall to block suspicious or unauthorized traffic.

48. How does Windows Firewall handle applications that require multiple network ports for communication, such as online games or peer-to-peer software?

Answer: Windows Firewall can dynamically allow or prompt for additional ports when applications require them, based on rule configurations.

49. Explain how to manage and troubleshoot Windows Firewall using the "wf.msc" management console.

Answer: The "wf.msc" console allows administrators to configure and troubleshoot Windows Firewall rules and settings through a graphical interface.

50. What is the role of "firewall security groups" in Windows Firewall with Advanced Security, and how are they used for rule management?

Answer: Firewall security groups provide a way to organize and manage firewall rules, making it easier to apply consistent policies.

Securing Windows Resources

1. What are the primary resources in a Windows environment that need to be secured, and why is resource security important?

Answer: Windows resources include files, folders, devices, and network shares. Resource security is crucial to protect sensitive data, ensure system integrity, and prevent unauthorized access.

2. Explain the concept of access control lists (ACLs) in the context of securing Windows resources. How do they determine who can access a resource and what actions they can perform?

Answer: ACLs are lists of permissions associated with resources. They specify which users or groups can access the resource and define the type of access, such as read, write, or execute.

3. What is the difference between NTFS and share permissions in Windows resource security, and how do they work together to control access to shared folders and files?

Answer: NTFS permissions are file system permissions that control access to files and folders on the local computer, while share permissions control access to shared folders over the network. They work together, and the most restrictive permission applies.

4. How can you encrypt files and folders in Windows, and what is the purpose of encryption in resource security?

Answer: Windows provides features like BitLocker and EFS (Encrypting File System) to encrypt files and folders. Encryption is used to protect data at rest, ensuring that even if unauthorized access occurs, the data remains secure.

5. Explain the benefits of using auditing in Windows to monitor and track resource access. What types of events can be audited, and how can the audit logs be used for security analysis?

Answer: Auditing allows tracking of various events, such as successful or failed access attempts to resources. Audit logs can be used to identify security breaches, track user activity, and ensure compliance with security policies.

6. What is the "Run as administrator" feature in Windows, and how does it impact resource security by allowing elevated privileges for certain tasks?

Answer: "Run as administrator" allows a user to run applications with elevated privileges, which can impact resource security by giving the user access to restricted resources. It should be used with caution.

7. How does User Account Control (UAC) enhance resource security in Windows, and what role does it play in preventing malicious software from making unauthorized changes?

Answer: UAC prompts users for permission when attempting actions that require administrative privileges. It prevents unauthorized changes and the execution of potentially harmful software.

8. Explain the concept of "least privilege" in Windows resource security and why it is a best practice.

Answer: "Least privilege" means users should have the minimum level of access necessary to perform their tasks. It is a best practice to reduce the potential impact of security breaches and limit unauthorized actions.

9. What is the purpose of using strong, complex passwords, and how do password policies in Windows contribute to resource security?

Answer: Strong, complex passwords are essential to prevent unauthorized access. Password policies in Windows enforce password complexity and expiration rules, enhancing resource security.

10. How can you restrict physical access to computer resources, such as servers or workstations, and why is physical security an integral part of resource protection in a Windows environment?

Answer: Physical access can be restricted through measures like locks, access control systems, and security badges. Physical security is crucial to prevent unauthorized individuals from tampering with or stealing computer resources, which can have a significant impact on overall security.

11. What are the key resources in a Windows environment that need to be secured?

Answer: Key resources include files, folders, registry keys, user accounts, system settings, applications, and network resources.

12. Explain the importance of resource security in a Windows environment.

Answer: Resource security is crucial for protecting sensitive data, maintaining system integrity, preventing unauthorized access, and ensuring regulatory compliance.

13. What are the fundamental principles of resource security in Windows?

Answer: The principles include authentication, authorization, audit, encryption, and least privilege.

14. What is the difference between authentication and authorization in resource security?

Answer: Authentication verifies a user's identity, while authorization determines what actions they are allowed to perform on resources once authenticated.

15. How do you enforce the principle of least privilege in Windows resource security?

Answer: Least privilege is enforced by granting users the minimum level of access needed to perform their tasks, reducing the risk of unauthorized actions.

16. Explain the role of Access Control Lists (ACLs) in resource security.

Answer:ACLs define permissions for users and groups on resources, specifying who can access, modify, or delete them.

17. What are some common security risks associated with improperly secured Windows resources?

Answer: Risks include data breaches, unauthorized access, data loss, malware infection, and compromised system integrity.

18. How can you secure a file or folder in Windows using NTFS permissions?

Answer: You can configure NTFS permissions by right-clicking on the file or folder, selecting "Properties," and using the "Security" tab to set permissions.

19. What is the difference between "Share" permissions and NTFS permissions, and why are both important in securing shared resources?

Answer: Share permissions control network access to shared resources, while NTFS permissions determine local access. Both are evaluated, with the most restrictive permissions applied.

20. Explain the concept of "effective permissions" in Windows resource security.

Answer: Effective permissions are the combined result of all permissions granted and denied to a user or group, determining what actions they can perform on a resource.

21. How do you audit resource access in Windows, and what is the purpose of auditing?

Answer: Auditing is enabled in resource properties, allowing administrators to track and review access to resources for security and compliance purposes.

22. What are the benefits of using encryption to secure Windows resources, and how does it work?

Answer: Encryption protects resource data by converting it into an unreadable format, making it inaccessible without the correct decryption key.

23. Explain the role of BitLocker in securing Windows resources.

Answer: BitLocker is used to encrypt the entire system drive, securing the data at rest and preventing unauthorized access.

24. What is Windows Defender SmartScreen, and how does it protect against malicious downloads and unsafe websites?

Answer: SmartScreen checks the reputation of websites and downloads, warning users about potentially harmful content.

25. How can you use Group Policy to enforce resource security settings across a network of Windows computers?

Answer: Group Policy allows administrators to define and enforce security settings for resource access and other configurations across a network.

26. What is the Windows Security Account Manager (SAM) database, and how does it play a role in securing user accounts and resource access?

Answer:SAM stores user account information and is used for local authentication on standalone Windows computers.

27. How can you enforce security settings and resource access control using Group Policy in a Windows domain environment?

Answer: Group Policy settings can be configured to manage resource security, access control, and other security-related configurations on domain-joined computers.

28. Explain the concept of "role-based access control" (RBAC) in resource security, and how it simplifies access management.

Answer:RBAC assigns permissions to roles rather than individual users, making access management more efficient and consistent.

29. What is "AppLocker," and how does it help control which applications can run on Windows systems?

Answer: AppLocker is a Windows feature that enforces application control policies to specify which applications are allowed to run on a system.

30. What is the Windows Credential Manager, and how does it improve user authentication and credential management?

Answer: Credential Manager stores and manages credentials securely, simplifying user access to resources without repeated login details.

31. How can you secure network shares and prevent unauthorized access to shared resources in Windows?

Answer: Network shares can be secured using both share permissions and NTFS permissions to control who can access and modify shared resources.

32. What is the principle of defense-in-depth, and how is it applied in securing Windows resources?

Answer: Defense-in-depth involves using multiple layers of security controls to protect resources against a variety of threats, enhancing security.

33. Explain the concept of "effective access denial" and how it is determined in Windows resource security.

Answer: Effective access denial is the result of a combination of permissions, including explicit "Deny" permissions, leading to a restriction of access.

34. How can you configure Windows Firewall to control network access to specific resources and applications?

Answer: You can create custom firewall rules to allow or block network traffic for specific resources and applications based on defined criteria.

35. What is the significance of the "Trusted Platform Module" (TPM) in securing Windows resources, and how does it enhance system security?

Answer:TPM is a hardware-based security component that provides secure storage of cryptographic keys and enhances security features like BitLocker.

36. Explain how to assign ownership of a file or folder in Windows, and why ownership is important for access control.

Answer: Ownership can be assigned in the "Security" tab of a file or folder's properties, allowing for control over access and resolution of permission conflicts.

37. How does "Active Directory" enhance resource security in a Windows domain environment?

Answer: Active Directory provides centralized user and group management, allowing administrators to enforce access controls and security policies across the network.

38. What is "Windows Information Protection" (WIP), and how does it safeguard data on Windows devices?

Answer:WIP separates personal and work-related data, encrypts business data, and enforces access controls to protect corporate information.

39. Explain the concept of "Share Permission" inheritance in Windows, and how it affects resource access control.

Answer: Share permission inheritance allows permissions set at a higher-level shared folder to flow down to its subfolders and files, simplifying access control.

40. What is the "Access Control List" (ACL), and how does it determine user and group access to Windows resources?

Answer:ACLs list permissions for users and groups, specifying who can access, modify, or delete resources, based on access control entries.

41. How can you restrict access to a specific set of IP addresses or IP ranges using Windows Firewall rules?

Answer: Custom firewall rules can be configured to allow or block traffic from specific IP addresses or ranges, providing granular access control.

42. Explain the role of the "Effective Permissions" tab in Windows resource security, and how it helps determine user access.

Answer: The "Effective Permissions" tab assists users and administrators in determining what actions they can perform on a resource based on their group memberships and permissions.

43. What are "Special Permissions" in Windows resource security, and how do they provide detailed access control?

Answer: Special permissions are fine-grained, allowing precise control over actions on resources, offering more detailed access control than standard permissions.

44. How can you configure auditing in Windows to track access to specific resources, and what is the purpose of auditing?

Answer: Auditing is enabled on resource properties, tracking and recording access to resources for security, compliance, and troubleshooting.

45. Explain the concept of "auditing logs" in resource security and how they help in monitoring and analyzing access events.

Answer: Auditing logs contain records of access events, allowing administrators to review and analyze who accessed resources and what actions they performed.

46. What is "traverse folder/execute file" permission, and how does it affect access to subfolders and files in Windows?

Answer:"Traverse folder/execute file" permission allows a user to navigate into a folder to access its subfolders, important for folder access.

47. How can you use Group Policy to enforce security settings for resources and access control across a Windows domain?

Answer: Group Policy settings allow administrators to define and enforce security settings for resource access control, user permissions, and other security-related configurations.

48. What is the role of "firewall stateful packet inspection," and how does it enhance network security in Windows Firewall?

Answer: Stateful packet inspection analyses network traffic and tracks connection states, allowing the firewall to block suspicious or unauthorized traffic.

49. Explain the concept of "firewall edge traversal" and how it affects network traffic in Windows Firewall.

Answer: Firewall edge traversal allows incoming network traffic to pass through the firewall when it reaches the edge of the network, ensuring it doesn't get blocked.

50. What is "File System Access Control Lists" (FACLs), and how do they help control access to resources in Windows?

Answer:FACLs are data structures that control access to resources, listing permissions for users and groups and specifying who can perform specific actions.

ONLINE RESOURCES

Practice Paper Link: https://forms.gle/pQ2J9MgnxuH5d5ey9

QR Code:

Video Link: https://www.youtube.com/playlist?list=PLzlh_31VWEFozRmqLl3gslnwb4K1uQ93M

QR Code:

Chapter 8 Windows Server and Enterprise Features

Introduction to Windows Server

1. What is Windows Server, and how does it differ from the Windows desktop operating system?

Answer: Windows Server is a specialized operating system designed for server applications and network services. It differs from the desktop version by focusing on stability, security, and scalability for managing network resources.

2. Explain the role of Windows Server in an organization's IT infrastructure, and why is it crucial for businesses of all sizes?

Answer: Windows Server acts as the backbone of an organization's IT infrastructure, providing essential services like file sharing, user authentication, and centralized management. It is crucial for ensuring the reliability and performance of critical business applications.

3. What are the core features and services provided by Windows Server, and how do they support various business needs?

Answer: Windows Server offers features such as Active Directory for user and group management, DNS for name resolution, DHCP for IP address assignment, and many others that support infrastructure, application, and data management requirements.

4. What is the role of Active Directory in Windows Server, and how does it simplify user and resource management in a networked environment?

Answer: Active Directory is a directory service that centralizes user and resource management. It simplifies tasks like user authentication, group policy enforcement, and resource access control in a networked environment.

5. Explain the concept of server roles in Windows Server and how they allow the server to perform specific functions or services.

Answer: Server roles are predefined configurations that enable a server to perform specific functions, such as being a web server, file server, or domain controller. They simplify the process of setting up and managing services.

6. What is the Windows Server Core installation option, and how does it differ from the full GUI installation? When might you choose one over the other?

Answer: The Windows Server Core installation omits the graphical user interface, reducing the server's footprint and attack surface. It is preferred for headless servers or those with minimal management needs, while the full GUI installation is useful when a graphical interface is required.

7. How does Windows Server support virtualization through technologies like Hyper-V, and what benefits does virtualization bring to an organization?

Answer: Windows Server with Hyper-V allows organizations to create and manage virtual machines (VMs). Virtualization enhances resource utilization, scalability, and flexibility by running multiple operating systems and applications on a single physical server.

8. Explain the significance of Windows Server's security features and best practices in maintaining a secure server environment.

Answer: Windows Server includes features like BitLocker, Windows Defender, and security policies to safeguard the server environment. Best practices involve regular updates, strong authentication, access controls, and monitoring for security threats.

9. What is Windows Server's role in data backup and disaster recovery, and how can organizations use it to ensure data availability and business continuity?

Answer: Windows Server provides backup and recovery features to protect critical data and enable business continuity. It allows organizations to schedule regular backups and recover data in case of hardware failures or disasters.

10. What are some common Windows Server editions, and how do they cater to different business needs, from small businesses to large enterprises?

Answer: Common Windows Server editions include Standard, Datacentre, and Essentials. Standard is suitable for small to medium-sized organizations, Datacentre is designed for data-intensive workloads, and Essentials is tailored for smaller businesses with limited IT resources. Each edition offers varying levels of features and licensing options.

11. What is Windows Server, and how does it differ from the Windows client operating system?

Answer: Windows Server is an operating system designed for server deployments. It offers features and capabilities for managing network resources, hosting services, and scaling for enterprise needs, while the client OS is designed for individual user workstations.

12. Explain the importance of Windows Server in an enterprise IT environment.

Answer: Windows Server is crucial for providing centralized management, network services, security, and scalability for enterprise organizations, supporting critical business operations.

13. What are the primary editions of Windows Server, and how do they differ from each other?

Answer: Windows Server editions include Essentials, Standard, Datacentre, and more. They differ in terms of licensing, features, and scalability. For example, Datacentre provides unlimited virtualization rights, while Standard has limitations.

14. How does Windows Server contribute to managing user accounts and permissions in a network environment?

Answer: Windows Server provides tools like Active Directory for user and group management, as well as Group Policy for defining access controls and permissions.

15. What role does Windows Server play in providing network services such as DNS and DHCP?

Answer: Windows Server can host services like DNS (Domain Name System) for name resolution and DHCP (Dynamic Host Configuration Protocol) for IP address allocation, helping to manage network infrastructure.

16. Explain the concept of a "domain controller" in Windows Server and its role in user authentication.

Answer: A domain controller is a server that hosts Active Directory and is responsible for authenticating users and managing user accounts, groups, and security policies within a domain.

17. What are the core components of Windows Server's network infrastructure services, and how do they contribute to network management?

Answer: Core components include DNS, DHCP, and WINS (Windows Internet Name Service) for name resolution and IP management, ensuring efficient network operation.

18. What is the role of the Windows Server "file server" role, and how does it facilitate centralized file storage and access for users?

Answer: The file server role allows Windows Server to act as a central repository for storing and sharing files and provides access control features to secure data.

19. Explain the concept of "active directory" in Windows Server and how it enhances user and resource management.

Answer: Active Directory is a directory service that stores information about network resources, user accounts, and group memberships. It simplifies resource management and enables single sign-on.

20. How does Windows Server support virtualization, and what is the role of Hyper-V in this context?

Answer: Windows Server provides virtualization capabilities through Hyper-V, allowing multiple virtual machines (VMs) to run on a single physical server, optimizing resource utilization and scalability.

21. What are the features of Windows Server's remote access and VPN services, and how do they enable remote connectivity for users and branch offices?

Answer: Remote access and VPN services in Windows Server provide secure, remote connections for users and branch offices, facilitating access to network resources.

22. Explain the concept of "failover clustering" in Windows Server and how it enhances system reliability and availability.

Answer: Failover clustering allows multiple servers to work together as a cluster. If one server fails, another takes over, ensuring high availability and fault tolerance.

23. What is Windows Server's role in web hosting and providing web services, and which features are commonly used for this purpose?

Answer: Windows Server can host websites and web applications using features like Internet Information Services (IIS) and the .NET Framework.

24. How does Windows Server support data backup and recovery?

Answer: Windows Server includes features like Windows Server Backup, Volume Shadow Copy Service (VSS), and Data Deduplication to facilitate data backup and recovery.

25. Explain the concept of "Group Policy" in Windows Server and its role in centralized system management and security.

Answer: Group Policy allows administrators to define and enforce security and management settings for users and computers across the network.

26. What is the purpose of Windows Server's "print server" role, and how does it facilitate print management in an organization?

Answer: The print server role centralizes print resource management, simplifying the administration of printers and print queues.

27. How does Windows Server support identity and access management for users and devices in a network environment?

Answer: Windows Server provides identity and access management through services like Active Directory, certificate services, and Azure Active Directory integration.

28. Explain the concept of "Windows Server Core" and its advantages in specific server deployments.

Answer: Windows Server Core is a minimal, command-line version of Windows Server, offering reduced attack surface and resource usage, making it suitable for specific server roles.

29. What is the role of Windows Server's "Network Policy Server" (NPS), and how does it enhance network security through authentication and authorization?

Answer: NPS is used for RADIUS-based authentication and authorization services, ensuring secure network access and controlling network policy enforcement.

30. How does Windows Server support cloud integration, and what role does it play in hybrid cloud environments?

Answer: Windows Server integrates with Azure and other cloud services, facilitating hybrid cloud deployments and offering a range of cloud-based solutions.

31. Explain the concept of "Windows Server Containers" and how they enhance application deployment and management.

Answer: Windows Server Containers are lightweight, isolated environments for running applications, enabling fast deployment, scalability, and resource isolation.

32. What is the purpose of Windows Server's "Windows Firewall with Advanced Security" and how does it protect the server and network?

Answer: Windows Firewall with Advanced Security provides advanced features for filtering network traffic, protecting the server from unauthorized access and threats.

33. What is "Windows Server Update Services" (WSUS), and how does it help in managing and deploying software updates in a network?

Answer: WSUS is used to manage, monitor, and deploy software updates for Microsoft products, ensuring system security and compliance.

34. Explain the role of "Remote Desktop Services" (RDS) in Windows Server and how it facilitates remote access to applications and desktops.

Answer: RDS allows users to access applications and desktops remotely, improving user productivity and enabling remote work scenarios.

35. What is the "Active Directory Certificate Services" (AD CS) role, and how does it enhance security through certificate management?

Answer: AD CS is used for managing digital certificates, providing secure authentication and encryption for network communications.

36. How does Windows Server provide security through features like BitLocker, Credential Guard, and Device Guard?

Answer: BitLocker encrypts data at rest, while Credential Guard and Device Guard enhance authentication and protect against malware and untrusted code execution.

37. Explain the concept of "Windows Event Logs" in Windows Server, and how they assist in monitoring and troubleshooting server issues.

Answer: Windows Event Logs record system events and errors, helping administrators monitor, diagnose, and resolve server-related issues.

38. What is "Windows Defender Antivirus," and how does it protect Windows Server from malware and security threats?

Answer: Windows Defender Antivirus provides real-time protection against malware and security threats, ensuring server security.

39. How does Windows Server support dynamic access control and claims-based authentication for resource access?

Answer: Dynamic access control and claims-based authentication allow administrators to define access policies based on user attributes and resource properties.

40. What is the role of "Network Load Balancing" (NLB) in Windows Server, and how does it enhance server performance and reliability?

Answer: NLB distributes network traffic across multiple servers, improving server performance and providing fault tolerance.

41. Explain the concept of "Windows Server backup" and its significance in protecting server data and system configurations.

Answer: Windows Server backup allows administrators to create and manage backups of system data and configurations, ensuring data recovery and system integrity.

42. What is the "Active Directory Federation Services" (AD FS) role in Windows Server, and how does it facilitate single sign-on and identity federation?

Answer: AD FS enables single sign-on and identity federation, allowing users to access multiple applications and services with a single set of credentials.

43. How can Windows Server be used for hosting virtual desktop infrastructure (VDI), and what are the advantages of this approach?

Answer: Windows Server can host virtual desktops, offering scalability, centralized management, and cost savings in VDI deployments.

44. Explain the concept of "Windows Storage Spaces" and its role in storage virtualization and management.

Answer: Windows Storage Spaces allows administrators to create virtualized storage pools and volumes, simplifying storage management and enhancing scalability.

45. What is the role of the "Windows Server Essentials" edition, and how does it cater to small businesses with limited IT resources?

Answer: Windows Server Essentials is designed for small businesses, offering simplified management, data protection, and remote access solutions.

46. How does Windows Server support software-defined networking (SDN) and enhance network flexibility and agility?

Answer: SDN in Windows Server provides a flexible, programmable network infrastructure, allowing dynamic management and automation of network resources.

47. Explain the concept of "Windows Subsystem for Linux" (WSL) and how it enables running Linux applications on Windows Server.

Answer: WSL allows running Linux applications on Windows Server, enhancing compatibility and flexibility for developers and administrators.

48. What is the "Windows Server AppFabric," and how does it facilitate building and managing composite applications?

Answer: Windows Server AppFabric is a set of middleware technologies that simplify building and managing composite applications, offering workflow and caching capabilities.

49. How does Windows Server support containerization and orchestration with technologies like Docker and Kubernetes?

Answer: Windows Server integrates with Docker containers and Kubernetes, providing a platform for containerized applications and scalable orchestration.

50. Explain the role of "Windows Server Manager" in centralizing server management and administration.

Answer: Windows Server Manager is a management tool that centralizes server administration tasks, making it easier to configure and monitor server roles and features.

Active Directory and Domain Services

1. What is Active Directory (AD)?

Answer: Active Directory is a directory service developed by Microsoft that stores information about objects on a network, including user accounts, groups, computers, and resources. It provides a centralized and secure way to manage and authenticate users and devices within a network.

2. What is the purpose of Domain Services in Active Directory?

Answer: Domain Services in Active Directory provide centralized authentication and authorization services within a network. They allow administrators to manage user accounts, group policies, and access controls across multiple computers and resources in a domain.

3. What is the difference between a domain and a forest in Active Directory?

Answer: A domain is a logical grouping of objects within an Active Directory network. A forest, on the other hand, is a collection of one or more domains that share a common schema, configuration, and directory information. Domains within a forest trust each other and share resources.

4. What is the Global Catalog in Active Directory?

Answer: The Global Catalog is a specialized domain controller in Active Directory that contains a partial replica of all objects from every domain within a forest. It is used for searching and locating objects across the entire forest, making it essential for certain directory-related operations.

5. What is the purpose of Organizational Units (OUs) in Active Directory?

Answer: Organizational Units are containers within a domain used to organize and manage objects. OUs allow for a hierarchical structure, making it easier to delegate administrative tasks and apply Group Policies to specific sets of objects.

6. Explain the difference between authentication and authorization in the context of Active Directory.

Answer: Authentication is the process of verifying the identity of a user or device, ensuring they are who they claim to be. Active Directory authenticates users during the login process. Authorization, on the other hand, determines the level of access and permissions granted to authenticated users or devices, based on their assigned rights and roles.

7. What is a Group Policy Object (GPO) in Active Directory?

Answer: A Group Policy Object (GPO) is a collection of settings that define the behaviour and configuration of user and computer accounts within a domain. GPOs are used to enforce security policies, manage desktop settings, and control various aspects of the Windows operating system.

8. How do you troubleshoot replication issues in Active Directory?

Answer: Troubleshooting replication issues in Active Directory involves using tools like Repadmin, DCDiag, and Event Viewer to identify and resolve problems with data synchronization between domain controllers. Common issues can include DNS problems, network connectivity issues, or AD database corruption.

9. Explain the concept of Trust relationships in Active Directory.

Answer: Trust relationships in Active Directory establish a secure connection between domains or forests, allowing users in one domain to access resources in another. There are one-way and two-way trusts, and trust types can be transitive or non-transitive, depending on the requirements of the organization.

10. What is the purpose of the Flexible Single Master Operations (FSMO) roles in Active Directory?

Answer: FSMO roles, also known as operations master roles, are specialized roles assigned to domain controllers that perform unique tasks within the Active Directory forest or domain. They are responsible for tasks like schema updates, domain naming operations, and handling password changes. Understanding FSMO roles is crucial for maintaining the health and functionality of the Active Directory environment.

Windows Server Roles and Features

1. What is a Windows Server role, and how does it differ from a feature?

Answer: In Windows Server, a role is a set of software programs and services that provide specific functionality, such as Active Directory, DNS, or Web Server. A feature, on the other hand, is a software component that supports a role or adds additional functionality to the server. Features are optional and can be installed as needed.

2. What is Active Directory Application Mode (ADAM), and how does it differ from Active Directory Lightweight Directory Services (AD LDS)?

Answer:ADAM is an earlier version of AD LDS, designed for directory-based applications. Both provide directory services but have different features and compatibility.

3. Explain the purpose of the Active Directory Domain Services (AD DS) role in Windows Server.

Answer: The Active Directory Domain Services role is responsible for directory services, authentication, and management of resources in a Windows network. It allows organizations to centralize user and computer account management, enforcing security policies and facilitating resource access.

4. What is the role of the DHCP Server in Windows Server, and why is it important?

Answer: The DHCP Server role automates the assignment of IP addresses, subnet masks, and other network configuration settings to client devices on a network. It ensures efficient IP address management, reduces manual configuration errors, and minimizes network downtime.

5. Explain the purpose of the File Server role in Windows Server.

Answer: The File Server role allows Windows Server to serve as a central repository for storing, managing, and sharing files and resources. It enables secure file access and collaboration, including support for features like shared folders and network-attached storage (NAS).

6. What is the Hyper-V role in Windows Server, and how does it relate to virtualization?

Answer: The Hyper-V role enables server virtualization, allowing multiple virtual machines to run on a single physical server. It is crucial for creating and managing virtualized environments, making efficient use of server hardware and resources.

7. What is the Web Server (IIS) role in Windows Server, and how is it used in web hosting?

Answer: The Web Server role, powered by Internet Information Services (IIS), allows Windows Server to host and serve web applications, websites, and services. It provides a platform for web developers to publish and manage web content and applications.

8. Explain the purpose of the DNS Server role in Windows Server.

Answer: The DNS Server role is responsible for resolving domain names to IP addresses, making it possible for clients to access resources using human-readable domain names. It's a fundamental role in network communication and internet connectivity.

9. What are Remote Desktop Services (RDS), and how does the RDS role benefit organizations?

Answer: Remote Desktop Services provide remote access and application virtualization capabilities. The RDS role enables organizations to centralize application management, improve remote access security, and provide a consistent user experience across various devices.

10. What is the Network Policy Server (NPS) role, and how does it enhance network security?

Answer: The Network Policy Server role in Windows Server is used for implementing network access policies and authentication. It is essential for enforcing security measures, such as 802.1X authentication, VPN access, and network authorization.

11. What are some tools and features used for managing and deploying Windows Server roles and features?

Answer: Windows Server provides various tools and features, including Server Manager, PowerShell, and Deployment Services, for managing and deploying roles and features. Server Manager offers a graphical interface, while PowerShell allows automation and scripting, and Deployment Services assist with network-based OS installations and role deployment.

12. What is Active Directory (AD), and what role does it play in a Windows network environment?

Answer: Active Directory is a directory service that stores information about network resources and user accounts, facilitating centralized management and authentication in a Windows network.

13. Explain the difference between a domain and a workgroup in the context of Windows networking.

Answer:A domain is a centralized network with a common security policy and directory, while a workgroup is a decentralized network with no central directory or security policy.

14. What is a Domain Controller (DC), and why is it a critical component of Active Directory?

Answer:A Domain Controller is a server that stores the Active Directory database and authenticates users. It's essential for user access and resource management in a domain.

15. What is a Forest in Active Directory, and how does it relate to Domains?

Answer:A Forest is a collection of one or more domains. Domains within a forest share a common schema and global catalog.

16. Explain the purpose of the Global Catalog in Active Directory.

Answer: The Global Catalog stores a partial copy of all objects in the forest, facilitating domain and forest-wide searches, especially during user authentication.

17. What are Organizational Units (OUs) in Active Directory, and how do they enhance organization and management of resources?

Answer:OUs are containers within a domain used to organize and manage resources, including user accounts, computers, and other objects.

18. What is Active Directory Trust, and how does it enable resource access between different domains and forests?

Answer: Trust relationships establish secure communication and resource access between domains and forests, allowing users to access resources in other domains.

19. Explain the concept of Group Policy in Active Directory and how it centralizes system management and security settings.

Answer: Group Policy allows administrators to define and enforce security and management settings for users and computers in a domain or Organizational Unit.

20. How can you create a new user account in Active Directory, and what attributes can be configured for a user account?

Answer: User accounts can be created using Active Directory Users and Computers, and attributes include username, password, display name, email address, and group memberships.

21. What is Active Directory Lightweight Directory Services (AD LDS), and how does it differ from traditional AD?

Answer:AD LDS is a lightweight version of AD designed for directory-based applications, offering directory services without the full AD features like domain controllers.

22. Explain the purpose of the Active Directory Schema, and why it should be carefully managed.

Answer: The Schema defines the structure and attributes of objects in AD. Managing it is critical as changes can affect the entire directory and should be done with caution.

23. What are the FSMO (Flexible Single Master Operations) roles in Active Directory, and why are they important?

Answer:FSMO roles are responsible for specific tasks in a domain, such as schema updates, domain naming, and RID allocation. They are critical for AD operation and integrity.

24. What is the Active Directory Recycle Bin, and how does it assist in object recovery and accidental deletion prevention?

Answer: The Recycle Bin allows the recovery of deleted AD objects and attributes, reducing the risk of permanent data loss.

25. How can you transfer FSMO roles between Domain Controllers, and what is the significance of role placement?

Answer:FSMO roles can be transferred using the Active Directory Users and Computers console. Role placement affects AD operations, and roles should be placed strategically.

26. What is the Global Catalog Server, and how does it differ from a standard Domain Controller?

Answer: The Global Catalog Server contains a partial copy of all objects in the forest, whereas a standard Domain Controller stores a complete copy of objects for its domain.

27. Explain the purpose of Active Directory Integrated DNS and how it simplifies DNS management.

Answer: Active Directory Integrated DNS stores DNS data within AD, allowing for secure and replicated DNS zone data management.

28. What is the Active Directory Certificate Services role, and how does it enhance security through certificate management?

Answer: Active Directory Certificate Services allows for secure issuance, management, and revocation of digital certificates, enhancing network security and authentication.

29. How does Active Directory contribute to secure and centralized user authentication in a Windows network environment?

Answer: Active Directory stores user account information and authentication data, allowing for single sign-on and secure access to resources.

30. Explain the process of joining a computer to an Active Directory domain, and the benefits of domain membership.

Answer: Joining a computer to a domain establishes trust with the domain controller, enabling centralized management, user authentication, and access control.

What are Group Policy Objects (GPOs), and how can they be linked to domains, OUs, and sites?

Answer:GPOs define group policy settings for users and computers. They can be linked to domains, OUs, and sites to apply configurations based on location and group memberships.

31. What is the purpose of Active Directory Sites and Services, and how does it optimize network traffic and resource access?

Answer: Active Directory Sites and Services manage network site configurations, optimizing resource access and replication traffic based on geographical locations.

32. Explain the difference between a forest, domain, and tree in Active Directory terminology.

Answer:A forest is a collection of domains with shared schema. A domain is a security boundary. A tree is a collection of domains with a contiguous namespace.

33. How can you delegate administrative tasks in Active Directory, and why is delegation important for role-based access control?

Answer: Delegation involves assigning specific administrative tasks to users or groups, ensuring role-based access control and minimizing security risks.

34. What is the Active Directory Migration Tool (ADMT), and how does it assist in migrating users, groups, and computers between domains?

Answer:ADMT simplifies the migration of objects between domains, including users, groups, and computers, while preserving their security identifiers.

35. Explain the concept of "Active Directory Sites" and their role in optimizing replication and resource access in a multi-site environment.

Answer: Active Directory Sites represent physical or logical network locations, allowing administrators to optimize replication and authentication traffic between sites.

36. What is Active Directory Federation Services (AD FS), and how does it facilitate single sign-on (SSO) across different applications and organizations?

Answer:AD FS allows users to access multiple applications and services using a single set of credentials, improving user experience and security.

37. What is the role of the RID Master FSMO role in Active Directory, and how does it manage security identifiers (SIDs)?

Answer: The RID Master allocates unique relative identifiers (RID) to domain controllers, ensuring that security identifiers (SIDs) remain unique within a domain.

38. How does Active Directory manage user passwords and account policies to enhance security and password management?

Answer: Active Directory enforces password policies, account lockout policies, and password changes, improving security and user account management.

39. What is the purpose of the PDC Emulator FSMO role in Active Directory, and how does it affect time synchronization in a domain?

Answer: The PDC Emulator maintains accurate time for the domain, ensuring synchronization between domain controllers and time-sensitive operations.

40. Explain the process of raising the functional level of a domain or forest, and what benefits it provides in Active Directory.

Answer: Raising the functional level enables access to advanced AD features and compatibility with newer Windows Server versions, enhancing functionality and security.

41. What is the purpose of Active Directory Rights Management Services (AD RMS), and how does it protect sensitive data and documents?

Answer:AD RMS provides information protection through encryption and access control, protecting sensitive data and documents from unauthorized access.

42. How can you recover a deleted object in Active Directory using the Recycle Bin, and what is the restoration process?

Answer: Deleted objects can be recovered using the Active Directory Recycle Bin feature by restoring them from the Deleted Objects container.

43. What is Active Directory Application Mode (ADAM), and how does it differ from Active Directory Lightweight Directory Services (AD LDS)?

Answer:ADAM is an earlier version of AD LDS, designed for directory-based applications. Both provide directory services but have different features and compatibility.

44. Explain the concept of "Active Directory Group Scope" and how it affects the scope of group membership.

Answer: Group scope defines the range of objects that a group can include as members, with options including universal, global, and domain local scopes.

45. What is the role of the Infrastructure Master FSMO role in Active Directory, and how does it maintain references between objects?

Answer: The Infrastructure Master updates references to objects within a domain, ensuring data consistency and object integrity.

46. How does Active Directory Certificate Services (AD CS) support Public Key Infrastructure (PKI) for secure communication and authentication?

Answer:AD CS provides certification authority services, allowing the issuance and management of digital certificates for secure communication and authentication.

47. Explain the concept of "Active Directory Domain Services Restore Mode" and when it is used for recovery.

Answer: Restore Mode allows administrators to perform authoritative restores of AD objects, recovering deleted or modified objects in specific scenarios.

48. What are "Shadow Groups" in Active Directory, and how are they used for resource access and role-based permissions?

Answer: Shadow groups are security groups that are dynamically populated based on specific criteria, simplifying role-based access control.

49. What is Active Directory Lightweight Directory Services (AD LDS) and its typical use cases in application and directory services?

Answer: AD LDS is used for directory-based applications where a lightweight directory service is required, such as in web applications or custom directory services.

50. How does Active Directory protect against common security threats, and what best practices should be followed to secure an Active Directory environment?

Answer: Active Directory provides security through authentication, access control, and encryption. Best practices include securing Domain Controllers, monitoring event logs, and implementing strong password policies.

Group Policy and Security Policies

1. What is Group Policy in the context of Windows systems administration?

Answer: Group Policy is a feature in Windows operating systems that allows administrators to manage and enforce specific settings, configurations, and security policies across a network of computers. It's a powerful tool for centralizing control in an Active Directory environment.

2. Explain the difference between Group Policy Objects (GPOs) and Security Policies.

Answer: Group Policy Objects (GPOs) are containers for various policy settings that can be applied to users and computers. Security Policies, on the other hand, are a subset of GPOs that focus specifically on security-related settings, such as password policies, account lockout policies, and user rights assignments.

3. What is the purpose of the Default Domain Policy in Active Directory?

Answer: The Default Domain Policy is a GPO that contains default settings for all user and computer accounts in a domain. It is often used to establish baseline security settings and policies for the entire domain.

4. How do you link a Group Policy Object to an Active Directory container, and what are the available scope levels for GPOs?

Answer: GPOs can be linked to Active Directory containers like sites, domains, and Organizational Units (OUs). The available scope levels are local, site, domain, and OU. GPOs are applied in a specific order, with the most specific (OU-level) GPO taking precedence over less specific ones.

5. What is Group Policy Inheritance, and how does it work in an Active Directory structure?

Answer: Group Policy Inheritance is the process by which GPOs are applied in a hierarchical manner in Active Directory. GPOs at the higher levels of the hierarchy (e.g., domain level) are inherited by lower-level containers (e.g., OUs). If there are conflicting settings, the GPO with the highest precedence takes effect.

6. Explain the importance of Group Policy filtering and Group Policy modeling.

Answer: Group Policy filtering allows administrators to specify which users or computers a GPO should apply to, increasing granularity and flexibility. Group Policy modeling is a tool for simulating the effects of GPOs on specific users and computers, helping administrators predict the outcomes of their policies.

7. What are some common security policies you can enforce using Group Policy?

Answer: Common security policies include password policies, account lockout policies, user rights assignments, audit policies, software restriction policies, and Windows Firewall settings, among others.

8. What is the purpose of Group Policy Preferences, and how do they differ from Group Policy settings?

Answer: Group Policy Preferences extend the functionality of Group Policy by allowing administrators to configure settings that users can change. Unlike traditional Group Policy settings, preferences are not enforced and can be overridden by the user.

9. What are Loopback Processing modes in Group Policy, and when are they used?

Answer: Loopback Processing modes, "Replace" and "Merge," control how GPOs are applied when a user logs into a computer. "Replace" replaces user settings with computer settings, while "Merge" combines both user and computer settings. Loopback Processing is often used in scenarios like kiosk computers or terminal servers.

10. How do you troubleshoot Group Policy issues in Windows?

Answer: Troubleshooting Group Policy issues involves using tools like Group Policy Results (GPResult), Group Policy Modeling, Event Viewer, and the Resultant Set of Policy (RSoP) tool. You should also check for issues with DNS, network connectivity, and conflicting GPOs.

11. What is Group Policy in Windows, and how does it facilitate centralized management of systems and users?

Answer: Group Policy is a feature that allows administrators to define and enforce system and user settings across a network.

12. What are the key benefits of using Group Policy in a Windows environment?

Answer: Benefits include centralized management, security, compliance, consistency, and the ability to control user and computer configurations.

13. Explain the difference between Local Group Policy and Domain Group Policy.

Answer: Local Group Policy applies settings to a single computer, while Domain Group Policy applies settings to all computers and users in a domain.

14. What is an Active Directory Group Policy Object (GPO), and how is it used to manage system configurations?

Answer:A GPO is a collection of settings that can be applied to users and computers in an Active Directory domain to manage their configurations.

15. How can you create a new Group Policy Object (GPO) in Windows Server?

Answer: New GPOs can be created using the Group Policy Management Console (GPMC) or Active Directory Users and Computers on a Windows Server.

16. What is the "Group Policy Inheritance" process, and how does it determine which GPO settings apply to a user or computer?

Answer: Group Policy Inheritance is the process by which settings from multiple GPOs are applied, with the most specific GPO taking precedence.

17. What is the "Group Policy Enforcement" feature in Windows, and when should it be used?

Answer: Group Policy Enforcement enforces GPO settings, preventing overrides by child OUs. It should be used when specific settings need to be maintained.

18. How do you troubleshoot Group Policy issues in Windows, and what tools are available for diagnosis?

Answer: Tools like the Group Policy Results wizard and Group Policy Modeling wizard in GPMC help troubleshoot GPO application issues.

19. What is the "Loopback Processing" mode in Group Policy, and how does it affect user and computer settings?

Answer: Loopback Processing mode determines whether user or computer settings from GPOs linked to the computer or user are applied when users log on.

20. Explain the concept of "Security Filtering" in Group Policy, and how it controls which users or groups receive GPO settings.

Answer: Security Filtering restricts the scope of a GPO by specifying which users or groups can apply the policy, based on their permissions.

21. What is the "WMI Filtering" feature in Group Policy, and how does it enable condition-based GPO application?

Answer:WMI Filtering allows GPOs to be applied based on Windows Management Instrumentation (WMI) queries, making GPO application conditional.

22. How does Group Policy refresh work in Windows, and at what intervals does it occur?

Answer: Group Policy refresh occurs at user logon and computer startup and then every 90 minutes (by default), with an additional 30-minute random offset.

23. Explain the significance of "Group Policy Preferences" and how they enhance GPO settings management.

Answer: Group Policy Preferences provide a user-friendly interface for configuring settings, allowing more granular control and additional options.

24. What is "Group Policy Central Store," and how does it standardize GPO settings across different versions of Windows?

Answer: The Central Store is a folder in SYSVOL that contains GPO Administrative Template files, ensuring consistent GPO settings across various Windows versions.

25. What is the "Group Policy Editor" (gpedit.msc), and how does it allow local configuration of Group Policy settings on a Windows computer?

Answer: The Group Policy Editor is a local tool used to configure local Group Policy settings on a Windows computer.

26. How can you restrict software installation using Group Policy, and what is the purpose of Software Restriction Policies?

Answer: Software Restriction Policies in GPOs can be used to control which software is allowed to run, preventing unauthorized applications from executing.

27. Explain the "Folder Redirection" feature in Group Policy, and how it helps manage user data and profiles.

Answer: Folder Redirection redirects specific user folders (e.g., My Documents) to a network location, allowing centralized management and backup of user data.

28. What are Group Policy Administrative Template files (ADMX/ADML), and how do they define policy settings for Windows components?

Answer:ADMX files contain policy settings, while ADML files provide language-specific definitions, allowing administrators to configure GPO settings.

29. What are the Group Policy settings for controlling Windows Firewall, and how can you use them to enhance network security?

Answer: Group Policy settings can be used to configure Windows Firewall rules, allowing administrators to control network access and security settings.

30. How does Group Policy assist in securing user accounts through password policies, account lockout policies, and Kerberos settings?

Answer: Group Policy allows administrators to enforce password policies, account lockout policies, and fine-tune Kerberos settings to enhance account security.

31. Explain the role of "Security Options" in Group Policy, and how it enhances system security by configuring various security settings.

Answer: Security Options in GPOs allow administrators to configure system security settings, including password policies, user rights, and security settings.

32. What are "Auditing Policies" in Group Policy, and how do they help monitor and track security events on Windows systems?

Answer: Auditing policies in GPOs define which security events are audited, enabling the monitoring and tracking of security-related events in the system.

33. What is the "Registry Policy Processing" feature in Group Policy, and how does it allow for registry-based settings configuration?

Answer: Registry Policy Processing enables the deployment and management of registry settings through GPOs, helping to configure various aspects of Windows.

34. How can you enforce data encryption and security using Group Policy, including BitLocker settings and EFS (Encrypting File System)?

Answer: Group Policy settings can be used to enforce BitLocker encryption and configure EFS settings to protect sensitive data and files.

35. What is the "User Rights Assignment" in Group Policy, and how does it grant or deny specific rights to users or groups on a Windows computer?

Answer: User Rights Assignment allows administrators to assign specific privileges or rights to users or groups, controlling their actions on the computer.

36. Explain the "Software Installation" feature in Group Policy, and how it enables the automated deployment of software applications to users and computers.

Answer: Software Installation in GPOs automates the deployment of software to users and computers, making it easier to manage software distribution.

37. How can you use Group Policy to restrict removable storage devices and control USB access on Windows computers?

Answer: Group Policy settings can be configured to restrict access to USB devices and control removable storage device usage.

38. What is the role of "Group Policy Preferences" in managing local user and group accounts on Windows computers?

Answer: Group Policy Preferences can be used to create, update, and manage local user and group accounts on Windows computers.

39. Explain the concept of "Public Key Policies" in Group Policy, and how it enhances certificate management and security.

Answer: Public Key Policies in GPOs allow administrators to manage certificate settings and control certificate enrollment and autoenrollment.

40. How does Group Policy help manage printer deployment and configuration on Windows clients?

Answer: Group Policy can be used to deploy and configure printers for users or computers, simplifying printer management in a network environment.

41. What is the "AppLocker" feature in Group Policy, and how does it control application access and execution?

Answer: AppLocker allows administrators to define and enforce policies that control which applications can run on Windows computers, enhancing security.

42. How can Group Policy be used to configure Internet Explorer settings for users and computers in a Windows domain?

Answer: Group Policy settings can be used to configure and enforce Internet Explorer settings, including security, proxy, and compatibility options.

43. Explain the "Power Options" settings in Group Policy and how they enable power management on Windows systems.

Answer: Power Options settings in GPOs allow administrators to manage power settings, screen timeouts, and energy-saving features on Windows systems.

44. What are "Administrative Templates" in Group Policy, and how do they provide a structured way to configure Windows settings?

Answer: Administrative Templates provide a structured way to configure Windows settings through GPOs, ensuring consistent policy implementation.

45. How can you use Group Policy to configure and manage Windows Updates on client computers in a network environment?

Answer: Group Policy settings can be used to specify how Windows Updates are installed and configured on client computers, ensuring timely and controlled updates.

46. What is "IP Security Policies" in Group Policy, and how does it allow the configuration of IPsec settings for secure network communications?

Answer: IP Security Policies in GPOs enable the configuration of IPsec settings, enhancing security and encryption for network communications.

47. Explain the concept of "Password Policy" in Group Policy and how it enforces password complexity and security.

Answer: Password Policy settings in GPOs enforce password complexity rules, minimum length, and other security-related settings for user accounts.

48. How does Group Policy enhance security by configuring Windows Defender settings, including real-time protection and malware scanning?

Answer: Group Policy settings can be used to configure and manage Windows Defender settings, enhancing security against malware and threats.

49. What are "Auditing Policies" in Group Policy, and how do they help monitor and track security events on Windows systems?

Answer: Auditing policies in GPOs define which security events are audited, enabling the monitoring and tracking of security-related events in the system.

50. Explain the "Printers" feature in Group Policy and how it simplifies printer management and deployment in a network.

Answer: The Printers feature in GPOs allows administrators to deploy and manage printers on user and computer clients, simplifying printer configuration.

ONLINE RESOURCES

Practice Paper Link: https://forms.gle/evDk49WbEQdxo7aS9

QR Code:

Video Link: https://www.youtube.com/playlist?list=PLzlh_31VWEFp__HhXBpd_P0eqLZTuNNvO

QR Code:

Chapter 9 Windows Scripting and Automation

Scripting with PowerShell

1. What is PowerShell, and how does it differ from traditional command-line interfaces?

Answer: PowerShell is a scripting language and shell developed by Microsoft. Unlike traditional command-line interfaces, PowerShell is object-oriented and enables administrators to work with structured data, making it more versatile and powerful for automation and administration tasks.

2. Explain the difference between cmdlets and scripts in PowerShell.

Answer: Cmdlets (commandlets) are built-in, single-function commands in PowerShell, while scripts are collections of PowerShell commands and logic that can be written and saved as reusable scripts. Cmdlets are typically used for one-time commands, while scripts provide more extensive automation and customization.

3. What is the significance of the "$_" variable in PowerShell scripting?

Answer:"$_" represents the current pipeline object in a PowerShell script or cmdlet. It allows you to work with objects one at a time as they move through the pipeline, making it an essential variable for many PowerShell operations.

4. How do you create and use variables in PowerShell, and what is the scope of a variable?

Answer: You create variables using the "$" symbol, and variables in PowerShell can have various scopes, such as script, global, local, or private. The scope defines where the variable can be accessed and modified.

5. What is the pipeline in PowerShell, and why is it crucial for automation?

Answer: The pipeline in PowerShell allows you to pass the output of one command (cmdlet) as input to another command, enabling you to chain commands together to perform complex operations. It's crucial for automation because it simplifies data processing and manipulation.

6. Explain the purpose of PowerShell modules and how to create and use them.

Answer: PowerShell modules are self-contained units of functionality that can be easily reused. They can contain functions, variables, and cmdlets. You can create and use modules to package and share PowerShell scripts and cmdlets across different systems.

7. What is the significance of execution policies in PowerShell, and how do they impact script execution?

Answer: Execution policies in PowerShell determine the level of security applied to script execution. They can be set to control which scripts are allowed to run on a system. Execution policies include "Restricted," "AllSigned," "RemoteSigned," and "Unrestricted."

8. What are some common methods for error handling and reporting in PowerShell scripts?

Answer: Common error handling techniques in PowerShell include using "Try...Catch" blocks, "Throw" statements to generate custom errors, and cmdlets like "Write-Host," "Write-Error," and "Write-Output" to provide feedback and error messages.

9. How do you schedule and automate PowerShell scripts to run at specified intervals in a Windows environment?

Answer: PowerShell scripts can be scheduled and automated using the Windows Task Scheduler or through scripts that run on a regular basis using scheduled tasks. You can also use PowerShell's "Scheduled Tasks" module for this purpose.

10. Explain the concept of remoting in PowerShell, and how does it facilitate managing remote systems?

Answer: Remoting in PowerShell allows you to run commands on remote computers. PowerShell remoting leverages protocols like WS-Management and WinRM to establish secure, authenticated connections to remote machines, making it a powerful tool for remote system administration.

11. What is Group Policy in Windows, and how does it facilitate centralized management of systems and users?

Answer: Group Policy is a feature that allows administrators to define and enforce system and user settings across a network.

12. What are the key benefits of using Group Policy in a Windows environment?

Answer: Benefits include centralized management, security, compliance, consistency, and the ability to control user and computer configurations.

13. Explain the difference between Local Group Policy and Domain Group Policy.

Answer: Local Group Policy applies settings to a single computer, while Domain Group Policy applies settings to all computers and users in a domain.

14. What is an Active Directory Group Policy Object (GPO), and how is it used to manage system configurations?

Answer:A GPO is a collection of settings that can be applied to users and computers in an Active Directory domain to manage their configurations.

15. How can you create a new Group Policy Object (GPO) in Windows Server?

Answer: New GPOs can be created using the Group Policy Management Console (GPMC) or Active Directory Users and Computers on a Windows Server.

16. What is the "Group Policy Inheritance" process, and how does it determine which GPO settings apply to a user or computer?

Answer: Group Policy Inheritance is the process by which settings from multiple GPOs are applied, with the most specific GPO taking precedence.

17. What is the "Group Policy Enforcement" feature in Windows, and when should it be used?

Answer: Group Policy Enforcement enforces GPO settings, preventing overrides by child OUs. It should be used when specific settings need to be maintained.

18. How do you troubleshoot Group Policy issues in Windows, and what tools are available for diagnosis?

Answer: Tools like the Group Policy Results wizard and Group Policy Modeling wizard in GPMC help troubleshoot GPO application issues.

19. What is the "Loopback Processing" mode in Group Policy, and how does it affect user and computer settings?

Answer: Loopback Processing mode determines whether user or computer settings from GPOs linked to the computer or user are applied when users log on.

20. Explain the concept of "Security Filtering" in Group Policy, and how it controls which users or groups receive GPO settings.

Answer: Security Filtering restricts the scope of a GPO by specifying which users or groups can apply the policy, based on their permissions.

21. What is the "WMI Filtering" feature in Group Policy, and how does it enable condition-based GPO application?

Answer:WMI Filtering allows GPOs to be applied based on Windows Management Instrumentation (WMI) queries, making GPO application conditional.

22. How does Group Policy refresh work in Windows, and at what intervals does it occur?

Answer: Group Policy refresh occurs at user logon and computer startup and then every 90 minutes (by default), with an additional 30-minute random offset.

23. Explain the significance of "Group Policy Preferences" and how they enhance GPO settings management.

Answer: Group Policy Preferences provide a user-friendly interface for configuring settings, allowing more granular control and additional options.

24. What is "Group Policy Central Store," and how does it standardize GPO settings across different versions of Windows?

Answer: The Central Store is a folder in SYSVOL that contains GPO Administrative Template files, ensuring consistent GPO settings across various Windows versions.

25. What is the "Group Policy Editor" (gpedit.msc), and how does it allow local configuration of Group Policy settings on a Windows computer?

Answer: The Group Policy Editor is a local tool used to configure local Group Policy settings on a Windows computer.

26. How can you restrict software installation using Group Policy, and what is the purpose of Software Restriction Policies?

Answer: Software Restriction Policies in GPOs can be used to control which software is allowed to run, preventing unauthorized applications from executing.

27. Explain the "Folder Redirection" feature in Group Policy, and how it helps manage user data and profiles.

Answer: Folder Redirection redirects specific user folders (e.g., My Documents) to a network location, allowing centralized management and backup of user data.

28. What are Group Policy Administrative Template files (ADMX/ADML), and how do they define policy settings for Windows components?

Answer:ADMX files contain policy settings, while ADML files provide language-specific definitions, allowing administrators to configure GPO settings.

29. What are the Group Policy settings for controlling Windows Firewall, and how can you use them to enhance network security?

Answer: Group Policy settings can be used to configure Windows Firewall rules, allowing administrators to control network access and security settings.

30. How does Group Policy assist in securing user accounts through password policies, account lockout policies, and Kerberos settings?

Answer: Group Policy allows administrators to enforce password policies, account lockout policies, and fine-tune Kerberos settings to enhance account security.

31. Explain the role of "Security Options" in Group Policy, and how it enhances system security by configuring various security settings.

Answer: Security Options in GPOs allow administrators to configure system security settings, including password policies, user rights, and security settings.

32. What are "Auditing Policies" in Group Policy, and how do they help monitor and track security events on Windows systems?

Answer: Auditing policies in GPOs define which security events are audited, enabling the monitoring and tracking of security-related events in the system.

33. What is the "Registry Policy Processing" feature in Group Policy, and how does it allow for registry-based settings configuration?

Answer: Registry Policy Processing enables the deployment and management of registry settings through GPOs, helping to configure various aspects of Windows.

34. How can you enforce data encryption and security using Group Policy, including BitLocker settings and EFS (Encrypting File System)?

Answer: Group Policy settings can be used to enforce BitLocker encryption and configure EFS settings to protect sensitive data and files.

35. What is the "User Rights Assignment" in Group Policy, and how does it grant or deny specific rights to users or groups on a Windows computer?

Answer: User Rights Assignment allows administrators to assign specific privileges or rights to users or groups, controlling their actions on the computer.

36. Explain the "Software Installation" feature in Group Policy, and how it enables the automated deployment of software applications to users and computers.

Answer: Software Installation in GPOs automates the deployment of software to users and computers, making it easier to manage software distribution.

37. How can you use Group Policy to restrict removable storage devices and control USB access on Windows computers?

Answer: Group Policy settings can be configured to restrict access to USB devices and control removable storage device usage.

38. What is the role of "Group Policy Preferences" in managing local user and group accounts on Windows computers?

Answer: Group Policy Preferences can be used to create, update, and manage local user and group accounts on Windows computers.

39. Explain the concept of "Public Key Policies" in Group Policy, and how it enhances certificate management and security.

Answer: Public Key Policies in GPOs allow administrators to manage certificate settings and control certificate enrollment and autoenrollment.

40. How does Group Policy help manage printer deployment and configuration on Windows clients?

Answer: Group Policy can be used to deploy and configure printers for users or computers, simplifying printer management in a network environment.

41. What is the "AppLocker" feature in Group Policy, and how does it control application access and execution?

Answer: AppLocker allows administrators to define and enforce policies that control which applications can run on Windows computers, enhancing security.

42. How can Group Policy be used to configure Internet Explorer settings for users and computers in a Windows domain?

Answer: Group Policy settings can be used to configure and enforce Internet Explorer settings, including security, proxy, and compatibility options.

43. Explain the "Power Options" settings in Group Policy and how they enable power management on Windows systems.

Answer: Power Options settings in GPOs allow administrators to manage power settings, screen timeouts, and energy-saving features on Windows systems.

44. What are "Administrative Templates" in Group Policy, and how do they provide a structured way to configure Windows settings?

Answer: Administrative Templates provide a structured way to configure Windows settings through GPOs, ensuring consistent policy implementation.

45. How can you use Group Policy to configure and manage Windows Updates on client computers in a network environment?

Answer: Group Policy settings can be used to specify how Windows Updates are installed and configured on client computers, ensuring timely and controlled updates.

46. What is "IP Security Policies" in Group Policy, and how does it allow the configuration of IPsec settings for secure network communications?

Answer:IP Security Policies in GPOs enable the configuration of IPsec settings, enhancing security and encryption for network communications.

47. Explain the concept of "Password Policy" in Group Policy and how it enforces password complexity and security.

Answer: Password Policy settings in GPOs enforce password complexity rules, minimum length, and other security-related settings for user accounts.

48. How does Group Policy enhance security by configuring Windows Defender settings, including real-time protection and malware scanning?

Answer: Group Policy settings can be used to configure and manage Windows Defender settings, enhancing security against malware and threats.

49. What are "Auditing Policies" in Group Policy, and how do they help monitor and track security events on Windows systems?

Answer: Auditing policies in GPOs define which security events are audited, enabling the monitoring and tracking of security-related events in the system.

50. Explain the "Printers" feature in Group Policy and how it simplifies printer management and deployment in a network.

Answer: The Printers feature in GPOs allows administrators to deploy and manage printers on user and computer clients, simplifying printer configuration.

Batch Scripting in Windows

1. What is a batch script, and how does it differ from other scripting languages?

Answer: A batch script is a text-based script in Windows that contains a series of commands executed by the Windows Command Prompt. Batch scripts are primarily used for automating repetitive tasks in a Windows environment. They differ from other scripting languages, such as PowerShell, in terms of syntax and capabilities.

2. What is the file extension for batch scripts in Windows, and why is it important?

Answer: Batch scripts in Windows typically have the ".bat" or ".cmd" file extension. This extension is essential because it tells the operating system that the file contains a batch script and should be executed accordingly.

3. Explain the difference between "echo" and "rem" in batch scripting.

Answer: "Echo" is a command used to display messages or variables on the screen, while "rem" is short for "remark" and is used for adding comments in a batch script. Comments are not displayed, and they are only for human readability.

4. How do you set environment variables in a batch script, and why are they useful?

Answer: Environment variables are set using the "set" command in a batch script. They are useful for storing and retrieving values that can be used throughout the script or by other processes and scripts. Environment variables are also used to customize the behaviour of the script.

5. What is conditional branching in batch scripting, and how is it achieved?

Answer: Conditional branching allows a batch script to make decisions based on the success or failure of previous commands. It is achieved using statements like "if," "else," and "goto," enabling the script to take different paths depending on certain conditions.

6. Explain the use of "for" loops in batch scripting.

Answer: "For" loops in batch scripting are used for iterating through lists of items or files. There are different types of "for" loops, such as "for /f" for processing text, "for /l" for numeric ranges, and "for %%var in (list)" for iterating through a specified list of items.

7. What is the purpose of the "call" command in batch scripts, and when should it be used?

Answer: The "call" command is used to run another batch script from within the current script. It's typically used to invoke a separate script or subroutine and return to the original script after execution.

8. How can you accept user input in a batch script, and what are some common validation techniques for user input?

Answer: User input can be accepted using the "set /p" command. Common validation techniques include checking for empty input, ensuring the input matches expected patterns, and performing range checks on numeric input.

9. What is the purpose of error handling in batch scripts, and how can it be achieved?

Answer: Error handling in batch scripts involves gracefully handling errors and unexpected conditions. It can be achieved using "if errorlevel," "goto," or by redirecting error messages to log files or the console.

10. How can you make batch scripts more modular and reusable?

Answer: Batch scripts can be made more modular and reusable by creating functions or subroutines using the "call" command. This allows you to encapsulate specific tasks in separate sections of the script, making it easier to maintain and reuse code.

11. What is a batch script in Windows, and how does it differ from other scripting languages?

Answer:A batch script is a text file that contains a sequence of Windows commands. It is executed by the Windows Command Prompt (cmd.exe) and is useful for automating tasks. Batch scripts differ from other scripting languages like PowerShell or Python in terms of syntax and capabilities.

12. What is the file extension typically used for batch scripts in Windows?

Answer: Batch scripts in Windows typically use the ".bat" or ".cmd" file extension.

13. How can you create a new batch script in Windows?

Answer: You can create a new batch script using a text editor like Notepad and then saving it with the ".bat" or ".cmd" file extension.

14. Explain the difference between a batch file and a batch script.

Answer:A batch file is the physical file that contains the batch script, while a batch script is the actual content or sequence of commands within the file.

15. What is the purpose of the "echo" command in a batch script, and how is it used?

Answer: The "echo" command is used to display text or messages on the screen. It's often used for providing output and feedback in batch scripts.

16. How can you add comments in a batch script to make it more readable and understandable?

Answer: Comments in batch scripts are added using the "rem" command followed by a space and the comment text. For example: **rem This is a comment**.

17. What is a batch script label, and how is it defined and used?

Answer:A label in a batch script is a marker that defines a specific point in the script. Labels are defined using a colon (e.g., **:labelname**) and are used with the "goto" command to direct the script's flow to that label.

18. Explain the purpose of the "set" command in a batch script and how it's used to define variables.

Answer: The "set" command is used to define and manipulate variables in a batch script. Variables store values that can be used throughout the script.

19. How can you use command-line arguments in a batch script to make it more flexible and dynamic?

Answer: Command-line arguments in batch scripts are represented by **%1**, **%2**, **%3**, and so on. They allow you to pass values to the script when it's executed.

20. What is conditional execution in batch scripting, and how are "if" statements used for decision-making?

Answer: Conditional execution in batch scripting involves using "if" statements to make decisions based on conditions. For example, you can use "if" to check if a file exists before performing an action.

21. Explain the purpose of the "for" loop in a batch script and how it's used to iterate through a list of items.

Answer: The "for" loop is used to iterate through a list of items, such as files, directories, or text. It allows you to perform actions on each item in the list.

22. How can you create and manage files and directories using batch scripts?

Answer: Batch scripts can create, delete, copy, move, and manage files and directories using commands like "mkdir," "rmdir," "copy," "move," and others.

23. What is input validation in batch scripting, and why is it important in writing reliable scripts?

Answer: Input validation is the process of verifying that user inputs are valid and within expected ranges. It's essential to prevent errors and ensure script reliability.

24. Explain the use of the "call" command in batch scripts and how it's used to invoke another batch script.

Answer: The "call" command is used to run another batch script from within the current script. It allows for modularity and reusability of code.

25. How can you pause the execution of a batch script to allow the user to review output or provide input?

Answer: You can use the "pause" command to pause the script's execution, displaying a "Press any key to continue..." message.

26. What is the purpose of error handling in batch scripting, and how can you handle errors gracefully?

Answer: Error handling in batch scripting involves checking for errors and taking appropriate actions when they occur. You can use "if" statements and "goto" labels to handle errors gracefully.

27. Explain the use of the "choice" command in batch scripts and how it allows users to make selections.

Answer: The "choice" command is used to create a menu in batch scripts, enabling users to make selections by pressing a corresponding key.

28. What is the purpose of the "shift" command in batch scripts, and how does it allow you to process multiple command-line arguments?

Answer: The "shift" command is used to shift the values of command-line arguments, allowing the script to process multiple arguments sequentially.

29. How can you redirect and capture the output of commands in a batch script, and why is it useful?

Answer: You can use redirection symbols like > and >> to redirect and capture the output of commands to files, making it useful for logging and analyzing script results.

30. Explain the use of environment variables in batch scripting, and how they provide system and user information.

Answer: Environment variables store system and user information that can be accessed and used within batch scripts. Common examples include **%USERNAME%** and **%COMPUTERNAME%**.

31. What is the purpose of the "choice" command in batch scripts, and how does it allow users to make selections?

Answer: The "choice" command allows batch scripts to present a menu to the user, where the user selects an option by pressing a corresponding key.

32. How do you create and use functions in batch scripts to modularize and reuse code?

Answer: Functions in batch scripts are defined using the **:label** syntax, and they allow you to create reusable blocks of code that can be called using the **call** command.

33. Explain how to use the "find" and "findstr" commands to search for text in files in a batch script.

Answer: The "find" and "findstr" commands are used to search for specific text within files. "find" is simpler, while "findstr" provides more advanced searching capabilities.

34. What are exit codes in batch scripts, and how can they be used to indicate the success or failure of a script or command?

Answer: Exit codes are numeric values that indicate the success or failure of a script or command. They are commonly checked using the **%errorlevel%** variable.

35. Explain how to create and use labels in batch scripts, and how they help with organizing and navigating the script.

Answer: Labels are created using the **:label** syntax and serve as markers for specific sections of a script. They are used with the **goto** command to navigate the script.

36. How can you use the "timeout" command in batch scripts to introduce delays or pauses in the script's execution?

Answer: The "timeout" command is used to introduce a time delay in the script's execution, providing a simple way to pause the script for a specified duration.

37. What is the "setlocal" and "endlocal" command pair in batch scripts, and how do they affect variable scope and environment?

Answer: The "setlocal" command is used to create a new environment in which variables are local. The "endlocal" command restores the previous environment, affecting variable scope.

38. Explain the use of the "xcopy" command in batch scripts and how it enables the copying of files and directories.

Answer: The "xcopy" command is used to copy files and directories, providing advanced options for copying, including subdirectories and file attributes.

39. What is the "choice" command in batch scripts, and how does it allow users to make selections?

Answer: The "choice" command enables the creation of menu-like selections within batch scripts, allowing users to choose options by pressing corresponding keys.

40. How can you use batch scripts to automate common system maintenance tasks, such as disk cleanup and backups?

Answer: Batch scripts can be used to automate tasks like disk cleanup, backups, and system maintenance by executing built-in Windows commands.

41. Explain the "goto" command in batch scripts and how it's used to direct the script's flow to specific labels.

Answer: The "goto" command is used to jump to a labeled section of a batch script, allowing for conditional branching and directing the flow of the script.

42. What is the "call" command in batch scripts, and how does it allow you to invoke other batch scripts or functions?

Answer: The "call" command is used to invoke other batch scripts or functions from within the current script, providing modularity and code reusability.

43. Explain the use of the "cls" command in batch scripts and how it clears the Command Prompt screen.

Answer: The "cls" command is used to clear the Command Prompt screen, making the output more readable and organized.

44. How can you use conditional statements like "if" and "else" in batch scripts to make decisions based on specific conditions?

Answer: Conditional statements like "if" and "else" are used to evaluate conditions and execute different commands based on the result.

45. What is the "goto :eof" command in batch scripts, and how does it indicate the end of a batch file or function?

Answer: The "goto :eof" command is used to mark the end of a batch file or function, allowing for clean termination of the script.

46. Explain the "choice" command in batch scripts and how it's used to create simple text menus for user interaction.

Answer: The "choice" command allows the creation of text menus that prompt the user to make a selection by pressing a corresponding key.

47. How do you set and manage environment variables in batch scripts, and why are they important for script flexibility?

Answer: Environment variables are set and managed using the "set" command. They provide a way to store and access dynamic values that enhance script flexibility.

48. What is the "del" command in batch scripts, and how does it allow you to delete files and directories?

Answer: The "del" command is used to delete files, while the "rmdir" command is used to delete directories in batch scripts.

49. Explain the use of the "start" command in batch scripts and how it can launch applications and processes.

Answer: The "start" command is used to launch external applications or processes from within a batch script, providing automation for various tasks.

50. How can you use the "for" loop in batch scripts to iterate through files, folders, or text lines, and what are common use cases for this loop?

Answer: The "for" loop in batch scripts allows you to iterate through files, folders, or text lines. Common use cases include batch renaming, processing files, and text manipulation.

Task Automation and Scheduled Tasks

1. What is task automation, and why is it important in IT operations?

Answer: Task automation involves using scripts, tools, or software to perform repetitive and manual tasks automatically. It is crucial in IT operations for improving efficiency, reducing human error, and ensuring consistency in various processes.

2. What are the benefits of using scheduled tasks in an operating system or server environment?

Answer: Scheduled tasks allow for the automated execution of scripts or programs at predefined times or based on specific triggers. Benefits include time savings, improved reliability, reduced human intervention, and better resource utilization.

3. How can you create a scheduled task in Windows, and what are the key parameters to configure when setting up a task?

Answer: In Windows, you can create a scheduled task using the Task Scheduler. Key parameters to configure include the program or script to run, when and how often the task should run, security settings, and any specific triggers or conditions.

4. What is the difference between "at" and "cron" scheduling in Windows and Unix/Linux systems?

Answer: "At" scheduling in Windows and "cron" scheduling in Unix/Linux are both used for task automation but differ in their syntax and capabilities. "At" is used for one-time tasks at specific times, while "cron" is more versatile, allowing for more complex and recurring schedules.

5. Explain the concept of "cron expressions" and how they are used in scheduled tasks.

Answer: "Cron expressions" are strings used in Unix/Linux systems to define schedules in a compact format. They consist of fields representing minutes, hours, days, months, and days of the week. By customizing these fields, you can create a wide range of scheduling options.

6. What are some common tasks that are suitable for automation with scheduled tasks, and how can they benefit an organization?

Answer: Common automated tasks include backups, system maintenance, log rotation, report generation, data synchronization, and security patching. Automation saves time, reduces errors, and ensures tasks are consistently executed.

7. What are some best practices for managing and monitoring scheduled tasks in a production environment?

Answer: Best practices include documenting tasks and schedules, setting up notifications for task status, ensuring that tasks run with the appropriate permissions, and regularly reviewing and optimizing scheduled tasks.

8. Explain the concept of "idempotent" tasks in task automation.

Answer: An idempotent task is one that can be safely executed multiple times without causing unintended side effects. In task automation, it's crucial to ensure that tasks are idempotent to prevent problems when tasks run more than once.

9. What are some tools and frameworks commonly used for advanced task automation and scheduling in an enterprise environment?

Answer: Common tools and frameworks include Microsoft System Center Orchestrator, Ansible, Puppet, Jenkins, and Apache Airflow. These platforms provide advanced automation and scheduling capabilities for complex enterprise tasks.

10. How can you secure and protect scheduled tasks from unauthorized access or tampering?

Answer: Scheduled tasks should be configured to run with the least privilege necessary, and access to task definitions should be restricted. Additionally, security measures like strong authentication and encryption should be used to protect task data and communication.

11. What is task automation, and why is it important in the context of system administration and daily tasks?

Answer: Task automation involves using scripts or tools to perform routine or repetitive tasks automatically. It's important for efficiency, consistency, and reducing human error.

12. Explain the purpose of the Windows Task Scheduler, and how does it help automate tasks?

Answer: The Windows Task Scheduler is a tool that allows users to schedule the execution of tasks or scripts at specific times or under certain conditions.

13. How can you open the Windows Task Scheduler, and what are the key components of its user interface?

Answer: You can open the Task Scheduler from the Control Panel or by running "taskschd.msc." Its key components include the Task Library, Task Scheduler Library, and the right-hand pane for task details.

14. What is a "task" in the context of the Windows Task Scheduler, and what types of actions can tasks perform?

Answer: A task is a unit of work scheduled by the Task Scheduler. Tasks can perform actions such as running programs, scripts, sending email, and displaying messages.

15. Explain the difference between a "basic task" and a "task created with the Create Task wizard" in the Task Scheduler.

Answer: A basic task is created using a simplified wizard for common tasks, while a task created with the Create Task wizard provides more advanced configuration options.

16. What are triggers in the Task Scheduler, and how do they determine when a task will run?

Answer: Triggers are conditions or events that initiate the execution of a task. They can be time-based (e.g., daily) or event-based (e.g., system startup).

17. How can you create a new scheduled task in the Task Scheduler, and what are the steps involved in the process?

Answer: You can create a new task by opening the Task Scheduler, selecting "Create Basic Task" or "Create Task," and following the wizard, which includes setting triggers, actions, and conditions.

18. Explain the concept of task conditions in the Task Scheduler and how they can control when a task is executed.

Answer: Task conditions specify additional requirements for task execution, such as only running when the computer is idle or when a specific network connection is available.

19. What is the Task Scheduler's "Actions" tab used for, and how can you specify what a task will do when it runs?

Answer: The "Actions" tab is used to define the specific actions a task will perform when executed. It can run a program, send an email, display a message, and more.

20. What are "settings" in the Task Scheduler, and how do they configure behaviour such as priority and error handling for tasks?

Answer: Settings in the Task Scheduler allow you to specify task behaviour, including priority, how to handle missed tasks, and what to do in case of task conflicts.

21. Explain the concept of "security options" in the Task Scheduler, and how they control who can create, modify, and run tasks.

Answer: Security options in the Task Scheduler determine the permissions and access levels for creating, modifying, and running tasks. They involve configuring users and groups with specific rights.

22. How can you manually run a scheduled task without waiting for its trigger event in the Task Scheduler?

Answer: You can manually run a scheduled task by selecting the task, right-clicking, and choosing "Run" from the context menu.

23. What is the "History" tab in the Task Scheduler, and why is it useful for tracking task execution and results?

Answer: The "History" tab records the execution history of tasks, including start times, results, and error codes. It's valuable for troubleshooting and auditing.

24. Explain the purpose of "exporting" and "importing" tasks in the Task Scheduler and how it allows for task transfer and backup.

Answer: Exporting tasks creates XML files that store task configurations, making it possible to import tasks on the same or different systems for transfer or backup.

25. How can you delete a scheduled task from the Task Scheduler, and what considerations should be made before deletion?

Answer: You can delete a task by selecting it and clicking "Delete" or by right-clicking and choosing "Delete" from the context menu. Consider backup and any dependencies before deletion.

26. What is the Task Scheduler "Library," and how does it organize and manage scheduled tasks?

Answer: The Task Scheduler Library is a folder structure where tasks are organized. It provides a structured view of tasks and allows for easy management.

27. Explain the use of the Task Scheduler command-line tool "schtasks" and how it allows for task management from the command prompt.

Answer:"schtasks" is a command-line tool that allows for creating, modifying, deleting, and querying scheduled tasks, offering automation and scripting capabilities.

28. How can you troubleshoot a task that failed to run in the Task Scheduler, and what tools are available for diagnostics?

Answer: You can use the "History" tab to view task execution details and error codes. Event Viewer and command-line tools like "schtasks" provide additional diagnostic capabilities.

29. What is the "Task Scheduler service" in Windows, and how does it facilitate the execution of scheduled tasks?

Answer: The Task Scheduler service is a system service that manages the execution of scheduled tasks, ensuring they run at the specified times or triggers.

30. Explain the role of "batch files" and "PowerShell scripts" in the automation of tasks through the Task Scheduler.

Answer: Batch files and PowerShell scripts are common choices for executing tasks via the Task Scheduler, as they can contain sequences of commands and actions.

31. How do you schedule a task to run with elevated privileges or as an administrator in the Task Scheduler?

Answer: You can set a task to run with elevated privileges by configuring it to run with the highest privileges in the "General" tab of the task properties.

32. What is the difference between "Allow task to be run on demand" and "Run task as soon as possible after a scheduled start is missed" in task properties?

Answer:"Allow task to be run on demand" allows manual execution, while "Run task as soon as possible after a scheduled start is missed" runs the task if a trigger is missed.

33. Explain how you can schedule a task to repeat at specific intervals or on specific days of the week or month.

Answer: You can use triggers like "Daily," "Weekly," or "Monthly" to set specific intervals or days for task repetition.

34. What is the "Idle Trigger" in the Task Scheduler, and how does it allow tasks to run when the computer is idle?

Answer: The "Idle Trigger" allows tasks to run when the computer is not in use, as determined by the system's idle state.

35. How can you set up email notifications for task execution in the Task Scheduler, and what settings are required for email notifications?

Answer: You can configure email notifications by specifying the SMTP server, sender and recipient email addresses, and authentication credentials in the task's "Actions" tab.

36. Explain the concept of "dependent tasks" in the Task Scheduler and how they allow for task execution based on the success or failure of other tasks.

Answer: Dependent tasks are tasks that rely on the outcome of another task. They can be set to execute only if the preceding task succeeds or fails.

37. What is the difference between "Start a program" and "Send an email" actions in the Task Scheduler's "Actions" tab?

Answer:"Start a program" executes a program or script, while "Send an email" sends an email notification when the task is triggered.

38. Explain the use of "Task Scheduler triggers" and how they determine when a task will be executed.

Answer: Task Scheduler triggers specify the conditions or events that initiate task execution, such as time-based triggers (e.g., daily) or event-based triggers (e.g., system startup).

39. How can you create a task that runs with specific network conditions or only when a particular network connection is available?

Answer: Network conditions can be set in the "Conditions" tab of the task properties, allowing tasks to run based on network availability.

40. What is the "Configure for" option in the Task Scheduler, and how does it affect task compatibility with different versions of Windows?

Answer: The "Configure for" option allows you to specify the Windows version for which the task is configured. It affects task compatibility when running on different Windows versions.

41. Explain how you can set a task to run only when a user is logged on or whether the user needs to be logged on at all.

Answer: The "Security Options" in the "General" tab allow you to specify whether the task runs only when a user is logged on or regardless of user login.

42. What is the "If the task is already running, then the following rule applies" option in the Task Scheduler, and how does it affect task execution?

Answer: This option allows you to specify how the Task Scheduler handles tasks that are already running when a new trigger occurs, including options to terminate or queue the task.

43. Explain the concept of "dynamic variables" in task actions and how they allow you to pass dynamic data to a task.

Answer: Dynamic variables, such as **%username%** and **%date%**, allow you to pass dynamic data to tasks for use in command-line arguments, filenames, and other settings.

44. What is the "Task Scheduler Library" in the Task Scheduler, and how does it help organize and manage scheduled tasks?

Answer: The Task Scheduler Library is a folder structure that organizes tasks into categories, making it easier to manage and locate tasks.

45. How can you prevent a scheduled task from running if the computer is on battery power, and what settings are required for this condition?

Answer: You can configure a task to run only when the computer is on AC power in the "Conditions" tab of the task properties.

46. Explain the use of "hidden" tasks in the Task Scheduler and why they may be configured as hidden.

Answer: Hidden tasks are not displayed in the Task Scheduler interface but can still run. They are often used for system maintenance and background tasks.

47. What is the "Idle Trigger" in the Task Scheduler, and how can it be used to run tasks when the computer is idle?

Answer: The "Idle Trigger" allows tasks to run when the computer is not in use, based on idle conditions defined by the system.

48. How can you schedule a task to wake up the computer from a sleep or hibernate state for execution?

Answer: In the "Conditions" tab of the task properties, you can check the option to "Wake the computer to run this task" to wake the computer for the task.

49. Explain how to configure a task to run with specific user credentials, such as an administrator or a different user account.

Answer: You can specify the user account and password for the task in the "General" tab under "Security Options."

50. What is the "On an event" trigger in the Task Scheduler, and how does it allow tasks to be triggered by specific system events?

Answer: The "On an event" trigger lets you configure tasks to run based on specific event log entries, allowing for event-driven automation.

ONLINE RESOURCES

Practice Paper Link: https://forms.gle/Tvp9tLKYVdgXSnfH7

QR Code:

Video Link: https://www.youtube.com/playlist?list=PLzlh_31VWEForjsPxTjus0FF9Q-7rN9LG

QR Code:

Chapter 10 Advanced Windows Topics

Windows Performance Monitoring

1. What is Windows Performance Monitoring, and why is it important for system administrators?

Answer: Windows Performance Monitoring is the process of observing, measuring, and analyzing system performance metrics and resource utilization on Windows systems. It is crucial for identifying performance issues, troubleshooting problems, and optimizing system performance.

2. What are some key performance metrics that Windows Performance Monitor can track?

Answer: Windows Performance Monitor can track metrics such as CPU utilization, memory usage, disk I/O, network bandwidth, process performance, and system counters like uptime, available storage, and page file usage.

3. Explain the difference between real-time monitoring and data logging in Windows Performance Monitoring.

Answer: Real-time monitoring provides immediate feedback on system performance, while data logging involves capturing performance metrics over time, allowing for historical analysis and trend identification.

4. What are "Performance Counters" in Windows, and how are they organized?

Answer: Performance Counters are specific metrics or statistics that Windows monitors to assess system performance. They are organized into categories, with each category containing related counters. For example, the "Processor" category includes counters like "% Processor Time" and "Processor Queue Length."

5. How can you configure alerts and notifications in Windows Performance Monitor to detect performance issues?

Answer: You can configure alerts and notifications by setting up Data Collector Sets in Windows Performance Monitor. When specific performance thresholds are exceeded, the system can trigger actions such as sending email notifications or writing events to the Windows Event Log.

6. Explain the purpose of the Windows Task Manager in performance monitoring, and what information does it provide?

Answer: The Windows Task Manager provides a real-time view of system performance and resource usage. It displays information on running processes, system performance graphs, and resource utilization (CPU, memory, disk, and network) for monitoring and troubleshooting purposes.

7. What is the "Performance Monitor" tool, and how can it be used to collect and analyze performance data?

Answer: Performance Monitor, also known as "PerfMon," is a built-in Windows tool that allows administrators to collect, view, and analyse performance data using performance counters. It can generate real-time graphs and log data for later analysis.

8. How does Windows Performance Monitoring help in capacity planning and resource allocation for an organization's IT infrastructure?

Answer: Windows Performance Monitoring provides historical data on resource utilization, helping organizations make informed decisions about resource allocation and capacity planning. By analyzing trends, administrators can predict when additional resources may be needed.

9. Explain the concept of "baseline performance" and why it is essential for performance monitoring.

Answer: A baseline performance is a set of performance metrics captured during normal operation. It serves as a reference point to identify deviations and abnormalities in system performance. It is crucial for detecting issues and optimizing system performance.

10. What are some third-party tools and software commonly used for advanced performance monitoring in Windows environments?

Answer: Common third-party tools include SolarWinds Orion, PRTG Network Monitor, Nagios, and Microsoft's System Center Operations Manager (SCOM). These tools offer advanced features and integration for comprehensive performance monitoring.

11. What is Windows Performance Monitoring, and why is it important for system administrators and IT professionals?

Answer: Windows Performance Monitoring involves tracking and analyzing system performance to ensure optimal operation, troubleshoot issues, and plan for system improvements.

12. What is the primary tool for Windows Performance Monitoring, and how can it be accessed in Windows?

Answer: The primary tool for Windows Performance Monitoring is the "Performance Monitor" (PerfMon), which can be accessed by running "perfmon.msc" or through the "Performance Monitor" application.

13. What is a performance counter in Windows, and how does it help in monitoring system performance?

Answer:A performance counter is a specific metric or measurement that reflects system performance, such as CPU usage, memory usage, disk activity, and network traffic.

14. How can you create a new data collector set in Performance Monitor, and what is its purpose?

Answer: You can create a new data collector set to collect and store performance data over time. It's used for performance analysis and troubleshooting.

15. What are "Performance Logs and Alerts" in Windows Performance Monitoring, and how do they help in collecting and storing performance data?

Answer: Performance Logs and Alerts are configurations for collecting and storing performance data. They define which counters to collect, sampling intervals, and log locations.

16. Explain the concept of "Performance Counters" and how they are categorized in Windows Performance Monitoring.

Answer: Performance Counters are measurements that monitor various aspects of system performance. They are categorized into groups like Processor, Memory, Disk, and Network.

17. What is the "System Monitor" in Performance Monitor, and how can it display real-time performance data?

Answer: The System Monitor displays real-time performance data by adding performance counters to the display. It provides a graphical view of system performance.

18. How can you use "Data Collector Sets" to schedule data collection and generate reports in Windows Performance Monitoring?

Answer: Data Collector Sets allow you to schedule data collection, set up alerts, and generate reports on system performance over specific time intervals.

19. Explain the concept of "Baseline Performance" and why it's important in Windows Performance Monitoring.

Answer: Baseline performance is a reference point that represents normal system operation. It's crucial for detecting deviations and identifying performance issues.

20. What are "Alerts" in Windows Performance Monitoring, and how can they be configured to notify administrators of performance issues?

Answer: Alerts are notifications triggered when performance counters reach specified thresholds. Administrators can configure them to receive notifications via email or other methods.

21. How can you identify performance bottlenecks using Windows Performance Monitoring, and what performance counters are commonly used for this purpose?

Answer: Performance bottlenecks can be identified by analyzing performance counters such as CPU utilization, memory usage, disk queue length, and network traffic.

22. Explain the use of "Data Collectors" in Windows Performance Monitoring and how they collect performance data for analysis.

Answer: Data Collectors are responsible for collecting specific performance data using performance counters and storing it for analysis in log files.

23. What is the "Resource Monitor" in Windows, and how does it provide real-time information on CPU, memory, disk, and network usage?

Answer: The Resource Monitor is a system tool that provides real-time information on CPU, memory, disk, and network usage, helping users identify resource-intensive processes.

24. How can you use Windows Performance Monitoring to monitor the performance of a specific application or service on your system?

Answer: You can set up custom Data Collector Sets to monitor the performance of specific applications or services by adding relevant performance counters.

25. What is the "Windows Event Log" in Windows Performance Monitoring, and how does it complement performance monitoring and troubleshooting?

Answer: The Windows Event Log records important system events, including performance-related events, which can provide context for performance monitoring and troubleshooting.

26. Explain the concept of "Performance Logs" and "Performance Alerts" in Windows Performance Monitoring and how they differ from each other.

Answer: Performance Logs collect and store performance data over time, while Performance Alerts trigger notifications based on predefined conditions.

27. How can you analyze performance data collected by Windows Performance Monitoring tools to identify and resolve performance issues?

Answer: You can analyze performance data by reviewing logs, identifying trends, comparing data to baselines, and using various analysis techniques to pinpoint performance issues.

28. What is "Remote Performance Monitoring," and how can you monitor the performance of remote computers using Performance Monitor?

Answer: Remote Performance Monitoring involves monitoring the performance of remote computers by connecting to them through the Performance Monitor's "Data Collector Set Properties."

29. Explain the concept of "Performance Baseline" and how it helps in understanding normal system behavior.

Answer:A performance baseline is a set of reference metrics that represent typical system performance. It aids in recognizing when performance deviates from the norm.

30. How can you configure Data Collector Sets to run in the background and collect performance data without user intervention?

Answer: You can configure Data Collector Sets to run as a scheduled task with specified triggers, allowing them to collect performance data without user intervention.

31. What is the role of "Performance Alerts" in Windows Performance Monitoring, and how can they be used to trigger actions when performance issues occur?

Answer: Performance Alerts allow you to define conditions that, when met, trigger actions such as logging an event, sending an email, or running a script in response to performance issues.

32. What is "Performance Counter Logging," and how does it differ from real-time monitoring in Performance Monitor?

Answer: Performance Counter Logging involves collecting performance data over time and storing it in log files for analysis, while real-time monitoring in Performance Monitor displays data as it occurs.

33. Explain the concept of "System Bottlenecks" in Windows Performance Monitoring and how to identify them using performance counters.

Answer: System bottlenecks are resource limitations that hinder system performance. Performance counters like disk queue length, CPU usage, and memory usage help identify bottlenecks.

34. What is the "Task Manager" in Windows, and how does it provide a quick overview of system performance and resource usage?

Answer: The Task Manager is a system tool that provides a snapshot of system performance, including CPU, memory, and disk usage, as well as running processes.

35. How can you set up automated performance data collection and analysis in Windows using PowerShell scripts and the Performance Counter cmdlets?

Answer: PowerShell scripts can automate data collection and analysis by using the Performance Counter cmdlets to query and store performance data.

36. Explain how "Pagefile Usage" can be monitored in Windows Performance Monitoring and why it's relevant for system performance.

Answer: Pagefile Usage measures the usage of virtual memory in Windows. Monitoring it is relevant for understanding memory usage and detecting potential memory issues.

37. What are some common performance counters for monitoring network activity in Windows Performance Monitoring?

Answer: Common network performance counters include "Network Interface," "Network Segment," "TCP/IP," and "Web Service" counters for tracking network usage and performance.

38. What is "disk queue length," and how does it relate to disk performance monitoring in Windows?

Answer: Disk queue length measures the number of requests waiting to be processed by the disk. It is a key indicator of disk performance and potential bottlenecks.

39. How can you determine the impact of specific applications or services on system performance by analyzing Windows Performance Monitoring data?

Answer: By isolating and examining performance data for specific applications or services, you can identify their impact on system resources and overall performance.

40. What is "Processor Time" in performance counters, and how does it measure CPU usage in Windows Performance Monitoring?

Answer:"Processor Time" measures the percentage of CPU utilization. It provides insights into the CPU's workload and whether it's a performance bottleneck.

41. Explain the role of "Performance Monitor Templates" in Windows Performance Monitoring and how they simplify the process of monitoring specific aspects of system performance.

Answer: Performance Monitor Templates are preconfigured sets of performance counters tailored for specific purposes. They simplify performance monitoring for specific scenarios.

42. How can you use Windows Performance Monitoring data to identify memory-related performance issues, such as excessive memory usage or memory leaks?

Answer: By analyzing memory-related performance counters like "Available Memory" and "Pagefile Usage," you can identify memory-related performance issues.

43. What is the "LogicalDisk" performance counter category, and how does it assist in monitoring disk performance?

Answer: The "LogicalDisk" category contains performance counters related to disk drives, including measures of disk activity, latency, and capacity.

44. Explain the role of "Sampling Interval" in Performance Counter logging and how it affects the accuracy of collected performance data.

Answer: The Sampling Interval determines how frequently performance data is collected. Smaller intervals provide more granular data but may result in larger log files.

45. How can you configure the Performance Monitor to display performance data in graphical format and use it for real-time monitoring?

Answer: You can add performance counters to the System Monitor and choose to display data in graphical format, allowing real-time monitoring of system performance.

46. What is "Page Faults/sec" in performance counters, and how does it relate to memory performance in Windows Performance Monitoring?

Answer:"Page Faults/sec" measures the rate at which data must be retrieved from the page file because it's not in physical memory, indicating memory performance issues.

47. How can you use Windows Performance Monitoring to track and optimize the performance of web servers and applications?

Answer: By monitoring relevant performance counters, such as those related to web services, you can track and optimize the performance of web servers and applications.

48. Explain the use of "Data Collector Set Templates" in Windows Performance Monitoring and how they simplify the process of creating data collector sets for specific scenarios.

Answer: Data Collector Set Templates provide predefined configurations for common scenarios, making it easier to create data collector sets tailored to specific monitoring needs.

49. What is "Network Bytes Total/sec," and how does it help in monitoring network performance in Windows Performance Monitoring?

Answer:"Network Bytes Total/sec" measures the rate at which data is transferred over the network, providing insights into network traffic and potential bottlenecks.

50. How can you configure Windows Performance Monitoring to automatically generate reports based on collected performance data, and what types of reports can be generated?

Answer: You can configure Data Collector Sets to automatically generate performance reports, including real-time reports and historical reports based on collected performance data.

Backup and Recovery Strategies

1. What is the importance of having a backup and recovery strategy for an organization's data and IT infrastructure?

Answer: A backup and recovery strategy is crucial to safeguard an organization's data and IT systems. It ensures data integrity, business continuity, and minimizes the impact of data loss or system failures.

2. Explain the difference between a backup and an archive.

Answer: A backup is a copy of data made for disaster recovery purposes, while an archive is a copy of data stored for long-term retention, often for compliance or historical purposes.

3. What is the "3-2-1 rule" in backup strategy, and why is it considered a best practice?

Answer: The "3-2-1 rule" suggests having three copies of data (original plus two backups), on two different media types, with one copy stored offsite. It's a best practice because it ensures redundancy, data availability, and protection against various types of data loss.

4. How can you determine the appropriate backup frequency and retention period for an organization's data?

Answer: Backup frequency and retention should be determined by accessing data importance, regulatory requirements, recovery time objectives (RTO), and recovery point objectives (RPO).

5. Explain the concept of full, incremental, and differential backups. When is each type commonly used?

Answer: Full backups copy all data, incremental backups copy only changed data since the last backup, and differential backups copy all changes since the last full backup. Full backups are typically used as a foundation, with incremental and differential backups used to reduce backup times and storage.

6. What is a disaster recovery plan, and how does it relate to backup and recovery strategies?

Answer: A disaster recovery plan is a documented strategy for resuming IT operations after a catastrophic event. It relies on backups and recovery strategies to restore systems and data to their previous state.

7. Explain the concept of "point-in-time recovery" and why it is essential for certain applications and data.

Answer: Point-in-time recovery refers to the ability to restore data to a specific moment in time. It is crucial for applications that require data consistency and integrity, such as databases.

8. How do backup and recovery strategies differ for physical servers versus virtualized environments?

Answer: Backup and recovery strategies for virtualized environments often involve capturing snapshots of virtual machines, whereas physical servers may rely on traditional backup methods. Recovery from snapshots is usually faster in virtualized environments.

9. What are the advantages and disadvantages of on-premises versus cloud-based backup solutions?

Answer: On-premises solutions provide more control but may be costlier and require maintenance. Cloud-based solutions offer scalability and accessibility but can lead to data sovereignty and security concerns.

10. How can you ensure the security and encryption of backup data to protect it from unauthorized access or data breaches?

Answer: Backup data should be encrypted during transmission and storage. Implement strong access controls, authentication, and encryption mechanisms to protect backup data from unauthorized access.

11. What is a backup strategy, and why is it important for Windows systems?

Answer: A backup strategy is a plan for regularly creating copies of data to ensure its availability in case of data loss or system failures. It is crucial for Windows systems to prevent data loss and minimize downtime.

12. What are the common backup types in Windows, and how do they differ?

Answer: Common backup types in Windows include Full, Incremental, and Differential backups. Full backups copy all selected data, Incremental backs up changes since the last backup, and Differential backups save changes since the last full backup.

13. Explain the 3-2-1 backup rule.

Answer: The 3-2-1 backup rule suggests having three copies of your data on two different types of media, with one copy stored offsite. This strategy enhances data protection.

14. What is Windows Shadow Copy, and how does it aid in recovery?

Answer: Windows Shadow Copy is a feature that creates point-in-time copies of files, allowing users to recover previous versions of files or restore system files to an earlier state.

15. What is the role of Volume Shadow Copy Service (VSS) in Windows backup and recovery?

Answer: VSS is responsible for creating consistent, point-in-time snapshots of volumes. Backup software uses VSS to ensure that backups do not interfere with open files and applications.

16. How does Windows Backup and Restore differ from third-party backup solutions?

Answer: Windows Backup and Restore is a built-in Windows feature for basic backup needs. Third-party solutions often offer more features, flexibility, and better integration with complex environments.

17. Explain the importance of disaster recovery planning for Windows systems.

Answer: Disaster recovery planning involves strategies for system recovery in case of catastrophic events. It is crucial for ensuring business continuity and data availability in extreme situations.

18. What is a System Restore Point in Windows, and how does it work?

Answer:A System Restore Point is a snapshot of a Windows system's state. It allows users to revert the system to a previous state, undoing recent changes and fixing issues.

19. What is Windows File History, and how can it be used for data recovery?

Answer: Windows File History is a feature that automatically backs up personal files to an external drive or network location. It allows users to restore previous versions of files.

20. Explain the role of the Windows Recovery Environment (WinRE) in system recovery.

Answer: WinRE is a minimal, pre-boot environment used to troubleshoot and repair Windows installations. It provides tools for system recovery and restoration.

21. What is the difference between Backup and System Image in Windows Backup and Restore?

Answer: Backup is used to back up selected files and folders, while System Image creates a complete copy of the system drive, including the operating system and all data.

22. What is BitLocker, and how does it contribute to data protection and recovery?

Answer: BitLocker is a disk encryption feature in Windows. It helps protect data by encrypting drives, making it more challenging for unauthorized users to access data, and is useful in recovery scenarios.

23. What is the purpose of Windows Event Logs in a backup and recovery scenario?

Answer: Windows Event Logs capture information about system events, errors, and application issues. They are valuable for diagnosing problems and determining the cause of system failures.

24. Explain the concept of Bare-Metal Recovery in Windows backup.

Answer: Bare-Metal Recovery is the process of restoring a system to a "bare-metal" state, meaning it includes the operating system, applications, and data. It's often used when a system has experienced a complete failure.

25. What is the role of the Windows Registry in system recovery, and how can it be backed up?

Answer: The Windows Registry stores system configuration settings. Backing it up is crucial because it can be restored to recover system settings in case of corruption or misconfiguration.

26. How does the Windows Task Scheduler play a role in automated backup tasks?

Answer: The Task Scheduler allows users to automate backup tasks, ensuring that backups are performed at specific times or intervals, reducing the risk of human error.

27. What are Volume-level and File-level backups, and when is each method appropriate?

Answer: Volume-level backups copy entire disk volumes, while file-level backups target specific files and folders. Volume-level backups are suitable for system recovery, while file-level backups are ideal for individual file restoration.

28. Explain the difference between on-site and off-site backups and their importance in a backup strategy.

Answer: On-site backups are stored in the same location as the source data, while off-site backups are stored at a separate location. Off-site backups protect against physical disasters that may affect the primary site.

29. What are the considerations for selecting backup hardware and storage media in a Windows environment?

Answer: Factors include capacity, speed, compatibility, redundancy, and scalability. Choosing the right hardware and storage media depends on the specific backup needs.

30. How can you ensure the security of backup data and prevent unauthorized access?

Answer: You can secure backup data by encrypting it, implementing access controls, storing backups in secure locations, and monitoring for security threats.

Windows Virtualization Technologies

1. What is virtualization, and how does it work in the context of Windows operating systems?

Answer: Virtualization is the process of creating virtual instances of computer systems, including hardware, operating systems, and software, on a single physical host. In Windows, this is achieved using virtualization technologies like Hyper-V.

2. Explain the role of Hyper-V in Windows virtualization.

Answer: Hyper-V is Microsoft's hypervisor-based virtualization technology that enables the creation and management of virtual machines (VMs) on Windows servers. It provides isolation and resource allocation for VMs.

3. What is the key difference between Type 1 and Type 2 hypervisors, and which category does Hyper-V belong to?

Answer: Type 1 hypervisors run directly on the physical hardware, while Type 2 hypervisors run on top of an existing operating system. Hyper-V is a Type 1 hypervisor because it runs directly on the hardware, providing better performance and isolation.

4. What are some benefits of virtualization in Windows environments, and how can it improve resource utilization?

Answer: Virtualization allows for better resource utilization, server consolidation, faster provisioning of new virtual machines, enhanced disaster recovery capabilities, and improved testing and development environments.

5. Explain the concept of "snapshot" in Hyper-V and its use in virtual machine management.

Answer:A snapshot is a point-in-time image of a virtual machine's state. Snapshots can be used for backup, rollback, and testing scenarios. They capture the VM's configuration, disk data, and memory state at a specific moment.

6. What are Integration Services (Integration Components) in Hyper-V, and why are they important for virtualized Windows guests?

Answer: Integration Services are a set of drivers and services that enhance the performance and functionality of Windows virtual machines. They enable features like time synchronization, mouse integration, and dynamic memory allocation.

7. How do you migrate or move virtual machines between Hyper-V hosts, and what considerations should be taken into account during the migration process?

Answer: Virtual machines can be migrated using techniques such as Live Migration or Quick Migration. Considerations include compatibility, network connectivity, and ensuring sufficient resources on the target host.

8. Explain the concept of a virtual switch in Hyper-V and how it connects virtual machines to the physical network.

Answer: A virtual switch is a software-based network switch that connects virtual machines to physical networks. It allows VMs to communicate with other VMs and with physical devices while providing network isolation and segmentation.

9. What is the purpose of Hyper-V checkpoints, and how do they differ from snapshots?

Answer: Hyper-V checkpoints (formerly called snapshots) capture a virtual machine's state and allow you to return to that state if needed. However, they are not recommended for production environments, as they do not capture data changes after the checkpoint is created.

10. How does Windows Subsystem for Linux (WSL) relate to virtualization in Windows, and what are its primary use cases?

Answer: WSL allows running Linux distributions alongside Windows in a virtualized environment. It is not a traditional virtualization solution but serves as a compatibility layer for running Linux tools and applications on a Windows host, making it useful for development and testing.

11. What is virtualization, and how does it work in the context of Windows?

Answer: Virtualization is the process of creating virtual instances of computer systems. In Windows, this is achieved through software called hypervisors, which allow multiple virtual machines (VMs) to run on a single physical server.

12. What are the primary benefits of using virtualization in a Windows environment?

Answer: Benefits of Windows virtualization include server consolidation, resource optimization, easier management, disaster recovery, and improved testing and development environments.

13. Explain the difference between Type 1 and Type 2 hypervisors.

Answer: Type 1 hypervisors run directly on the host's hardware (bare-metal), while Type 2 hypervisors run on a conventional operating system. Windows Hyper-V is an example of a Type 1 hypervisor.

14. What is Windows Hyper-V, and how does it compare to other virtualization platforms?

Answer: Windows Hyper-V is a Type 1 hypervisor developed by Microsoft. It is known for its integration with Windows Server and offers features such as live migration and dynamic memory allocation.

15. Describe the concept of a virtual machine (VM) and its key components.

Answer: A VM is a software-based emulation of a physical computer. Key components include a virtual processor, memory, storage, and network adapters.

16. How does Windows Hyper-V handle hardware virtualization support, and why is it important?

Answer: Windows Hyper-V uses hardware-assisted virtualization (e.g., Intel VT-x/AMD-V) to improve VM performance and isolation. It allows VMs to run with minimal overhead.

17. What are Integration Services in Hyper-V, and why are they essential for VM performance?

Answer: Integration Services are a set of drivers and services that enhance VM performance and functionality. They enable features like time synchronization and network optimizations.

18. Explain the concept of live migration in Windows Hyper-V.

Answer: Live migration allows you to move a running VM from one host to another without causing downtime. This ensures high availability and load balancing.

19. What is the difference between checkpoint and backup in Windows Hyper-V?

Answer: A checkpoint captures the state of a VM at a specific point in time and can be used for recovery or testing. A backup is a full copy of VM data and is more comprehensive for disaster recovery.

20. How do you allocate resources (CPU, RAM, disk space) to virtual machines in Hyper-V?

Answer: Resources are allocated using settings in the VM configuration, including virtual processors, memory, and attaching virtual hard disks.

21. What is the role of Virtual Switches in Hyper-V networking, and how do they work?

Answer: Virtual Switches allow VMs to communicate with each other and the host system. They act as a bridge between the physical network and VMs, and can be configured with different network profiles.

22. Explain the concept of containers in Windows and how they differ from VMs.

Answer: Containers are lightweight, isolated instances of applications and their dependencies. Unlike VMs, they share the host OS kernel, resulting in less overhead and faster startup times.

23. What are the licensing considerations for Windows VMs in a virtualized environment?

Answer: Licensing can be complex and depends on the edition of Windows Server and the type of licensing (e.g., per-core, per-VM, or CAL-based). It's crucial to comply with Microsoft's licensing terms.

24. What is the difference between Hyper-V Generation 1 and Generation 2 VMs?

Answer: Generation 1 VMs emulate traditional hardware, while Generation 2 VMs use modern UEFI firmware and offer various performance and security enhancements.

25. Explain the role of the Virtual Machine Connection tool in managing Hyper-V VMs.

Answer: The Virtual Machine Connection tool allows administrators to connect directly to a VM's console for management and troubleshooting.

26. How can you back up and restore virtual machines in Hyper-V for disaster recovery?

Answer: Hyper-V offers features like Export and Import for VM backups, but third-party backup solutions are often preferred for comprehensive and automated backup and recovery.

27. What is the purpose of the Hyper-V Manager and System Center Virtual Machine Manager (SCVMM) in VM management?

Answer: Hyper-V Manager is a basic management tool, while SCVMM is a more advanced solution for managing multiple Hyper-V hosts and VMs in a centralized manner.

28. How can you secure virtual machines in a Windows Hyper-V environment?

Answer: Security measures include keeping VMs up to date, applying access controls, using encryption, and regularly reviewing and hardening the virtualization infrastructure.

29. Explain the concept of Nested Virtualization in Windows Hyper-V.

Answer: Nested Virtualization allows you to run Hyper-V within a Hyper-V VM, enabling scenarios like testing and development of virtualization solutions within VMs.

30. What is the significance of dynamic memory in Hyper-V, and when is it useful?

Answer: Dynamic memory allocation allows VMs to use memory resources more efficiently by adjusting the memory allocation based on the VM's workload. It's useful for optimizing resource utilization.

Cloud Integration and Windows Azure

1. What is Microsoft Azure, and how does it fit into the broader concept of cloud computing?

Answer: Microsoft Azure is a cloud computing platform and service offered by Microsoft. It provides a wide range of cloud-based services, including infrastructure as a service (IaaS), platform as a service (PaaS), and software as a service (SaaS). Azure enables organizations to build, deploy, and manage applications and services in the cloud.

2. Explain the difference between on-premises, hybrid, and fully cloud-based deployments in the context of Azure.

Answer: On-premises refers to deploying applications and services on local servers and infrastructure, while a hybrid deployment combines on-premises and cloud resources. Fully cloud-based deployments use Azure as the primary platform for all services and applications, with no on-premises infrastructure.

3. What is Azure Virtual Machines (VMs), and how can they be used for cloud integration and scalability?

Answer: Azure VMs are scalable, on-demand virtual machines that run in the Azure cloud. They can be used to host a wide variety of applications, enabling cloud integration and scalability by adjusting resources as needed to meet demand.

4. What are Azure Functions, and how do they facilitate serverless computing and integration?

Answer: Azure Functions are serverless compute services that allow you to run event-driven code without managing infrastructure. They are suitable for tasks like data processing, automation, and integration, and they scale automatically as needed.

5. Explain Azure Logic Apps and their role in cloud-based integration scenarios.

Answer: Azure Logic Apps are a cloud-based service for creating workflows that integrate with various services and systems. They enable organizations to automate business processes, connect applications, and streamline data flow between different platforms.

6. What are Azure Active Directory and how do they contribute to identity and access management in the cloud?

Answer: Azure Active Directory (Azure AD) is Microsoft's cloud-based identity and access management service. It provides features for authentication, authorization, and directory services, making it integral for securing access to Azure resources and applications.

7. What is Azure DevOps, and how does it support application development and deployment in Azure?

Answer: Azure DevOps is a set of development tools and services that support application lifecycle management, including planning, development, testing, and deployment. It helps organizations build, test, and deploy applications efficiently in Azure.

8. What is Azure Data Factory, and how does it help in data integration and transformation in the cloud?

Answer: Azure Data Factory is a cloud-based data integration service used to create, schedule, and manage data-driven workflows. It allows organizations to move data between supported data stores, transform data, and monitor data pipelines in Azure.

9. What is Azure API Management, and how does it simplify the management and publication of APIs?

Answer: Azure API Management is a service that helps organizations create, publish, and manage APIs. It provides features for security, rate limiting, analytics, and developer portal management, making it easier to expose and manage APIs.

10. Explain the role of Azure Resource Manager (ARM) in managing Azure resources and supporting infrastructure as code (IaC).

Answer: Azure Resource Manager is the control plane for managing Azure resources. It allows you to create, deploy, update, and delete resources as a group. ARM templates enable the implementation of infrastructure as code (IaC) principles by defining the desired state of Azure resources in a declarative format.

11. What is cloud integration, and why is it important for businesses?

Answer: Cloud integration refers to the process of connecting on-premises or cloud-based systems and services to work together seamlessly. It's crucial for businesses to enhance productivity, scalability, and flexibility.

12. Explain the role of Microsoft Azure in cloud integration.

Answer: Microsoft Azure is a cloud platform that provides a wide range of services, including integration services like Azure Logic Apps and Azure Service Bus, to connect and extend on-premises and cloud applications.

13. What is Azure Logic Apps, and how does it enable workflow automation?

Answer: Azure Logic Apps is a cloud-based service for creating workflows and integrating applications and services. It enables users to automate tasks and integrate systems with a visual designer.

14. Describe the difference between Azure Logic Apps and Azure Functions.

Answer: Azure Logic Apps are used for building workflows, while Azure Functions are event-driven, serverless compute services. Functions are used for executing code in response to specific events or triggers.

15. How does Azure Service Bus facilitate communication between applications and services?

Answer: Azure Service Bus is a messaging service that enables reliable and asynchronous communication between distributed applications. It supports queues, topics, and subscriptions.

16. What are Azure Data Factory and Azure Data Factory Data Flow?

Answer: Azure Data Factory is a cloud-based data integration service for creating, scheduling, and orchestrating data pipelines. Data Flow is a feature that enables data transformations within Data Factory.

17. Explain the concept of hybrid cloud integration and its benefits.

Answer: Hybrid cloud integration combines on-premises and cloud-based resources, providing businesses with greater flexibility, scalability, and cost efficiency.

18. How does Azure Hybrid Integration Services help with hybrid cloud scenarios?

Answer: Azure Hybrid Integration Services includes tools like Azure BizTalk Services and Azure VPN Gateway, allowing businesses to integrate on-premises systems with Azure services.

19. What is Azure API Management, and how does it enable API integration?

Answer: Azure API Management is a service that provides capabilities for creating, publishing, and managing APIs. It allows organizations to expose their APIs securely and manage their usage.

20. Explain the purpose of Azure Functions Proxies in API management.

Answer: Azure Functions Proxies allow developers to create custom APIs that can transform or redirect incoming requests to different backend services, making it a powerful tool for API integration.

21. How does Azure App Service facilitate web app integration with Azure resources?

Answer: Azure App Service is a platform for building and hosting web applications. It can be easily integrated with various Azure resources and services through configuration settings.

22. What is Azure Key Vault, and how does it enhance security in cloud integration?

Answer: Azure Key Vault is a service for securely managing keys, secrets, and certificates. It enhances security by **providing a central repository for managing sensitive information used in cloud integration.**

23. Explain the role of Azure Event Grid in event-driven integration.

Answer: Azure Event Grid is a service for managing and routing events from various Azure services. It enables event-driven integration by providing a way to respond to events in near real-time.

24. What is Azure Logic Apps Enterprise Integration Pack, and when is it used?

Answer: The Azure Logic Apps Enterprise Integration Pack is an add-on for Logic Apps that enables B2B integration by supporting EDI (Electronic Data Interchange) and XML transformation.

25. How can you ensure data security and compliance when integrating on-premises systems with Azure?

Answer: Data security and compliance can be ensured through encryption, access controls, compliance certifications, and data governance policies.

26. What are the advantages of using Azure Integration Runtime in Azure Data Factory?

Answer: Azure Integration Runtime enables data movement between various data stores in Data Factory. It offers better connectivity options, scalability, and performance optimizations.

27. Explain the use of Azure Logic Apps connectors and triggers.

Answer: Connectors are pre-built integrations with various services and systems. Triggers are events that initiate the execution of a Logic App workflow.

28. What is the Azure Functions Consumption Plan, and when is it a suitable choice for integration?

Answer: The Azure Functions Consumption Plan is a serverless hosting option. It's suitable for integration when you need to handle variable workloads and only want to pay for the resources consumed during execution.

29. How does Azure Monitor help with the monitoring and management of cloud integration solutions?

Answer: Azure Monitor provides insights into the performance, health, and operation of your integrated solutions, helping you detect and respond to issues effectively.

30. Explain how Azure Stack fits into the concept of hybrid cloud integration.

Answer: Azure Stack is an extension of Azure that allows organizations to run Azure services on their own infrastructure. It supports hybrid cloud integration by providing consistent services and APIs on-premises and in the cloud.

ONLINE RESOURCES

Practice Paper Link: https://forms.gle/UrhJrtAfGCVdLoYT6

QR Code:

Video Link: https://www.youtube.com/playlist?list=PLzlh_31VWEFrf6dXDqR3bXIpEWP1OaIES

QR Code:

Chapter 11 Windows Aministration

User Account Management

1. What is User Account Management, and why is it important in a Windows environment?

Answer: User Account Management involves creating, configuring, and maintaining user accounts on a Windows system. It's essential for controlling access, ensuring security, and managing user privileges.

2. How do you create a new user account in Windows, and what information is required during the process?

Answer:A new user account can be created through the Control Panel or settings. Typically, you need to provide a username, password, and account type (e.g., Administrator or Standard User).

3. What are the different types of user accounts in Windows, and what are their primary roles?

Answer: Windows offers three main types of user accounts: Administrator (full control), Standard User (limited privileges), and Guest (restricted access). These roles determine the level of control and permissions a user has.

4. Can you explain the purpose of a User Group in Windows, and how does it simplify User Account Management?

Answer: User Groups allow you to group users with similar permissions and apply policies to multiple users simultaneously. They simplify User Account Management by streamlining access control.

5. How do you modify user account settings, such as password, account type, or name, in Windows?

Answer: User account settings can be modified through the Control Panel or the User Accounts section in settings, allowing changes to username, password, and account type.

6. Explain the difference between a local user account and a domain user account in Windows.

Answer:A local user account is specific to a single computer, while a domain user account is part of a network domain and can access resources across multiple computers in a domain.

7. What is the purpose of a user profile in Windows, and where are user profiles stored?

Answer: User profiles store user-specific settings and configurations. In Windows, user profiles are typically stored in the "C:\Users" folder.

8. How can you delete a user account in Windows, and what are the considerations when doing so?

Answer: User accounts can be deleted through the Control Panel. Care should be taken when deleting accounts, as it can result in data loss and access issues.

9. Explain the concept of user permissions and access control in Windows, and how are they related to User Account Management?

Answer: User permissions define what actions a user can perform on a system or its resources. Access control, managed through user accounts and groups, enforces these permissions.

10. How can you enforce strong password policies for user accounts in Windows, and why is this important for security?

Answer: Strong password policies can be configured through Group Policy settings. They are vital for security because they help protect user accounts from unauthorized access and data breaches.

11. What is the Windows Administrator account, and how does it differ from other user accounts?

Answer: The Administrator account is a built-in, superuser account with full control over the system. It differs from regular user accounts by having unrestricted access.

12. How can you reset a user's password in Windows if they forget it or need a password change?

Answer: Passwords can be reset by an Administrator through the Control Panel or Local Users and Groups (lusrmgr.msc) for local accounts. Domain users can reset their passwords using domain services or an Administrator's assistance.

13. What is the purpose of User Rights in Windows, and how can they be managed to enhance User Account Management?

Answer: User Rights are specific privileges assigned to user accounts or groups, allowing them to perform certain actions. They can be managed through Group Policy settings to enhance security and access control.

14. How do you disable or enable a user account in Windows, and what are the reasons for doing so?

Answer: User accounts can be disabled or enabled through the Control Panel or Active Directory for domain accounts. Disabling an account prevents login, which is useful for security or temporary user account suspension.

15. What is User Lockout in Windows, and why is it implemented for User Account Management?

Answer: User Lockout is a security feature that temporarily disables an account after a specified number of failed login attempts, helping protect against unauthorized access and brute force attacks.

16. Can you explain the concept of User Authentication in Windows, and how does it verify user identities?

Answer: User Authentication is the process of verifying a user's identity. In Windows, it's achieved through username and password verification, often against a domain controller.

17. How can you configure a user's home directory in Windows, and why is it important for User Account Management?

Answer: Home directories provide users with a private space to store their files and settings. They can be configured through user account properties and are essential for personalization and data management.

18. What are the security implications of using "Guest" accounts in Windows, and how can they be managed effectively?

Answer: Guest accounts should be used with caution, as they can pose security risks. To manage them effectively, set appropriate permissions and restrictions on Guest accounts.

19. How can you enforce user account policies, such as account lockout, password complexity, and logon hours, in Windows?

Answer: User account policies can be enforced through Group Policy settings, which allow administrators to define account lockout thresholds, password complexity requirements, and logon hour restrictions.

20. What is User Account Control (UAC) in Windows, and how does it enhance security for User Account Management?

Answer:UAC is a security feature that prompts users for confirmation before performing actions that require Administrator privileges. It helps prevent unauthorized or unintentional system changes.

System Configuration and Maintenance

1. What is System Configuration in Windows, and how can it be accessed?

Answer: System Configuration (msconfig) is a utility in Windows used to manage system startup and configuration settings. It can be accessed by typing "msconfig" into the Run dialog or searching for it in the Start menu.

2. How can you configure the Windows boot options using System Configuration?

Answer: In System Configuration, navigate to the "Boot" tab, where you can select the desired boot options, such as Safe Mode or booting with minimal services.

3. Explain the purpose of the Windows Registry and its role in system configuration and maintenance.

Answer: The Windows Registry stores configuration settings and options for the operating system and applications. It is essential for maintaining and configuring various aspects of the system.

4. What are Windows Services, and how can you manage them for system configuration and maintenance?

Answer: Windows Services are background processes that can be managed through the Services application (services.msc) to control system components and features. This is important for system configuration and maintenance.

5. How can you configure Windows Update settings to ensure that your system remains up to date with the latest updates and patches?

Answer: Windows Update settings can be configured through the Control Panel. You can choose automatic updates, scheduled updates, and configure update preferences.

6. What is the Windows Task Scheduler, and how can it be used for system maintenance and automation?

Answer: The Task Scheduler allows users to schedule tasks and processes, automating system maintenance and other actions. It can be accessed through the Control Panel.

7. How can you create a system restore point in Windows, and when is it useful for system maintenance?

Answer: System restore points can be created through the System Properties dialog. They are useful for undoing system changes and recovering from issues that may arise during system maintenance.

8. What is Disk Cleanup in Windows, and how can it help with system maintenance?

Answer: Disk Cleanup is a utility for removing unnecessary files from the system to free up disk space. It helps in maintaining system performance and storage capacity.

9. How can you use the Windows Resource Monitor for system performance monitoring and troubleshooting?

Answer: The Resource Monitor provides real-time information about system performance, including CPU, memory, disk, and network usage, making it a valuable tool for system maintenance and troubleshooting.

10. Explain the importance of driver updates in system maintenance and how they can be managed in Windows.

Answer: Driver updates are crucial for maintaining hardware compatibility and system stability. They can be managed through Device Manager or by downloading updated drivers from the manufacturer's website.

11. What is the Windows Event Viewer, and how can it be used for system maintenance and troubleshooting?

Answer: The Event Viewer records system events, errors, and warnings. It is a valuable tool for diagnosing issues and performing system maintenance by analyzing event logs.

12. How can you configure and monitor system security settings in Windows for ongoing system maintenance?

Answer: System security settings can be configured through the Security and Maintenance section in the Control Panel. Regular monitoring and updates are essential for system maintenance.

13. What is the Windows Reliability Monitor, and how does it aid in system maintenance and troubleshooting?

Answer: The Reliability Monitor provides a timeline of system events and issues, making it easier to identify problems and maintain system reliability.

14. How can you use the Windows System File Checker (sfc) for system maintenance, and what does it check for?

Answer: The System File Checker checks and repairs corrupted or missing system files, contributing to system maintenance and stability. It can be run from the Command Prompt with "sfc /scannow."

15. How can you optimize system performance in Windows through the use of disk defragmentation and disk cleanup tools?

Answer: Disk defragmentation rearranges data on the hard drive for improved performance, while disk cleanup removes unnecessary files. Both are essential for system maintenance.

16. What is the Windows Reliability and Performance Monitor, and how can it help with system maintenance and performance analysis?

Answer: The Reliability and Performance Monitor provides detailed information about system performance and reliability, making it a valuable tool for maintaining and troubleshooting the system.

17. How can you configure power management settings in Windows to conserve energy and enhance system maintenance?

Answer: Power management settings can be configured through the Power Options in the Control Panel. They allow you to specify sleep, hibernate, and display settings to conserve energy.

18. Explain the role of System Restore in Windows and how it can be used for system maintenance and recovery.

Answer: System Restore allows users to revert the system to a previous state in case of issues. It is a valuable tool for system maintenance and recovery.

19. What is the Windows Action Center, and how does it assist in system maintenance and security monitoring?

Answer: The Action Center is a central location for system maintenance and security alerts. It provides notifications and recommendations to address system issues and maintain security.

20. How can you schedule automatic maintenance tasks in Windows to keep the system optimized and up to date?

Answer: Automatic maintenance tasks can be scheduled through the Action Center settings. These tasks include updates, security scans, and performance optimizations to maintain the system.

ONLINE RESOURCES

Practice Paper Link: https://forms.gle/6zDdE5ngCsWBNbRY8

QR Code:

Video Link: https://www.youtube.com/playlist?list=PLzlh_31VWEFriWXKGNXPdCy1Egd8jbSaC

QR Code:

Chapter 12 Windows architecture

Kernel and Operating System Components

1. What is the role of the operating system kernel in a Windows environment?

Answer: The operating system kernel is the core component responsible for managing hardware resources, executing processes, and providing essential services to user applications.

2. Can you explain the key responsibilities of the Windows kernel?

Answer: The Windows kernel manages memory, I/O operations, device drivers, system calls, process scheduling, and security, ensuring the efficient operation of the operating system.

3. What is the difference between the user mode and kernel mode in Windows?

Answer: User mode is where application code runs, while kernel mode is where the core operating system code and device drivers run. Access to hardware and sensitive resources is restricted to kernel mode for security and stability.

4. How does the Windows kernel manage system memory, and what is the role of the Memory Manager?

Answer: The Memory Manager handles memory allocation and management, including virtual memory, page file management, and physical RAM control to ensure efficient use of system resources.

5. What are device drivers, and how do they interact with the Windows kernel?

Answer: Device drivers are software components that allow the operating system to communicate with hardware devices. They are loaded into the kernel and provide a standardized interface for hardware interaction.

6. Explain the concept of a system call in Windows, and why are they important for application development?

Answer: System calls are APIs that allow user applications to request services from the operating system kernel. They are essential for developers to interact with low-level operating system functions.

7. What is the Windows Registry, and how does it play a role in the functioning of the operating system?

Answer: The Windows Registry is a hierarchical database used for storing system and application configuration settings. It provides a central repository for various configuration data accessed by the kernel and applications.

8. How does the Windows Task Manager help users and administrators interact with the kernel and manage system resources?

Answer: The Task Manager provides a user-friendly interface to view and manage running processes, monitor system performance, and terminate unresponsive applications, interacting with the kernel to control processes.

9. What is process scheduling, and how does the Windows kernel manage it?

Answer: Process scheduling is the kernel's responsibility for allocating CPU time to different processes. The Windows kernel uses various scheduling algorithms to manage multitasking and ensure fairness among running processes.

10. What are interrupt service routines (ISRs), and how do they relate to the Windows kernel?

Answer: ISRs are functions that handle hardware interrupts generated by hardware devices. The Windows kernel calls the appropriate ISR to respond to hardware events.

11. How does the Windows kernel handle system crashes and errors, and what is the role of the Blue Screen of Death (BSOD)?

Answer: The kernel has error-handling mechanisms to respond to system crashes, and the BSOD is a screen displayed when a critical system error occurs. It provides diagnostic information and helps analyze the cause of the crash.

12. What is the purpose of the Windows Event Viewer, and how does it help with system monitoring and troubleshooting?

Answer: The Event Viewer is a tool for viewing and analyzing event logs generated by the Windows kernel and applications. It assists in monitoring system events, diagnosing issues, and troubleshooting errors.

13. Can you explain the concept of I/O request packets (IRPs) and their role in managing input and output operations in Windows?

Answer: IRPs are data structures used to manage I/O operations between the kernel and device drivers. They carry information about I/O requests and help coordinate data transfer.

14. How does the Windows kernel manage hardware interrupts and handle priorities among different hardware devices?

Answer: The kernel uses interrupt controllers to prioritize and manage hardware interrupts. These controllers ensure that high-priority hardware events are serviced first.

15. What is the Windows Plug and Play (PnP) system, and how does it relate to the kernel's management of hardware devices?

Answer: PnP is a system that allows the kernel to dynamically recognize and configure hardware devices. The kernel communicates with PnP components to manage hardware changes and device recognition.

16. How does the Windows kernel ensure system security, including user authentication and access control?

Answer: The kernel enforces security policies, manages user access rights, and ensures authentication through mechanisms like Access Control Lists (ACLs) and Security Identifiers (SIDs).

17. What is the Windows System Service Table (SST) and its significance in the kernel's interaction with user processes?

Answer: The SST is a table that contains function pointers to system services. It plays a critical role in enabling user processes to request services from the kernel through system calls.

18. How does the kernel handle power management, including sleep, hibernation, and device power states, in a Windows environment?

Answer: The kernel manages power states and sleep modes by coordinating with device drivers and power management policies to conserve energy while maintaining system responsiveness.

19. What is the Windows Boot Manager, and how does it interact with the kernel during system startup?

Answer: The Boot Manager is a component responsible for loading the operating system. It hands control to the kernel when the system starts, initiating the boot process.

20. Can you explain the concept of the HAL (Hardware Abstraction Layer) in Windows, and how it contributes to the kernel's portability across different hardware platforms?

Answer: The HAL is a layer that abstracts hardware-specific functions, making the kernel more portable. It allows the same kernel to work on different hardware platforms by isolating hardware dependencies.

Windows File System and Storage

1. What is the default file system used by Windows for most storage devices?

Answer: The default file system used by Windows is NTFS (New Technology File System).

2. How does NTFS differ from FAT32, and what are the advantages of using NTFS?

Answer: NTFS supports larger file sizes and offers advanced security features and file compression, while FAT32 has limitations in these areas. NTFS is the preferred choice for modern Windows systems.

3. What is the purpose of the Master File Table (MFT) in the NTFS file system?

Answer: The MFT is a database that stores information about all files and directories on an NTFS volume, including file attributes and metadata.

4. How can you compress files and folders in NTFS, and what are the implications of compression on performance and storage space?

Answer: Compression can be enabled in NTFS using the built-in feature. It can save storage space but may slightly impact read/write performance due to the need for on-the-fly compression and decompression.

5. What is the Windows Registry, and where is it located in the file system?

Answer: The Windows Registry is a hierarchical database used to store system and application settings. It is stored in files located in the %SystemRoot%\System32\Config directory.

6. Explain the purpose of the Recycle Bin in Windows and how it manages deleted files.

Answer: The Recycle Bin acts as a temporary storage for deleted files and allows users to recover them if needed. When files are deleted, they are moved to the Recycle Bin, and users can restore or permanently delete them from there.

7. How can you manage disk partitions and volumes in Windows?

Answer: Disk Management is a built-in Windows tool that allows users to create, resize, delete, and format partitions or volumes on their hard drives.

8. What is the purpose of Disk Quotas in Windows file systems, and how do they work?

Answer: Disk Quotas are used to limit the amount of disk space a user can consume. Administrators can set quotas on individual users or directories to prevent excessive storage usage.

9. What is the difference between a hard link and a symbolic link in Windows file systems?

Answer: A hard link is a reference to the same file on disk, while a symbolic link is a pointer to another file or directory. Changes to the original file affect hard links, but symbolic links can point to files or directories in different locations.

10. How do you defragment and optimize disks in Windows, and why is this important for storage performance?

Answer: The built-in tool, Disk Defragmenter (or Optimize Drives in modern Windows), is used to reorganize data on disks, reducing file fragmentation and improving read/write performance.

11. Explain the purpose of the Windows System Restore feature and how it affects the file system.

Answer: System Restore allows users to revert the system's state to a previous point in time. It affects the file system by restoring system and registry files to their previous state.

12. How does BitLocker enhance data security in Windows, and what types of storage devices can it encrypt?

Answer: BitLocker is used for full-disk encryption and protects data on storage devices like hard drives, SSDs, and USB drives. It enhances data security by encrypting the entire disk, preventing unauthorized access to data.

13. What is Storage Spaces in Windows, and how does it allow for data redundancy and fault tolerance?

Answer: Storage Spaces is a feature that allows users to pool drives together and create storage spaces with features like mirroring or parity for data redundancy and fault tolerance.

14. How can you recover deleted files or previous versions of files in Windows without using the Recycle Bin?

Answer: You can use the "Previous Versions" feature to recover previous versions of files or restore deleted files by right-clicking on the file or folder and selecting "Restore previous versions."

15. What is the purpose of the Windows Libraries feature, and how can it help organize files and folders?

Answer: Windows Libraries allow users to organize and access files from multiple locations in one central place. They help streamline file management by presenting a unified view of data.

16. How can you use the Windows Robocopy command for file copying and synchronization?

Answer: Robocopy is a command-line tool used for robust file copying and synchronization in Windows. It can mirror directories, preserve file attributes, and handle network file transfers.

17. What is the purpose of the Windows Hosts file, and where is it located in the file system?

Answer: The Hosts file is used to map hostnames to IP addresses. It is located in the %SystemRoot%\System32\drivers\etc directory and can be used for DNS resolution overrides.

18. How can you check disk health and diagnose disk-related issues in Windows?

Answer: Windows provides the "Check Disk" utility (chkdsk) to scan and repair file system errors and bad sectors on a disk. This tool can help identify and resolve disk issues.

19. What is the difference between a dynamic disk and a basic disk in Windows, and when might you choose one over the other?

Answer: Dynamic disks offer more advanced features like software RAID and volume spanning. Basic disks are simpler and are typically used for standard storage. The choice depends on the specific requirements and capabilities needed for a storage solution.

20. How can you use Windows Group Policy to control file and folder access and security?

Answer: Windows Group Policy can be used to set access control policies, restrict access to files and folders, and enforce security settings, providing centralized management of file and folder security.

Networking and Security Layers

1. What are the key networking and security layers in a Windows environment?

Answer: The key networking and security layers in Windows include the physical layer, data link layer, network layer, transport layer, application layer, and security layers for access control and data protection.

2. Explain the role of the physical layer in networking and security in Windows.

Answer: The physical layer deals with the physical transmission of data, such as through cables or wireless signals, and includes considerations like cable quality, connectors, and signal strength.

3. How does the data link layer contribute to network security in a Windows environment?

Answer: The data link layer ensures reliable data transmission over a network. It's responsible for MAC addresses, which are used in access control to prevent unauthorized access to the network.

4. What are some common network protocols used in the network layer in Windows networking?

Answer: Common network layer protocols in Windows include IP (Internet Protocol), ICMP (Internet Control Message Protocol), and routing protocols like OSPF and BGP.

5. How does Windows implement network security at the transport layer, and what is its primary function?

Answer: The transport layer provides end-to-end communication, ensuring data integrity and reliability. Windows uses protocols like TCP (Transmission Control Protocol) and UDP (User Datagram Protocol) at this layer, with security features like Windows Firewall controlling access and filtering at this level.

6. Explain the role of the Windows Firewall in securing a Windows environment.

Answer: Windows Firewall is a software-based firewall that controls incoming and outgoing network traffic, allowing administrators to configure rules to filter and secure network traffic based on ports, applications, and IP addresses.

7. How does Windows implement security at the application layer for network communication?

Answer: Windows can use secure communication protocols like HTTPS, SSH, and FTPS at the application layer to ensure data protection and authentication.

8. What is the purpose of Access Control Lists (ACLs) in Windows networking and security?

Answer: ACLs are used to define and enforce access control policies, specifying which users or systems are allowed to access specific network resources and services.

9. How can you secure remote access to a Windows network, and what technologies are commonly used?

Answer: Technologies like VPN (Virtual Private Network), RDP (Remote Desktop Protocol), and DirectAccess can be used to secure remote access to Windows networks, ensuring data encryption and secure authentication.

10. What are the benefits of using Network Address Translation (NAT) in a Windows environment, and how does it enhance security?

Answer: NAT allows multiple devices on a local network to share a single public IP address. This provides a level of security by hiding internal network structures from external threats.

11. Explain the concept of Virtual LANs (VLANs) in Windows networking and security.

Answer: VLANs segment a physical network into logical subnetworks. This enhances security by isolating network traffic and limiting communication between different VLANs.

12. How can you protect sensitive data in transit in a Windows network environment?

Answer: Data can be protected in transit through the use of encryption protocols like SSL/TLS for web traffic, IPSec for secure communication, and SMB encryption for file sharing.

13. What is a DMZ (Demilitarized Zone) in network security, and how is it implemented in Windows environments?

Answer: A DMZ is a separate network segment that contains systems exposed to the internet. In Windows, this can include web servers or application gateways. It's implemented using firewall rules and network segmentation.

14. How does Windows implement port security to enhance network security?

Answer: Port security in Windows involves configuring switches to limit the number of devices that can connect to a switch port and restricting MAC addresses, preventing unauthorized devices from connecting.

15. What is the role of network segmentation in Windows security, and how is it achieved?

Answer: Network segmentation divides a network into smaller, isolated segments to limit the spread of malware and unauthorized access. This is achieved through VLANs, routers, and firewalls.

16. Explain the concept of Intrusion Detection Systems (IDS) and Intrusion Prevention Systems (IPS) in Windows security.

Answer: IDS monitors network traffic for signs of suspicious activity, while IPS not only detects but also actively blocks or mitigates threats. Both are used to enhance network security.

17. How does Windows implement IP filtering, and why is it important for network security?

Answer: Windows IP filtering involves defining rules to allow or block traffic based on IP addresses or port numbers. It's important for restricting access to services and resources.

18. What is Network Access Control (NAC) in Windows security, and how does it work?

Answer: NAC verifies the security posture of devices before granting network access. In Windows, this can be done through solutions like Network Policy Server (NPS) and Network Access Protection (NAP).

19. How can Windows Active Directory be used to control network access and enhance security?

Answer: Active Directory provides centralized user authentication, authorization, and access control, allowing administrators to manage network access effectively.

20. What are the key principles of a defense-in-depth strategy for Windows network security?

Answer: Defense-in-depth involves using multiple layers of security, including firewalls, access control, encryption, and monitoring, to create a robust security posture.

21. How does Windows implement DNS security features to protect against DNS-based attacks?

Answer: Windowsimplements DNS Security Extensions (DNSSEC) to authenticate and verify DNS data, preventing DNS spoofing and cache poisoning attacks.

22. What are the security implications of running services such as SMB (Server Message Block) in a Windows environment, and how can they be secured?

Answer: Running services like SMB can pose security risks. To secure them, it's essential to keep them up to date, apply proper access controls, and use SMB encryption.

23. Explain the role of Windows Network Policy Server (NPS) in network security.

Answer: NPS is used for RADIUS-based authentication, authorization, and accounting in Windows networks, allowing granular control over network access.

24. How can Windows BitLocker be used to enhance data security over the network?

Answer: BitLocker is used to encrypt data on Windows devices and can protect data in transit when used in conjunction with other security measures.

25. What are common security challenges related to Wi-Fi networks in a Windows environment, and how can they be addressed?

Answer: Challenges include Wi-Fi password security, rogue access points, and encryption. These can be addressed through strong Wi-Fi security practices, regularly changing Wi-Fi passwords, and using WPA3 encryption.

26. How can Windows implement security measures to protect against DDoS (Distributed Denial of Service) attacks on a network?

Answer: Measures include using DDoS mitigation services, traffic filtering, and increasing network capacity to absorb attacks.

27. What are some best practices for securing remote desktop services in a Windows environment?

Answer: Best practices include changing default ports, enabling Network Level Authentication (NLA), and restricting RDP access to authorized users and IP addresses.

ONLINE RESOURCES

Practice Paper Link: https://forms.gle/BLdTFTfhLtyRsZxq7

QR Code:

Video Link: https://www.youtube.com/playlist?list=PLzlh_31VWEFq9vYdcksqfqkFl4zG3h_4F

QR Code:

Chapter 13 Windows cyber security

Security Policies and Best Practice

1. What is a security policy in the context of Windows?

Answer: A security policy in Windows is a set of rules and guidelines that define how to protect computer systems, networks, and data from unauthorized access and threats.

2. Why are security policies important in a Windows environment?

Answer: Security policies are crucial for ensuring the confidentiality, integrity, and availability of data and resources, as well as compliance with industry regulations and legal requirements.

3. What are the key components of a typical security policy for Windows?

Answer: A security policy typically includes access control, password policies, encryption standards, user privileges, audit and monitoring procedures, and incident response guidelines.

4. How do you enforce password complexity in a Windows environment?

Answer: Password complexity can be enforced by setting Group Policy to require a minimum length, a mix of uppercase and lowercase characters, numbers, and special symbols in passwords.

5. What is the principle of least privilege, and why is it important in Windows security?

Answer: The principle of least privilege means granting users the minimum level of access they need to perform their job. This minimizes the risk of privilege escalation and unauthorized access to resources.

6. What is BitLocker and how does it enhance Windows security?

Answer: BitLocker is a disk encryption feature in Windows that helps protect data by encrypting the entire disk. It provides a higher level of data security in case of loss or theft of the device.

7. How can you secure Remote Desktop Protocol (RDP) in Windows?

Answer: You can secure RDP by configuring network-level authentication (NLA), using strong passwords, and restricting RDP access to authorized users and IP addresses.

8. What are some best practices for securing Active Directory in Windows?

Answer: Best practices include regular patching, limiting physical access to domain controllers, implementing strong password policies, and monitoring Active Directory for unusual activities.

9. How often should security audits and vulnerability assessments be conducted in a Windows environment?

Answer: Security audits and vulnerability assessments should be conducted regularly, ideally on a quarterly or annual basis, and after significant system changes or incidents.

10. Explain the importance of regular software patch management in Windows security.

Answer: Regular patch management ensures that known vulnerabilities are addressed promptly, reducing the risk of exploitation by attackers.

11. What is the difference between antivirus and antimalware software, and why should both be used in a Windows environment?

Answer: Antivirus software primarily focuses on detecting and preventing traditional viruses, while antimalware software is more comprehensive, addressing a wider range of malicious software. Using both enhances overall security.

12. How can you ensure physical security of Windows servers and workstations?

Answer: Physical security measures may include locking server rooms, using access control systems, and installing security cameras to prevent unauthorized physical access.

13. What are some common social engineering attacks, and how can Windows users be trained to recognize and prevent them?

Answer: Common social engineering attacks include phishing, pretexting, and baiting. Training users to recognize suspicious emails and websites and to verify the identity of individuals requesting information can help prevent these attacks.

14. How do you manage third-party software updates in a Windows environment to enhance security?

Answer: Using a software update management system, like WSUS (Windows Server Update Services), can help automate and control third-party software updates to ensure they are current and secure.

15. What is the role of incident response in Windows security, and how should it be structured?

Answer: Incident response involves identifying, mitigating, and recovering from security incidents. It should be structured with clear roles and responsibilities, a defined incident classification system, and well-documented procedures.

16. How do you secure wireless networks in a Windows environment?

Answer: Securing wireless networks involves using strong encryption (e.g., WPA2 or WPA3), changing default credentials, hiding SSIDs, and limiting access to authorized devices.

17. What is the purpose of a firewall in a Windows security policy?

Answer: A firewall is used to control incoming and outgoing network traffic based on an organization's previously established security policies, helping to prevent unauthorized access and protect against external threats.

18. How do you secure sensitive data stored on Windows servers or in the cloud?

Answer: Securing sensitive data involves encrypting it, using access controls, and implementing data loss prevention (DLP) policies. Additionally, regular data backups are crucial to recover from data breaches.

19. What is the role of security awareness training for employees in Windows security?

Answer: Security awareness training helps employees recognize security threats, avoid common pitfalls, and follow security policies to protect company assets and data.

20. How do you manage and secure privileged accounts in Windows Active Directory?

Answer: Managing privileged accounts includes restricting their use to authorized personnel, implementing multi-factor authentication, and regularly auditing and monitoring their activities.

21. What are some best practices for securely disposing of hardware and data in a Windows environment?

Answer: Best practices include securely wiping data from devices before disposal, physically destroying storage media when necessary, and maintaining records of hardware disposal to comply with data protection regulations.

22. How can Windows Event Logs be utilized for security monitoring and incident detection?

Answer: Windows Event Logs can be configured to track security-related events, and tools like SIEM (Security Information and Event Management) can be used to analyze these logs for signs of security incidents.

23. What is the importance of regular system backups in Windows security?

Answer: Regular backups are essential for data recovery in the event of security incidents or system failures, ensuring business continuity and minimizing data loss.

24. How do you implement a network segmentation strategy in a Windows environment to enhance security?

Answer: Network segmentation involves dividing a network into smaller, isolated segments to limit the spread of malware and unauthorized access. Using firewalls and access controls is key to its implementation.

25. What are the key elements of a disaster recovery plan (DRP) in Windows security?

Answer: A DRP should include backup and restoration procedures, a communication plan, a list of critical systems, and predefined roles and
responsibilities for incident response.

26. How can Windows Group Policy be used to enforce security policies across a network?

Answer: Group Policy allows you to centrally manage user and computer settings in a Windows environment, including security policies, ensuring consistency and adherence to security standards.

27. What is the importance of continuous monitoring and assessment in Windows security?

Answer: Continuous monitoring helps identify and address security weaknesses, threats, and vulnerabilities in real-time, improving the overall security posture of a Windows environment.

28. How do you handle security incidents, and what steps should be taken during an incident response?

Answer: Handling security incidents involves identifying the incident, containing it, eradicating the root cause, recovering systems, and conducting a post-incident analysis to prevent future incidents.

29. What is the role of encryption in Windows security, and what are the different encryption methods available?

Answer: Encryption helps protect data at rest and in transit. Different encryption methods include BitLocker for disk encryption and protocols like TLS for secure communication.

30. How do you keep security policies up to date in a Windows environment to adapt to evolving threats and regulations?

Answer: Keeping security policies up to date involves regular reviews and revisions, monitoring emerging threats, and staying informed about changes in relevant laws and regulations, such as GDPRor HIPAA.

Threat Detection and Response

1. What is threat detection and response in the context of Windows security?

Answer: Threat detection and response involves identifying, analyzing, and mitigating security threats and incidents in a Windows environment to prevent or minimize their impact.

2. Can you explain the differences between threat detection and threat prevention in Windows security?

Answer: Threat detection is the process of identifying and confirming the presence of a threat, while threat prevention aims to stop threats from occurring in the first place. Detection is reactive, while prevention is proactive.

3. What is the role of Windows Defender in threat detection and response on Windows systems?

Answer: Windows Defender is Microsoft's built-in antivirus and antimalware solution that detects and responds to malware threats, suspicious files, and behaviours on Windows systems.

4. How does Windows Firewall contribute to threat detection and response on a Windows network?

Answer: Windows Firewall helps control incoming and outgoing network traffic, limiting exposure to threats. It can be configured to log network activity, aiding in threat detection.

5. What is the importance of log analysis in threat detection for Windows environments?

Answer: Log analysis helps in identifying suspicious activities and security incidents by reviewing logs of events like failed logins, system changes, and access attempts.

6. How can Windows Event Logs be used for threat detection and response?

Answer: Windows Event Logs record system and security-related events. By monitoring these logs, one can detect signs of potential security threats or incidents.

7. What is SIEM, and how does it enhance threat detection and response in Windows environments?

Answer: SIEM (Security Information and Event Management) systems collect, correlate, and analyze security-related data from various sources, providing real-time threat detection and response capabilities.

8. Describe the key indicators of compromise (IOCs) in the context of Windows threat detection.

Answer: IOCs are specific pieces of information or patterns that may indicate a security breach, such as unusual network traffic, file changes, or unauthorized access.

9. How can Windows Group Policy be leveraged to enhance threat detection and response?

Answer: Group Policy can be used to enforce security settings and restrictions, helping to prevent or limit the impact of security threats in a Windows environment.

10. What are the primary challenges in identifying and responding to insider threats in a Windows environment?

Answer: Insider threats can be challenging to detect as insiders have legitimate access. Monitoring user behaviour and access patterns, along with regular audits, can help identify such threats.

11. Explain the concept of "zero-day vulnerabilities" in the context of Windows threat detection and response.

Answer: Zero-day vulnerabilities are security flaws in software or systems for which no patches or updates are available. Detecting and responding to threats exploiting these vulnerabilities is critical.

12. What is a Security Information Sharing and Analysis Center (ISAC), and how does it benefit threat detection and response in Windows environments?

Answer: ISACs facilitate information sharing and collaboration among organizations to detect and respond to cyber threats collectively, improving threat intelligence.

13. How can endpoint detection and response (EDR) solutions enhance threat detection on Windows endpoints?

Answer: EDR solutions offer advanced threat detection and response capabilities, allowing real-time monitoring of endpoints for suspicious activities and behaviours.

14. What role do threat intelligence feeds play in Windows threat detection and response?

Answer: Threat intelligence feeds provide information about emerging threats, helping security teams identify and respond to new and evolving attack techniques.

15. Explain the importance of a well-defined incident response plan in Windows threat detection and response.

Answer: An incident response plan outlines the steps to take when a security incident is detected, ensuring a coordinated and effective response.

16. How can a Windows environment benefit from automated threat detection and response tools?

Answer: Automated tools can rapidly identify and respond to threats, reducing response times and minimizing the potential impact of security incidents.

17. What is the role of user and entity behaviour analytics (UEBA) in threat detection for Windows environments?

Answer: UEBA solutions analyse user and entity behaviours to detect anomalies and potential threats, helping to identify insider threats and advanced attacks.

18. How do you prioritize threats and incidents when responding to security alerts in a Windows environment?

Answer: Threats should be prioritized based on their severity, potential impact, and the value of the assets they may compromise.

19. What is the difference between reactive and proactive threat detection and response in a Windows environment?

Answer: Reactive detection responds to known threats, while proactive detection focuses on identifying vulnerabilities and threats before they are exploited.

20. What are some common indicators of malware infection on a Windows system, and how can they be detected and mitigated?

Answer: Common indicators include unusual network traffic, system slowdowns, unexpected pop-ups, and changes in system files. Detecting these indicators involves using antivirus software and conducting malware scans.

21. How can Windows operating system updates and patch management contribute to threat detection and response?

Answer: Keeping systems up to date with security patches helps to eliminate known vulnerabilities that attackers may exploit, reducing the likelihood of successful threats.

22. What is the role of honeypots and deception technology in Windows threat detection and response?

Answer: Honeypots and deception technology create decoy systems that attract attackers, allowing security teams to study their tactics and identify threats.

23. How do you handle a ransomware incident in a Windows environment, and what steps should be taken in response?

Answer: Response to a ransomware incident includes isolating affected systems, assessing data integrity, reporting the incident, and deciding whether to pay the ransom (not recommended) or restore from backups.

24. Explain the concept of security orchestration, automation, and response (SOAR) in the context of Windows threat detection and response.

Answer: SOAR platforms enable security teams to automate response actions and orchestrate workflows for efficient threat detection and response.

25. What is the difference between a false positive and a false negative in threat detection, and how can they impact the response process?

Answer: A false positive is an alert indicating a threat that does not exist, while a false negative is a failure to detect a real threat. False positives can waste resources, and false negatives can result in security breaches.

26. How can machine learning and artificial intelligence be used to enhance threat detection and response in a Windows environment?

Answer: Machine learning and AI can analyze large volumes of data to identify patterns and anomalies, improving the accuracy and speed of threat detection.

27. What steps should be taken during a post-incident analysis in a Windows environment, and why is it important?

Answer: Post-incident analysis involves reviewing the incident, identifying root causes, and implementing measures to prevent similar incidents in the future. It helps in strengthening security.

28. How do you manage and share threat intelligence with other organizations in a Windows environment to improve collective threat detection and response?

Answer: Threat intelligence sharing can be achieved through ISACs, threat sharing platforms, and trusted partnerships, which facilitate the exchange of threat data and insights.

29. What is the role of threat hunting in threat detection, and how can it complement traditional threat response methods in Windows environments?

Answer: Threat hunting involves proactively searching for hidden threats within a network. It complements traditional threat response by identifying threats that may not trigger alerts.

30. How can you stay updated on emerging threats and best practices for threat detection and response in the Windows environment?

Answer: Staying updated involves continuous learning, attending security conferences, subscribing to threat intelligence feeds, and participating in security communities to stay informed about the latest threats and solutions.

ONLINE RESOURCES

Practice Paper Link: https://forms.gle/zbWRkrWJ66ctFWSX8

QR Code:

Video Link: https://www.youtube.com/playlist?list=PLzlh_31VWEFqGuV-smm29oqzv-noha0JD

QR Code:

ADDITIONAL RESOURCES

: https://www.youtube.com/playlist?list=PLzlh_31VWEFpI_Mce_W-LNgZNq97wd3XY

QR Code:

In this book

Welcome to "Windows Operating System Interview Questions & Answers" your comprehensive guide to mastering Windows Operating System. This book offers a blend of theoretical knowledge and practical applications, designed to cater to learners at all levels. Whether you are a student or a professional, you'll find essential tools and resources to enhance your expertise and achieve your learning goals in this transformative field. Dive in and explore the innovations driving industries forward.

YouTube Videos Playlists for all Chapters

CHAPTER 1: https://www.youtube.com/playlist?list=PLzlh_31VWEFqAd8JlYri0rF5l14cV1XoS

QR Code:

CHAPTER 2: https://www.youtube.com/playlist?list=PLzlh_31VWEFpUeiz4FrASN1AU0es5WtcH

QR Code:

CHAPTER 3: https://www.youtube.com/playlist?list=PLzlh_31VWEFqTwNl_4muKAGq-SKyrURId

QR Code:

CHAPTER 4: https://www.youtube.com/playlist?list=PLzlh_31VWEFpo9PFaPd2wDiw1-6o7lNrI

QR Code:

CHAPTER 5: https://www.youtube.com/playlist?list=PLzlh_31VWEFou_X2dK5vqoy4Wl8kvm_bZ

QR Code:

CHAPTER 6: https://www.youtube.com/playlist?list=PLzlh_31VWEFqJYVteDLCTUIa-YtXJfu36

QR Code:

CHAPTER 7: https://www.youtube.com/playlist?list=PLzlh_31VWEFozRmqLl3gslnwb4K1uQ93M

QR Code:

CHAPTER 8: https://www.youtube.com/playlist?list=PLzlh_31VWEFp__HhXBpd_P0eqLZTuNNvO

QR Code:

CHAPTER 9: https://www.youtube.com/playlist?list=PLzlh_31VWEForjsPxTjus0FF9Q-7rN9LG

QR Code:

CHAPTER 10: https://www.youtube.com/playlist?list=PLzlh_31VWEFrf6dXDqR3bXIpEWP1OaIES

QR Code:

CHAPTER 11: https://www.youtube.com/playlist?list=PLzlh_31VWEFriWXKGNXPdCy1Egd8jbSaC

QR Code:

CHAPTER 12: https://www.youtube.com/playlist?list=PLzlh_31VWEFq9vYdcksqfqkFl4zG3h_4F

QR Code:

CHAPTER 13: https://www.youtube.com/playlist?list=PLzlh_31VWEFqGuV-smm29oqzv-noha0JD

QR Code: